SELECTED WORKS OF MAO TSE-TUNG

毛澤東

SELECTED WORKS

of

MAO TSE-TUNG

Volume One

LONDON
LAWRENCE & WISHART LTD
1954

First Published 1954

PRINTED AND BOUND IN GREAT BRITAIN
BY JARROLD AND SONS LTD, NORWICH

CONTENTS

PERIOD OF THE FIRST REVOLUTIONARY CIVIL WAR

PERIOD OF THE SECOND REVOLUTIONARY CIVIL WAR

PUBLISHER'S NOTE

This English edition of *The Selected Works of Mao Tse-tung* will occupy five volumes, and is based on the Chinese Edition in four volumes, the first volume of which appeared in 1951, edited by a Commission of the Central Committee of the Chinese Communist Party. The translation of the first volume is from the fourth printing of the second Chinese edition, People's Publishing House, Peking, July 1952. The explanatory note at the head of each article is translated from the Chinese edition. Explanatory notes are added at the end of the volume: some of these are translated from the Chinese edition, others have been added by the translators.

The contents of the entire Selection are arranged in chronological order, and are further divided according to the five historical periods which the Chinese Communist Party has gone through since its foundation in 1921. The first volume covers the first two periods: the period of the foundation of the Communist Party and of the First Revolutionary Civil War (1921–1927), and the period of the Second Revolutionary Civil War (1927–1936).

Editions of *Selected Works of Mao Tse-tung* have appeared previously in various places, but as none of them had been attended to by the author, their arrangement was haphazard and their text disfigured by errors, while certain important writings were omitted. The Chinese editors made every effort to include in the present edition the important writings not included in the other editions. And the author himself went over all the articles, making certain verbal changes here and there, and, in a few cases, revising or amplifying certain passages.

The present selection is, however, still far from adequate. As the archives of revolutionary literature were either destroyed deliberately by the Kuomintang reactionaries or dispersed and lost during the years of war, it was not possible to collect all that Mao Tse-tung had written, especially the numerous letters and telegrams which form a considerable part of his writings.

According to the author's wishes, some articles which have been widely circulated (*e.g. Rural Surveys*) were omitted, and for the same reason only Chapter I ("A Brief Conclusion on our Work in the Past") of *On Economic and Financial Problems* was included.

PERIOD
OF THE FIRST
REVOLUTIONARY CIVIL WAR

ANALYSIS OF THE CLASSES IN CHINESE SOCIETY

This article was written in 1926 to combat two deviations then existing in the Party—"Right" opportunism represented by Ch'en Tu-hsiu and "Left" opportunism represented by Chang Kuo-t'ao. One paid attention only to the Kuomintang-Communist co-operation and the other only to the labour movement, but both forgot the peasants. Although both brands of opportunists were keenly aware of the insufficiency of the revolutionary forces, neither knew where to look for reinforcements and for broad masses of allies. Comrade Mao Tse-tung pointed out that the Chinese proletariat had in the peasantry its staunchest and most numerous ally, and thus solved the problem concerning the chief ally in the Chinese revolution. At the same time he foresaw that the national bourgeoisie, as a wavering class, would split up during a revolutionary upsurge, with its right wing going over to the imperialist camp. The events of 1927 confirmed his judgment.

Who are our enemies, and who are our friends? This question is one of primary importance in the revolution. All past revolutionary struggles in China achieved very little, basically because the revolutionaries were unable to unite their real friends to attack their real enemies. A revolutionary party is the guide of the masses, and no revolution ever succeeds when the revolutionary party leads it astray. To make sure that we will not lead our revolution astray but will achieve positive success, we must pay attention to uniting our real friends to attack our real enemies. To distinguish real friends from real enemies, we must make a general analysis of the economic status of the various classes in Chinese society and of their respective attitudes towards the revolution.

What are the conditions of the various classes in Chinese society?

The landlord and comprador classes. In economically backward and semi-colonial China the landlords and compradors are completely the vassals of the international bourgeoisie, depending upon imperialism for their existence and development. These classes represent the most backward and the most reactionary relations of production in China and hinder the development of her productive forces. Their existence is incompatible with the objectives of the Chinese revolution. This is especially true of the big landlords and big compradors who always side with imperialism and form the extreme counter-revolutionary group. They are politically represented by the *Etatistes*[1] and the right wing of the Kuomintang.

The middle class. This class represents China's capitalist relations of production in town and country. The middle class, by which is chiefly meant the national bourgeoisie, is contradictory in its attitudes towards the Chinese revolution: when it suffers from the blows of foreign capital and the oppression of the warlords, it feels the need of a revolution and favours the revolutionary movement against imperialism and the warlords; but when the proletariat at home takes a militant part in the revolution and the international proletariat abroad gives its active support, so that it senses the threat to the realisation of its desire to develop as a class into the status of a big bourgeoisie, it becomes sceptical about the revolution. Politically it stands for the establishment of a state under the rule of a single class, the national bourgeoisie.

A self-styled "true disciple" of Tai Chi-t'ao[2] wrote in the *Chen Pao*,[3] Peking: "Raise your left fist to knock down imperialism and your right fist to knock down the Communist Party." This remark depicts the dilemma and quandary of this class. This class objects to the Kuomintang's Principle of the People's Welfare being interpreted according to the theory of the class struggle, and objects to the Kuomintang's alliance with Russia and inclusion of Communists[4] and left-wingers. But its aim of establishing a state under its own rule is impracticable, because the present world situation is one in which the two big forces, revolution and counter-revolution, are engaged in the final struggle. Two huge banners have been raised by these two huge forces: One is the red banner of revolution which the Third International holds aloft, rallying all the oppressed classes of the world, and the other is the white banner of counter-revolution which the League of Nations hold aloft, rallying all the counter-revolutionary elements of the world. The intermediate class will beyond doubt rapidly fall apart, some sections turning left and joining the ranks of the revolution and others turning right and joining the ranks of the counter-revolution; there is no room for any to remain "independent". Therefore the idea cherished by the Chinese middle class of an "independent" revolution in which it would play the leading role is a mere illusion.

The petty bourgeoisie. Owner-peasants,[5] master handicraftsmen and the petty intellectuals—students, primary and middle school teachers, lower government functionaries, office clerks, small lawyers and petty traders—all belong to this category. On account of its size and its class character, this class deserves great attention. The owner-peasants and the master handicraftsmen are both engaged in small-scale production. Although the various strata of this class have the same petty-bourgeois economic status, they nevertheless fall into three different groups.

The first group consists of those who have some surplus money and grain, *i.e.* people who, by their manual or mental labour, have an annual surplus over and above what they need for their own support. Such people are very eager about getting rich and worship Marshal Chao[6] most devotedly; though without any illusions about amassing a great fortune, they constantly desire to climb up to the position of the middle class. At the sight of small capitalists who command people's respect their mouths water copiously. They are timid, afraid of government officials, and also a bit afraid of the revolution. Since their economic status is quite close to that of the middle class, they more or less believe in the latter's propaganda and adopt a sceptical attitude towards the revolution. This group is a minority among the petty bourgeoisie and constitutes its right wing.

The second group consists of those who in the main are economically self-supporting. People of this group differ greatly from the people of the first group in that, though they also want to become rich, Marshal Chao never allows them to, and moreover in recent years, victimised by the oppression and exploitation of the imperialists, the warlords, the feudal landlords and the big comprador bourgeoisie, they feel that the world now is no longer what it was. They feel that if they put in now only the same amount of labour as before, they will be unable to maintain their standard of living. They can maintain their standard of living only by increasing their working hours, getting up earlier and finishing work later, and redoubling their efforts at their jobs. They begin to be somewhat abusive, calling the foreigners "foreign devils", the warlords "money-grabbing commanders", and the local bullies and bad gentry "the heartless rich". Merely feeling uncertain of the success of the movement against the imperialists and the warlords (the reason being that the foreigners and the warlords have so much power behind them), they refuse to join it rashly and remain neutral, but they never oppose the revolution. This group is very numerous, making up about one-half of the petty bourgeoisie.

The third group consists of those whose standard of living is being reduced. Many of this group, who belonged on the whole to the so-called prosperous families in the past, are going through a gradual change in their condition—from that of being barely able to hold on to their wealth to that of living in more and more reduced circumstances. At the end of each year, on settling their accounts, they are horrified, exclaiming, "What! Another deficit!" Because such people have seen better days and are now going downhill with every passing year, their debts mounting and their life becoming more and more miserable, they "shudder as if with cold" at the thought of the future. Spiritually they suffer very much because they have in mind the contrast between the past and the present. Such people are quite important in the revolutionary movement, constitute a mass following of no small number and form the left wing of the petty bourgeoisie.

In normal times the three above-mentioned groups of the petty bourgeoisie differ in their attitude towards the revolution; but in times of war, that is, in a revolutionary upsurge when the dawn of victory is discernible, not only the left wing but the middle group of this class may also join the revolution— and even its right wing, swept along by the great revolutionary tide of the proletariat and the left wing of the petty bourgeoisie, cannot but attach itself to the revolution. From the experience of the May 30 Movement[7] in 1925 and the peasant movement in various places, we can see that this judgment is correct.

The semi-proletariat. What is called the semi-proletariat here consists of five categories: (1) the overwhelming majority of the semi-tenant peasants,[8] (2) poor peasants, (3) handicraftsmen, (4) shop assistants[9] and (5) pedlars. The overwhelming majority of the semi-tenant peasants, together with the poor peasants, constitute a very large section of the masses in the countryside. The "peasant problem" is essentially their problem. The semi-tenant peasants, the poor peasants and the handicraftsmen are all engaged in production on yet a smaller scale than the petty bourgeoisie. Although both the overwhelming majority of the semi-tenant peasants and the poor peasants belong to the semi-proletariat, yet according to their economic conditions they can be further divided into three grades, upper, middle and lower.

The life of the semi-tenant peasants is harder than that of the owner-peasants because every year they are short of about half the food they need, and must rent land from others, sell part of their labour power, or engage in petty trading to make up the shortage. Between spring and summer, before the green corn grows and after the white crop is consumed, they borrow money at exorbitant interest and buy grain at high prices; compared with the lot of the owner-peasants who need no help from others, theirs is of course harder, though still better than that of the poor peasants. For the poor peasants own no land, and, for their year's ploughing and sowing, receive only half the harvest or even less, while the semi-tenant peasants, though they receive only half or less than half of the harvest of the land rented from others, can nevertheless keep the entire crop from the land owned by themselves. The revolutionary qualities of the semi-tenant peasants are therefore superior to those of the owner-peasants, but inferior to those of the poor peasants.

The poor peasants are tenant-peasants in the countryside, exploited by the landlords. According to their economic status, they can again be divided into two sections. One section of the poor peasants own comparatively adequate farm implements and a proportional amount of funds. Such peasants can get half the product of their year's toil; to make up the deficit they can cultivate side-crops, catch fish and crayfish, raise chickens and pigs, or sell part of their labour power, thus

2

eking out a living and hoping to tide over the year amid
want and hardships. Therefore their life is harder than that of
the semi-tenant peasants, but better than that of the other
section of the poor peasants. Their revolutionary qualities
are superior to those of the semi-tenant peasants, but inferior
to those of the other section of the poor peasants. As to the
other section of the poor peasants, they possess neither adequate
farm implements nor funds; they have not enough manure,
reap but a poor harvest from their land, and, with little left
after the payment of the land rent, have even greater need to
sell part of their labour power. During lean seasons and hard
times they appeal to relatives and friends, borrowing a few
tou or *sheng*[10] of grain to tide over three or five days, and their
debts pile up like the load on the backs of draught oxen.
They are among the most hard-pressed of the peasants, and
very receptive to revolutionary agitation.

The handicraftsmen are classed with the semi-proletariat
because, though they possess some simple means of production
and moreover follow a sort of liberal profession, they are often
forced to sell part of their labour power and are somewhat
similar in economic status to the poor peasants in the countryside. As a result of their heavy family burdens and the disparity between their earnings and the cost of living, they also
on the whole resemble the poor peasants in constantly feeling
the pressure of poverty and threat of unemployment.

Shop assistants are employees in commercial establishments,
who have to defray their family expenses with their meagre
pay; while prices rise with every passing year, their pay is
raised usually once in several years, and any casual conversation with them is an occasion for them to ventilate their
endless grievances. They are not much different in status from
the poor peasants and handicraftsmen and are very receptive
to revolutionary agitation.

The pedlars, whether carrying their wares around on a pole
or setting up stalls along the street, have but small capital,
make but a meagre profit, and do not earn enough to feed and
clothe themselves. They are not much different in status from
the poor peasants and likewise need a revolution that will
change the existing state of affairs.

The proletariat. The modern industrial proletariat in China numbers about two million. As China is economically backward the number of her modern industrial proletariat is not large. The majority of the approximately two million industrial workers are engaged in five industries—railways, mining, maritime transport, textiles and shipbuilding—and are enslaved in large numbers in enterprises owned by foreign capital. The industrial proletariat, though small in number, is nevertheless the representative of China's new productive forces and the most progressive class in modern China, and has become the leading force in the revolutionary movement. If we look at the strength it showed in the strike movements of the last four years, such as the seamen's strike, [11] the railway strike, [12] the strikes in the Kailan and Tsiaotso coal-mines, [13] the Shameen strike [14] and the general strikes in Shanghai and Hongkong after the May 30 Movement, [15] we can immediately realise the importance of the position of the industrial proletariat in the Chinese revolution. The first reason why the industrial workers can hold such a position is their concentration. No other section of the people is so concentrated. The second reason is their low economic status. They are particularly able to fight because, deprived of all means of production and left with nothing but their hands, they have despaired of ever becoming rich and are subjected to the most ruthless treatment by the imperialists, the warlords and the bourgeoisie. The strength of the city coolies is also well worth attention. They are mostly stevedores and rickshawmen, but with them belong also sewage carters and street cleaners. Having nothing but their hands, they are similar in economic status to the industrial workers, but they are less concentrated and play a less important role in production.

There is as yet little modern capitalist farming in China. What is called the rural proletariat consists of farm labourers hired by the year, the month or the day. Having neither land nor farm implements, nor even the least amount of funds, they can only sell their labour power to make a living. Compared with other workers, they work the longest hours, on the lowest pay, and under the worst conditions, and with the least security of employment. Such people find themselves the most hard-pressed in the villages, and hold a position in the peasant movement as important as the poor peasants.

In addition to these, there is a fairly large number of *lumpen*-proletarians, that is, peasants who have lost their land and handicraftsmen who have lost all opportunity of employment. They lead the most precarious kind of life. They have formed secret societies in various places—for instance, the Triune Society in Fukien and Kwangtung; the Society of Brothers in Hunan, Hupeh, Kweichow and Szechwan; the Society of Big Swords in Anhwei, Honan and Shantung; the Society of Rational Life in Chihli and the three north-eastern provinces;[16] and the Blue Band in Shanghai and elsewhere[17]—all these have been their mutual-aid organisations in political and economic struggle. To assign these people to their proper role is one of China's difficult problems. Able to fight very bravely but apt to be destructive, they can become a revolutionary force when properly guided.

From the above it can be seen that all those in league with imperialism—the warlords, the bureaucrats, the compradors, the big landlords and the reactionary section of the intelligentsia dependent on them—are our enemies. The industrial proletariat is the leading force in our revolution. All sections of the semi-proletariat and the petty bourgeoisie are our closest friends. As to the vacillating middle class, its right wing may become our enemy and its left wing may become our friend, but we must be constantly on our guard towards the latter and not allow it to create confusion in our front.

March 1926.

REPORT OF AN INVESTIGATION INTO THE PEASANT MOVEMENT IN HUNAN

This article was written in reply to criticisms made both inside and outside the Party against the peasants' revolutionary struggles in 1926–7. Comrade Mao Tse-tung went to Hunan and spent thirty-two days making investigations and then wrote this report. The Right opportunists in the Party, headed by Ch'en Tu-hsiu, were unwilling to accept Comrade Mao's views and persisted in their erroneous opinions. Their chief mistake was that, scared by the reactionary current of the Kuomintang, they dared not support the great revolutionary struggles of the peasants that had broken out or were breaking out. To appease the Kuomintang, they preferred to desert the peasantry, the chief ally in the revolution, and thus landed the working class and the Communist Party in helpless isolation. The Kuomintang took advantage of this weakness of the Communist Party and was emboldened in the summer of 1927 to betray the revolution, launch its campaign to "purge the party", and make war against the people.

THE IMPORTANCE OF THE PEASANT PROBLEM

During my recent visit to Hunan[1] I conducted an investigation on the spot into the conditions in the five counties of Siangtan, Siangsiang, Hengshan, Liling and Changsha. In the thirty-two days from January 4 to February 5, in villages and in county towns, I called together for fact-finding conferences experienced peasants and comrades working for the peasant movement, listened attentively to their reports and collected a lot of material. Many of the hows and whys of the peasant movement were quite the reverse of what I had heard from the gentry in Hankow and Changsha. And many strange things there were that I had never seen or heard of before. I think these conditions exist in many other places.

All kinds of arguments against the peasant movement must be speedily set right. The erroneous measures taken by the revolutionary authorities concerning the peasant movement must be speedily changed. Only thus can any good be done for the future of the revolution. For the rise of the present peasant movement is a colossal event. In a very short time, in China's central, southern and northern provinces, several hundred million peasants will rise like a tornado or tempest, a force so extraordinarily swift and violent that no power, however great, will be able to suppress it. They will break all trammels that now bind them and rush forward along the road to liberation. They will send all imperialists, warlords, corrupt officials, local bullies and bad gentry to their graves. All revolutionary parties and all revolutionary comrades will stand before them to be tested, and to be accepted or rejected as they decide.

To march at their head and lead them? Or to follow at their rear, gesticulating at them and criticising them? Or to face them as opponents?

Every Chinese is free to choose among the three alternatives, but circumstances demand that a quick choice be made.

GET ORGANISED!

The peasant movement in Hunan, so far as it concerns the counties in the central and southern sections of the province, where the movement is already developed, can be roughly divided into two periods.

The first period was the period of organisation, extending from January to September of last year. In this period, there was the stage from January to June—a stage of underground activities, and the stage from July to September when the revolutionary army expelled Chao Heng-t'i[2]—a stage of open activities. In this period, the membership of the peasant association totalled only 300,000–400,000, and the masses it could directly lead numbered but little more than a million; as there was hardly any struggle in the rural areas, very little criticism of the association was heard. Since its members served as guides, scouts and carriers, the officers in the Northern Expedition Army even had a good word or two for the peasant association.

The second period was the period of revolutionary action, extending from last October to this January. The membership of the peasant association jumped to two million and the masses over whom it could exercise direct leadership increased to ten million people. As the peasants mostly entered only one name for each family when joining the association, a membership of two million therefore means a mass following of about ten million. Of all the peasants in Hunan, almost half are organised. In counties like Siangtan, Siangsiang, Liuyang, Changsha, Liling, Ningsiang, Pingkiang, Siangyin, Hengshan, Hengyang, Leiyang, Chen and Anhwa, nearly all the peasants have rallied organisationally in the association and followed its leadership. The peasants, with their extensive organisation, went right into action and within four months brought about a great and unprecedented revolution in the countryside.

DOWN WITH THE LOCAL BULLIES AND BAD GENTRY! ALL POWER TO THE PEASANT ASSOCIATION!

The peasants attack as their main targets the local bullies and bad gentry and the lawless landlords, hitting in passing against patriarchal ideologies and institutions, corrupt officials in the cities and evil customs in the rural areas. In force and momentum, the attack is like a tempest or hurricane; those who submit to it survive and those who resist it perish. As a result, the privileges which the feudal landlords have enjoyed for thousands of years are being shattered to pieces. The dignity and prestige of the landlords are dashed to the ground. With the fall of the authority of the landlords, the peasant association becomes the sole organ of authority, and what people call "All power to the peasant association" has come to pass. Even such a trifle as a quarrel between man and wife has to be settled at the peasant association. Nothing can be settled in the absence of people from the association. The association is actually dictating in all matters in the countryside, and it is literally true that "whatever it says, goes". The public can only praise the association and must not condemn it. The local bullies and bad gentry and the lawless landlords have been totally deprived of the right to have their say, and no one dares mutter the word "No". To be safe from the power and pressure of the peasant association, the first-rank local bullies and bad gentry fled to Shanghai; the second-rank ones to Hankow; the third-rank ones to Changsha; and the fourth-rank ones to the county towns; the fifth-rank ones and even lesser fry can only remain in the countryside and surrender to the peasant association.

"I'll donate ten dollars, please admit me to the peasant association", one of the smaller gentry would say.

"Pshaw! Who wants your filthy money!" the peasants would reply.

Many middle and small landlords, rich peasants and middle peasants, formerly opposed to the peasant association, now seek admission in vain. Visiting various places, I often came across such people, who solicited my help. "I beg", they would say, "the committeeman from the provincial capital to be my guarantor."

The census book compiled by the local authorities under the Manchu régime consisted of a regular register and a special register; in the former honest people were entered, and in the latter burglars, bandits and other undesirables. The peasants in some places now use the same method to threaten people formerly opposed to the association: "Enter them in the special register!"

Such people, afraid of being entered in the special register, try various means to seek admission to the association and do not feel at ease until, as they eagerly desire, their names are entered in its register. But they are as a rule sternly turned down, and so spend their days in a constant state of suspense; barred from the doors of the association, they are like homeless people. In short, what was generally sneered at four months ago as the "peasants' gang" has now become something most honourable. Those who prostrated themselves before the power of the gentry now prostrate themselves before the power of the peasants. Everyone admits that the world has changed since last October.

"AN AWFUL MESS!" AND "VERY GOOD INDEED!"

The revolt of the peasants in the countryside disturbed the sweet dreams of the gentry. When news about the countryside reached the cities, the gentry there immediately burst into an uproar. When I first arrived in Changsha, I met people from various circles and picked up a good deal of street gossip. From the middle strata upwards to the right-wingers of the Kuomintang, there was not a single person who did not summarise the whole thing in one phrase: "An awful mess!" Even quite revolutionary people, carried away by the opinion of the "awful mess" school which prevailed like a storm over the whole city, became downhearted at the very thought of the conditions in the countryside, and could not deny the word "mess". Even very progressive people could only remark, "Indeed a mess, but inevitable in the course of the revolution". In a word, nobody could categorically deny the word "mess".

But the fact is, as stated above, that the broad peasant masses have risen to fulfil their historic mission, that the democratic forces in the rural areas have risen to overthrow the rural feudal power. The patriarchal-feudal class of local bullies, bad gentry and lawless landlords has formed the basis of autocratic government for thousands of years, the cornerstone of imperialism, warlordism and corrupt officialdom. To overthrow this feudal power is the real objective of the national revolution. What Dr. Sun Yat-sen wanted to do in the forty years he devoted to the national revolution but failed to accomplish, the peasants have accomplished in a few months. This is a marvellous feat which has never been achieved in the last forty or even thousands of years. It is very good indeed. It is not "a mess" at all. It is anything but "an awful mess".

"An awful mess"—that is obviously a theory which, in line with the interests of the landlords, aims at combating the rise of the peasants, a theory of the landlord class for preserving the old order of feudalism and obstructing the establishment of a new order of democracy, and a counter-revolutionary theory. No revolutionary comrade should blindly repeat it. If you have firmly established your revolutionary viewpoint and have furthermore gone the round of the villages for a look, you will feel overjoyed as never before. There, great throngs of tens of thousands of slaves, *i.e.* the peasants, are overthrowing their cannibal enemies. Their actions are absolutely correct; their actions are very good indeed! "Very good indeed!" is the theory of the peasants and of all other revolutionaries. Every revolutionary comrade should know that the national revolution requires a profound change in the countryside. The Revolution of 1911[3] did not bring about this change, hence its failure. Now the change is taking place, which is an important factor necessary for completing the revolution. Every revolutionary comrade must support this change, or he will be taking the counter-revolutionary stand.

THE QUESTION OF "GOING TOO FAR"

There is another section of people who say, "although the peasant association ought to be formed, it has gone rather too far in its present actions". This is the opinion of the middle-of-the-roaders. But how do matters stand in reality? True, the peasants do in some ways "act unreasonably" in the countryside. The peasant association, supreme in authority, does not allow the landlords to have their say and makes a clean sweep of all their prestige. This is tantamount to trampling the landlords underfoot after knocking them down. The peasants threaten: "Put you in the special register"; they impose fines on the local bullies and bad gentry and demand contributions; they smash their sedan-chairs. Crowds of people swarm into the homes of the local bullies and bad gentry who oppose the peasant association, slaughtering their pigs and consuming their grain. They may even loll for a minute or two on the ivory beds of the young mesdames and mademoiselles in the families of the bullies and gentry. At the slightest provocation they make arrests, crown the arrested with tall paper-hats, and parade them through the villages: "You bad gentry, now you know who we are!" Doing whatever they like and turning everything upside down, they have even created a kind of terror in the countryside. This is what some people call "going too far", or "going beyond the proper limit to right a wrong", or "really too outrageous".

The opinion of this group, reasonable on the surface, is erroneous at bottom.

First, the things described above have all been the inevitable results of the doings of the local bullies and bad gentry and lawless landlords themselves. For ages these people, with power in their hands, tyrannised over the peasants and trampled them underfoot; that is why the peasants have now risen in such a great revolt. The most formidable revolts and the most serious troubles invariably occur at places where the local bullies and bad gentry and the lawless landlords were the most ruthless in their evil deeds. The peasants' eyes are perfectly discerning. As to who is bad and who is not, who is the most ruthless and who is less so, and who is to be severely punished and who is to be dealt with lightly, the peasants keep perfectly clear accounts and very seldom has there been any discrepancy between the punishment and the crime.

Secondly, a revolution is not the same as inviting people to dinner, or writing an essay, or painting a picture, or doing fancy needlework; it cannot be anything so refined, so calm and gentle, or so mild, kind, courteous, restrained and magnanimous.[4] A revolution is an uprising, an act of violence whereby one class overthrows another. A rural revolution is a revolution by which the peasantry overthrows the authority of the feudal landlord class. If the peasants do not use the maximum of their strength, they can never overthrow the authority of the landlords which has been deeply rooted for thousands of years. In the rural areas, there must be a great, fervent revolutionary upsurge, which alone can arouse hundreds and thousands of the people to form a great force. All the actions mentioned above, labelled as "going too far", are caused by the power of the peasants, generated by a great, fervent, revolutionary upsurge in the countryside. Such actions were quite necessary in the second period of the peasant movement (the period of revolutionary action). In this period, it was necessary to establish the absolute authority of the peasants. It was necessary to stop malicious criticisms against the peasant association. It was necessary to overthrow all the authority of the gentry, to knock them down and even trample them underfoot. All actions labelled as "going too far" had a revolutionary significance in the second period. To put it bluntly, it was necessary to bring about a brief reign of terror in every rural area; otherwise one could never suppress the activities of the counter-revolutionaries in the countryside or overthrow the authority of the gentry. To right a wrong it is necessary to exceed the proper limits, and the wrong cannot be righted without the proper limits being exceeded.[5]

The opinion of this school that the peasants are "going too far" is on the surface different from the opinion of the other school mentioned earlier that the peasant movement is "an awful mess", but in essence it adheres to the same viewpoint, and is likewise a theory of the landlords which supports the interests of the privileged classes. Since this theory hinders the rise of the peasant movement and consequently disrupts the revolution, we must oppose it resolutely.

THE SO-CALLED "MOVEMENT OF THE RIFFRAFF"

The right wing of the Kuomintang says, "The peasant movement is a movement of the riffraff, a movement of the lazy peasants". This opinion has gained much currency in Changsha. I went to the countryside and heard the gentry say, "It is all right to set up the peasant association, but the people now running it are incompetent; better put others on the job." This opinion and the dictum of the right wing come to the same thing; both admit that the peasant movement may be carried on (as the peasant movement has already risen, no one dares say that it shouldn't); but both regard the people leading the movement as incompetent and hate particularly those in charge of the associations at the lower levels, labelling them "riffraff". In short, all those who were formerly despised or kicked into the gutter by the gentry, who had no social standing, and who were denied the right to have a say, have now, to everyone's surprise, raised their heads. They have not only raised their heads, but have also taken power into their hands. They are now running the township peasant associations (peasant associations at the lowest level), which have been turned into a formidable force in their hands. They raise their rough, blackened hands and lay them on the gentry. They bind the bad gentry with ropes, put tall paper-hats on them and lead them in a parade through the villages. (This is called "parading through the township" in Siangtan and Siangsiang, and "parading through the fields" in Liling.) Every day the coarse, harsh sound of their denunciation assails the ears of the gentry. They are giving orders and directions in all matters. They rank above everybody else, they who used to rank below everybody else— that is what people mean by "upside down".

VANGUARD OF THE REVOLUTION

When there are two opposite approaches to a thing or a kind of people, there will be two opposite opinions. "An awful mess" and "very good indeed", "riffraff" and "vanguard of the revolution", are both suitable examples.

We have seen the peasants' accomplishment of a revolutionary task for many years left unaccomplished, and their important contributions to the national revolution. But have all the peasants taken part in accomplishing such a great revolutionary task and in making important contributions? No. The peasantry consist of three sections—the rich peasants, the middle peasants and the poor peasants. The circumstances of the three sections differ, and so do their reactions to the revolution. In the first period, what reached the ears of the rich peasants was that the Northern Expedition Army had met with a crushing defeat in Kiangsi, that Chiang Kai-shek had been wounded in the leg[6] and had flown back to Kwangtung,[7] and that Wu P'ei-fu[8] had recaptured Yochow. So they thought that the peasant association certainly could not last long and that the Three People's Principles[9] could never succeed, because such things were never heard of before. The officials of a township peasant association (generally of the so-called "riffraff" type), bringing the membership register and entering the house of a rich peasant, would say to him, "Please join the peasant association." How would the rich peasant answer? "Peasant association? For years I have lived here and tilled the fields; I have not seen anything like the peasant association but I get along all the same. You had better give it up!"—this from a moderate rich peasant. "What peasant association? Association for having one's head chopped off—don't get people into trouble!"—this from a violent rich peasant.

Strangely enough, the peasant association has now been established for several months, and has even dared to oppose the gentry. The gentry in the neighbourhood have been arrested by the association and paraded through the villages because they refused to surrender their opium-smoking kits. In the county towns, moreover, prominent members of the gentry have been put to death, such as Yen Yung-ch'iu of Siangtan and Yang Chih-tse of Ningsiang. At the meeting celebrating the anniversary of the October Revolution, the anti-British rally and the grand celebration of the victory of the Northern Expedition, at least ten thousand peasants in every county, carrying big and small banners, with poles and hoes thrown in, marched in demonstrations in great columns like rolling waves. When all this happened, the rich peasants began to feel perplexed. In the grand celebration of the victory of the Northern Expedition, they learnt that Kiu-kiang[10] had been taken, that Chiang Kai-shek had not been wounded in the leg and that Wu P'ei-fu had been finally defeated. Furthermore, "Long live the Three People's Principles!" "Long live the peasant association!" and "Long live the peasants!" were clearly written on the "decrees on red and green paper" (posters). "'Long live the peasants!' Are these people to be regarded as emperors?"[11] The rich peasants were greatly puzzled.

So the peasant association put on grand airs. People from the association said to the rich peasants, "We'll enter you in the special register", or, "In another month, the admission fee will be ten dollars!" It was only in these circumstances that the rich peasants tardily joined the peasant association,[12] some paying fifty cents or a dollar (the regular fee being only one hundred cash), others securing admission only after people had put in a good word for them at their request. There are also quite a number of die-hards who, even up to the present, have not joined the association. When the rich peasants join the association they generally enter the name of some old man of sixty or seventy of their family, for they are always afraid of "the drafting of the adult males".[13] After joining the association they never work for it enthusiastically. They remain inactive throughout.

How about the middle peasants? Their attitude is vacillating. They think that the revolution will not do them much good. They have rice in their pots and are not afraid of bailiffs knocking at their doors at midnight. They too, judging a thing by whether it ever existed before, knit their brows and think hard: "Can the peasant association really stand on its own feet?" "Can the Three People's Principles succeed?" Their conclusion is, "Afraid not". They think that all these things depend entirely on the will of Heaven; "To run a peasant association? Who knows if Heaven wills it or not?" In the first period, people from the peasant association, registers in hand, would enter the house of a middle peasant and say to him, "Please join the peasant association!" "No hurry!" replied the middle peasant. It was not until the second period, when the peasant association enjoyed great power, that the middle peasants joined up. In the association they behave better than the rich peasants, but are as yet not very active, and still want to wait and see. It is certainly necessary for the peasant association to explain a good deal more to the middle peasants in order to get them to join.

The main force in the countryside which has always put up the bitterest fight is the poor peasants. Throughout both the period of underground organisation and that of open organisation, the poor peasants have fought militantly all along. They accept most willingly the leadership of the Communist Party. They are the deadliest enemies of the local bullies and bad gentry and attack their strongholds without the slightest hesitation. They say to the rich peasants: "We joined the peasant association long ago, why do you still hesitate?" The rich peasants answer in a mocking tone, "You people have neither a tile over your head nor a pinpoint of land beneath your feet, what should have kept you from joining!" Indeed, the poor peasants are not afraid of losing anything. Many of them really have "neither a tile over their head nor a pinpoint of land beneath their feet"—what should have kept them from joining the association?

According to a survey of Changsha county, the poor peasants comprise 70 per cent of the rural population; the middle peasants, 20 per cent; and the rich peasants and landlords, 10 per cent. The poor peasants who comprise 70 per cent can be subdivided into two groups, the utterly impoverished[14] and the less impoverished. The completely dispossessed, *i.e.* those who have neither land nor money, and who, without any means of livelihood, are forced to leave home and become mercenary soldiers, or hired labourers, or tramp about as beggars—all belong to the "utterly impoverished" and comprise

20 per cent. The partly dispossessed, *i.e.* those who have
a little land or a little money, but consume more than they
receive and live in the midst of toil and worry all the year
round, *e.g.* the handicraftsmen, tenant-peasants (except the
rich tenant-peasants) and semi-tenant peasants—all belong
to the "less impoverished"[15] and comprise 50 per cent. This
enormous mass of poor peasants, altogether comprising 70 per
cent of the rural population, are the backbone of the peasant
association, the vanguard in overthrowing the feudal forces,
and the foremost heroes who have accomplished the great
revolutionary undertaking left unaccomplished for many years.
Without the poor peasants (the "riffraff" as the gentry call
them) it would never have been possible to bring about in the
countryside the present state of revolution, to overthrow the
local bullies and bad gentry, or to complete the democratic
revolution. Being the most revolutionary, the poor peasants
have won the leadership in the peasant association. Almost all
the posts of chairmen and committee members in the peasant
associations at the lowest level were held by poor peasants in
both the first and second periods (of the officials in the township
associations in Hangshan the utterly impoverished comprise
50 per cent, the less impoverished comprise 40 per cent, and
the impoverished intellectuals comprise 10 per cent). This
leadership of the poor peasants is absolutely necessary. Without
the poor peasants there can be no revolution. To reject them
is to reject the revolution. To attack them is to attack the
revolution. Their general direction of the revolution has never
been wrong.

They have hurt the dignity of the local bullies and bad
gentry. They have beaten the big and small local bullies and
bad gentry to the ground and trampled them underfoot. Many
of their deeds in the period of revolutionary action, described
as "going too far", were in fact the very needs of the revolution.
Some of the county governments, county headquarters of the
party[16] and county peasant associations in Hunan have committed a number of mistakes; there are even some which at the
request of the landlords sent soldiers to arrest the lower officials
of the peasant associations. Many chairmen and committeemen of the township associations are imprisoned in the jails

in Hengshan and Siangsiang. This is a serious mistake, which greatly encourages the arrogance of the reactionaries. To judge whether or not it is a mistake, one need only see how, as soon as the chairmen and committeemen of the peasant associations are arrested, the local lawless landlords are elated and reactionary sentiments grow. We must oppose such counter-revolutionary calumnies as "riffraff movement" and "movement of the lazy peasants" and must be especially careful not to commit the mistake of helping the local bullies and bad gentry to attack the poor peasants.

As a matter of fact, although some of the poor peasant leaders certainly had shortcomings in the past, most of them have reformed themselves by now. They are themselves energetically prohibiting gambling and exterminating banditry. Where the peasant association is powerful, gambling and banditry have vanished. In some places it is literally true that people do not pocket articles dropped on the road and that doors are not bolted at night. According to a survey of Hengshan, 85 per cent of the poor peasant leaders have now turned out to be quite reformed, capable and energetic. Only 15 per cent of them retain some bad habits. They can only be regarded as "the few undesirables", and we must not echo the local bullies and bad gentry in condemning indiscriminately everybody as "riffraff". To tackle this problem of "the few undesirables", we can only, on the basis of the association's slogan of strengthening discipline, carry on propaganda among the masses and educate the undesirables themselves, so that the discipline of the association may be strengthened; but we must not wantonly send soldiers to make arrests, lest we should undermine the prestige of the poor peasantry and encourage the arrogance of the local bullies and bad gentry. This is a point we must particularly attend to.

FOURTEEN GREAT DEEDS

People criticise the peasant association for having done many evil things. I have already pointed out that the peasants' attacks on the local bullies and bad gentry are perfectly revolutionary actions and are in no way open to criticism. But the peasants have done many things, and in order to answer people's criticisms we must closely examine all their activities one by one to find out what exactly they have done. After classifying and summarising their activities in the last few months, I found that they have, under the leadership of the peasant associations, performed the following fourteen great deeds.

I. ORGANISING THE PEASANTS INTO THE PEASANT ASSOCIATION

This is the first great deed performed by the peasants. In counties like Siangtan, Siangsiang and Hengshan, nearly all the peasants are organised—there are almost no peasants in any remote corner who have not risen—this is the first grade. In some counties, like Yiyang and Hwajung, the majority of the peasants is organised, while the minority remains unorganised—this is the second grade. In some counties, like Chengpu and Lingling, only a minority has been organised, while the majority remains unorganised—this is the third grade. In many counties in western Hunan, dominated by Yuan Tzu-ming,[17] the peasants remain completely unorganised because the propaganda of the peasant association has not reached them—this is the fourth grade. In general, the counties in central Hunan, with Changsha as the centre, are the most advanced; those in southern Hunan come second; while western Hunan is only beginning to get organised.

According to the provincial peasant association's statistical survey of last November, organisations were set up in thirty-seven out of the province's seventy-five counties, totalling a membership of 1,367,727. Of this number about one million were organised during last October and November when the power of the association flourished, while up to last September there were only 300,000–400,000. Another two months, December and January, have now elapsed, and the peasant movement continues its brisk growth. By the end of January the membership must have reached at least two million. As a family, which averages five persons, generally enters only one name, there should be a mass following of about ten million. Such an amazingly accelerating expansion is the reason why the local bullies and bad gentry as well as the corrupt officials have been isolated, why the general public has been astonished to see that the present world is so completely different from the past, and why a great revolution has come to pass in the countryside. This is the first great deed which the peasants have accomplished under the leadership of the peasant association.

2. DEALING POLITICAL BLOWS AGAINST THE LANDLORDS

After the peasants are organised, the first thing they do is to smash the political prestige and power of the landlord class, especially of the local bullies and bad gentry, *i.e.* to overthrow the power of the landlords so far as their social position in the countryside is concerned, and to foster the growth of the power of the peasants. This is a most serious and vital struggle. It is the central struggle in the second period, the period of revolutionary action. Without victory in this struggle, no victory will be possible in any economic struggle, such as the struggle for reducing rent and interest or for securing land and other means of production. In many places in Hunan, like Siangsiang, Hengshan and Siangtan, this of course no longer presents any problem, since the power of the landlords has been completely overthrown and the peasants have become the sole authority. But in counties like Liling there are still some places (like the western and southern districts of Liling) where, as the actual political struggle has not been intense, the landlords are surreptitiously opposing the peasants, though they seem to be less powerful than the latter. In such places it cannot yet be said that the peasants have won their political victory, and they must wage more vigorous political struggles until the power of the landlords is completely overthrown.

The peasants deal political blows to the landlords in the following ways.

Auditing of Accounts. Most of the local bullies and bad gentry are guilty of embezzling the public funds under their management and their accounts are not in order. Now the peasants have used the auditing of accounts as a lever to overthrow a great many local bullies and bad gentry. In many places auditing committees are set up for the specific purpose of settling with the local bullies and bad gentry, who shudder at the mere sight of the officers of such committees. Auditing campaigns like these have been carried out extensively in all counties where the peasant movement has risen, and their significance lies not so much in recovering the funds as in exposing the crimes of the local bullies and bad gentry and knocking them down from their political as well as social position.

Fining. Embezzlement exposed through auditing, past misdeeds of oppressing the peasants, present activities to undermine the peasant association, violation of the ban on gambling or refusal to surrender opium-smoking kits—on such charges the peasants resolve to fine this local bully so much or that representative of the bad gentry so much, and the sum may range from tens to thousands of dollars. Naturally, those who have been fined by the peasants lose face completely.

Contributions. Raising funds among the rich and brutal landlords for the relief of the poor, for the organisation of co-operatives and of rural credit agencies, or for other purposes. Such contributions are also a form of punishment, though milder than fines. There are also quite a number of landlords who, in order to avoid trouble, have made voluntary contributions to the peasant associations.

Minor protests. In case a person undermines the peasant association by word or deed, and his offence is a minor one, a large number of people rally together and swarm into his house to make a mild protest. As a result, he usually has to write a "cease-and-desist pledge", stating explicitly that henceforth he will stop defaming the peasant association by word or deed.

Major demonstrations. A big crowd is rallied to demonstrate against a local bully or one of the bad gentry who is hostile to the association. They take their meals at his house, slaughtering his pigs and consuming grain as a matter of course; quite a few such cases have occurred. Recently at Makiaho, Siangtan, a crowd of fifteen thousand paid such a punitive visit to six families of the bad gentry; they stayed four days and slaughtered more than 130 pigs. After such demonstrations, the peasants usually impose fines.

Parades through the villages in tall paper-hats. Such things have been staged many times in various places. The local bullies and bad gentry are crowned with tall paper-hats which bear legends like "Local bully so and so" or "So and so, one of the bad gentry". They are led on a rope and escorted by big crowds both in front of and behind them. Sometimes gongs are beaten and flags waved to attract attention. This form of punishment, more than any other, makes the local bullies and bad gentry shudder with fear. He who has once been crowned with the tall paper-hat loses face for ever and can never hold up his head again. Thus many of the wealthy would rather pay a fine than wear the tall paper-hat. But put it on they must, if the peasants insist. One township peasant association was very ingenious; it arrested an obnoxious member of the gentry and announced that he was to be crowned with the tall paper-hat that very day. He turned blue with fear. But then the association decided to put the whole thing off. For they argued that if he were crowned that day, he would become quickly resigned to his fate and would not be troubled any more with his guilt; it would be better to let him go home and crown him some other day. This man, not knowing when he would be made to put on the hat, stayed at home in daily suspense, fidgeting about and starting at every sound.

Imprisonment in the county jail. This is a heavier punishment than wearing the tall paper-hat. The local bullies and bad gentry are arrested and sent to the county jail to be locked up, and the county magistrate is asked to sentence them. The people sent to prison now are different from those in the past: formerly it was the gentry who sent the peasants to jail, and now it is the other way round.

Banishment. The peasants do not want to banish those among the local bullies and bad gentry who are notorious for their crimes and wrong-doing, but to arrest or kill them. Afraid of being arrested or killed, they run away. In the counties where the peasant movement is well developed almost all the prominent local bullies and bad gentry have fled, and consequently are as good as banished. Among them, those of the first rank have fled to Shanghai; the second, to Hankow; the third, to Changsha; and the fourth, to the county towns. Those who fled to Shanghai are the safest. Some of those who fled to Hankow,

like the three from Hwajung, were eventually captured and
brought back. Even those who fled to Changsha go in fear
of being apprehended at any moment by students in the
provincial capital who hail from the counties. I myself saw
two of them arrested when I was in Changsha. Those who fled
to the county towns are after all only in the fourth rank, and,
as the peasants have many sources of information, can be easily
tracked down. Once, when the Hunan Provincial Government
found itself in straitened circumstances, its financial authorities
laid the blame on the peasants for having banished the wealthy
people and so made it difficult to raise money; this again gives
us some idea of the way the local bullies and bad gentry are
no longer tolerated at home.

Shooting. This punishment was invariably meted out to the
most notorious of the local bullies and bad gentry on the
demand of the peasants together with the people generally.
For example, Yang Chih-tse of Ningsiang, Chou Chia-kan of
Yoyang, and Fu Tao-nan and Sun Po-chu of Hwajung were
shot by the government at the insistence of the peasants and
the people generally. The peasants shot Yen Yung-ch'iu of
Siangtan on their own responsibility after they and the general
public had compelled the magistrate to agree to taking him
out of prison. Liu Chao of Ningsiang was killed by the peasants
themselves. P'eng Chih-fan of Liling and Chou T'ien-chueh
and Ts'ao Yun of Yiyang will be executed pending the decision
of the "special court for local bullies and bad gentry". The
execution of one of such notorious local bullies and bad gentry
has its repercussions throughout the whole county, and is very
effective in eradicating the remaining evils of feudalism. Scores
or at least a few of such notorious local bullies and bad gentry
are to be found in every county, and the only effective way of
suppressing the reactionaries is to execute in every county at
least those of them whose crimes and wrong-doing are most
serious. When the local bullies and bad gentry were at the
height of their power, they themselves killed peasants without
batting an eyelid. Ho Mai-ch'uan, head of the defence corps of
the town of Sinkang, Changsha county, was in charge of the
corps for ten years; the poor peasants who died at his hands
numbered almost a thousand, and this he euphemistically

described as "execution of bandits". T'ang Chun-yen and Lo Shu-lin, heads of the defence corps of the town of Yintien in my native county, Siangtan, killed more than fifty and buried four alive in fourteen years since 1913. Of the more than fifty they murdered, the first two were perfectly innocent beggars. T'ang said, "Let me kill two beggars to start the business!" and alas! two poor wretches lost their lives. Such being the atrocities of the local bullies and bad gentry as well as the White terror created by them in the rural areas, how can one say that the peasants should not now rise and shoot a handful of them and create a little terror in suppressing the counter-revolutionaries?

3. DEALING ECONOMIC BLOWS AGAINST THE LANDLORDS

Bans on sending grain out of the area, on forcing up the price of grain, and on hoarding and speculation. This is a great event in the economic struggle of the Hunan peasants in recent months. From last October up to the present, the poor peasants have prevented the outflow of the grain of the landlords and rich peasants and have placed a ban on forcing up the price of grain and on hoarding and speculation. As a result, the poor peasants have achieved their objectives completely: the ban on the outflow of grain is watertight, grain prices have fallen and hoarding and speculation have disappeared.

Ban on increasing rents and deposits;[18] *propaganda for reducing rents and deposits.* In July and August last year when the peasant association was still weak, the landlords, in accordance with their old idea that exploitation cannot be too heavy, one after another notified their tenant-peasants of an increase in rent and deposit. By October, however, with the tremendous growth in the power of the association, the peasants rose unanimously in protest and the landlords were so scared they dropped the matter. Since November last year, the peasants, having grown stronger than the landlords, have gone a step farther to agitate for reductions in rents and deposits. What a pity, they say, that the peasant association was not strong enough when the rent was being paid last autumn, otherwise it would have been reduced then. The peasants are carrying out a big campaign to have rent reduced this autumn, and the landlords are trying to ascertain how the reductions will be carried out. Reduction in deposit is under way in Hengshan and other counties.

Ban on cancelling leases. In July and August last year there were still many cases of leases being cancelled and farms re-let by the landlords. After October nobody dared cancel the leases any more. Now cancelling leases and re-letting farms are out of the question; the only problem that remains to some extent unsettled is whether a lease can be cancelled if the landlord wants to cultivate the land himself. In certain places even this is not allowed by the peasants. In other places, while this is permissible, there arises the problem of the tenant-peasants becoming unemployed. No uniform settlement has yet been found for this problem.

Reduction of interest. Interest has generally been reduced in Anhwa, and similar reductions are being effected in other counties. But wherever the peasant association is powerful, moneylending has virtually disappeared from the countryside, as the landlords have completely "stopped lending" for fear of "socialisation of property". What is called reduction of interest is at present confined to old loans. Not only is the interest on old loans reduced, but the creditor is even forbidden to press for the repayment of the principal. The poor peasant would say, "Don't blame it on me. It's too old an affair and I'll pay it next year!"

4. OVERTHROWING THE FEUDAL RULE OF THE LOCAL BULLIES AND BAD GENTRY—THE *TU* AND *T'UAN*

The old *tu* and *t'uan* (*i.e.* the districts and township) organs of political power, especially those at the *tu* level which is next to the county level, used to be almost entirely in the hands of the local bullies and bad gentry. The *tu* had under its jurisdiction a population of from ten to fifty or sixty thousand, an independent armed force, namely, the defence corps, independent power in fiscal collection which included the acreage levy,[19] and independent judicial power which included arrest, imprisonment, trial and punishment of the peasants at its own discretion. The bad gentry in such a body were virtually kings in the countryside. The peasants paid comparatively little heed to the president, the military governor[20] or the county magistrate, for their real "chiefs" were these kings in the countryside; when these men hummed through their noses, the peasants knew that they must watch their step. As a consequence of the present revolt in the countryside, the power and prestige of the landlord class has been largely overthrown, and such organs of rural administration dominated by the local bullies and bad gentry have naturally collapsed. The chiefs of the *tu*'s and *t'uan*'s all steer clear of the people now and dare not face them. They refer all local matters to the peasant association, and put people off with the remark, "It's none of my business".

Whenever their conversation touches on the chiefs of the *tu*'s and *t'uan*'s the peasants say indignantly, "That bunch! They are down and out now!"

The phrase "down and out" certainly describes the fate of the old organs of rural administration in places over which the tempest of revolution has swept.

5. OVERTHROWING THE LANDLORDS' ARMED FORCES AND BUILDING UP THE PEASANTS' ARMED FORCES

The armed forces of the landlord class in Hunan were smaller in the central part of the province than in its western and southern parts. With an average of 600 rifles in each county, there are altogether 45,000 rifles in seventy-five counties, and there may, in fact, be even more. In the southern and central parts where the peasant movement is most developed, *e.g.* in the counties of Ningsiang, Pingkiang, Liuyang, Changsha, Liling, Siangtan, Siangsiang, Anhwa, Hengshan and Hengyang, because the peasants have risen with tremendous momentum, the landlords cannot hold their own and their armed forces have largely capitulated to the peasant association and are now upholding the interests of the peasants. A small number of the landlords' armed forces, *e.g.* in counties like Paoking, are taking a neutral stand but are inclined to capitulate. Another small section of them, *e.g.* in the counties of Ichang, Linwu and Kiaho, are opposing the peasant associations, but the peasants are now dealing out blows to them and may before long wipe them out. The armed forces thus taken over from the reactionary landlords will all be reorganised into the house-to-house regular militia[21] and placed under the new organs of rural self-government—organs of rural self-government under the political power of the peasantry. Taking over these old armed forces is one way in which peasants' armed forces are being built up.

There is also another means by which armed forces are being built up, namely, the "spear corps" of the peasant association. Such spears—a weapon with a pointed, double-edged blade mounted on a long shaft—number 100,000 in the county of Siangsiang alone. Other counties like Saingtan, Hengshan, Liling and Changsha have each 70,000–80,000 or 50,000–60,000, or 30,000–40,000 spears. In all counties where the peasant movement is afoot, the spear corps is growing rapidly. These peasants armed with spears form the house-to-house emergency militia. This vast force of spears is larger than the old armed forces mentioned above and is an armed force freshly formed, at the sight of which the local bullies and bad gentry tremble with fear. The revolutionary authorities in Hunan should see to it that such armed forces are built up on a really large scale among the more than twenty million peasants in the seventy-five counties—that every peasant, whether young or in his prime, possesses a spear, and that no restriction is placed on possessing one, as though that were something dreadful. Anyone who is afraid of such spear corps is a coward indeed! Only the local bullies and bad gentry are afraid of them, revolutionaries should not be.

6. OVERTHROWING THE POLITICAL POWER OF HIS EXCELLENCY THE COUNTY MAGISTRATE AND HIS BAILIFFS

That the county government cannot become clean until the peasants have risen was proved some time ago in Haifeng, Kwangtung. Now we have sufficient proof of this, particularly in Hunan. In a county dominated by the local bullies and bad gentry, the magistrate, no matter who he is, almost without exception turns out to be a corrupt official. In a county where the peasants have risen there is clean government, no matter who is in charge. In the counties I visited the magistrates have to consult the peasant association on everything. In a county where the power of the peasants is at its height, the word of the peasant association "works instant miracles". If the peasant association demands the arrest of a local bully or one of the bad gentry in the morning, the magistrate dares not delay it till noon; if it demands the arrest by noon, he dares not postpone it till the afternoon.

When the power of the peasants was just beginning to grow in the countryside, the magistrate and the local bullies and bad gentry collaborated to deal with the peasants. When the peasants' power rose and became equal to that of the landlords, the magistrate tried to ingratiate himself with both the land-lords and the peasants, accepting some of the peasant associa-tion's suggestions while rejecting others. The above remark that the word of the peasant association "works instant miracles" holds true only after the power of the landlords is completely overthrown by that of the peasants. At present the govern-mental situation in counties like Siangsiang, Siangtan, Liling and Hengshan is as follows:

(1) *Everything is decided by the joint council of the magistrate and the revolutionary mass organisations.* The council is convened by the magistrate and held at his office. It is called in some counties the "joint council of the public organisations and government bodies", and in others the "council of county affairs". The people who attend it are, besides the magistrate himself, the representatives of the county peasant association, the county trade union council, the county chamber of commerce, the county women's association, the county school teachers' and staff members' association, the county student association and the county headquarters of the Kuomintang.[22] What influ-ences the magistrate at such a council meeting is the opinion of the mass organisations, and he invariably does what he is told. Therefore, the adoption in Hunan of the democratic committee system for the county government organisation should not present much of a problem. The present county governments are already quite democratic both in form and in substance. And this situation has been brought about only in

the last two or three months, that is, after the peasants had risen all over the countryside and overthrown the power of the local bullies and bad gentry. The magistrates, seeing that their old stand-bys had fallen and that they could not retain their posts without new stand-bys, began to curry favour with the mass organisations; hence the situation as described.

(2) *The judicial assistant has scarcely any cases to handle.* The judicial system in Hunan remains one in which the county magistrate is concurrently in charge of judicial affairs with a judicial assistant helping him during trials. To become rich, the magistrate and his underlings relied entirely on collecting taxes and levies, on procuring men and provisions for the troops, and on extorting money in civil and criminal lawsuits by confounding right and wrong, the last being the most regular and reliable source of their income. In the last few months, with the downfall of the local bullies and bad gentry, all pettifogging lawyers have disappeared. Moreover the peasants' problems, big and small, are all settled in the peasant associations at various levels. Thus the judicial assistant in the county government simply has nothing to do. The judicial assistant in Siangsiang told me, "When there was no peasant association, the county government received on the average sixty petitions a day for civil and criminal suits; since it appeared, the county government has received only an average of four or five a day." Thus the purses of the magistrate and his underlings cannot but remain empty.

(3) *The armed guards, the policemen and the magistrate's bailiffs all watch their step and dare not go to the countryside to practise rackets and extortions.* In the past people in the countryside were afraid of the city people; now the city people are afraid of the people in the countryside. In particular, the fierce jackals kept by the county government—the policemen, the armed guards and the bailiffs—are afraid of going to the countryside, and when they do go there, they no longer dare practise their rackets and extortions. They all tremble at the sight of the peasants' spears.

7. OVERTHROWING THE CLAN AUTHORITY OF THE ELDERS AND
ANCESTRAL TEMPLES, THE THEOCRATIC AUTHORITY OF THE CITY
GODS AND LOCAL DEITIES, AND THE MASCULINE AUTHORITY OF
THE HUSBANDS

A man in China is usually subjected to the domination of
three systems of authority: (1) the system of the state (political
authority), ranging from the national, provincial and county
government to the township government; (2) the system of the
clan (clan authority), ranging from the central and branch
ancestral temples to the head of the household; and (3) the
system of gods and spirits (theocratic authority), including the
system of the nether world ranging from the King of Hell to
the city gods and local deities, and that of supernatural beings
ranging from the Emperor of Heaven to all kinds of gods and
spirits. As to women, apart from being dominated by the three
systems mentioned above, they are further dominated by men
(the authority of the husband). These four kinds of authority—
political authority, clan authority, theocratic authority and the
authority of the husband—represent the whole ideology and
institution of feudalism and patriarchy, and are the four great
cords that have bound the Chinese people and particularly the
peasants. We have already seen how the peasants are overthrowing the political authority of the landlords in the countryside. The political authority of the landlords is the backbone
of all other systems of authority. Where it has already been
overthrown, clan authority, theocratic authority and the
authority of the husband are all beginning to totter. Where the
peasant association is powerful, the clan elders and administrators of temple funds no longer dare oppress members of the clan
or embezzle the funds. The bad clan elders and administrators
have been overthrown as local bullies and bad gentry. No
ancestral temple dare any longer, as it used to do, inflict cruel
corporal and capital punishments like "beating", "drowning",
and "burying alive". The old rule that forbids women and
poor people to attend banquets in the ancestral temple has also
been broken. On one occasion the women of Paikwo, Hengshan, marched into their ancestral temple, sat down on the
seats and ate and drank, while the grand patriarchs could only

look on. At another place the poor peasants, not admitted to the banquets in the temples, swarmed in and ate and drank their fill, while the frightened local bullies, bad gentry and gentlemen in long gowns all took to their heels.

Theocratic authority begins to totter everywhere as the peasant movement develops. In many places the peasant associations have taken over the temples of the gods as their offices. Everywhere they advocate the appropriation of temple properties to maintain peasant schools and to defray association expenses, calling this "public revenue from superstition". Forbidding superstition and smashing idols has become quite the vogue in Liling. In its northern districts the peasants forbade the festival processions in honour of the god of pestilence. There were many idols in the Taoist temple on Fupo hill, Lukow, but they were all piled up in a corner to make room for the district headquarters of the Kuomintang, and no peasant raised any objection. When a death occurs in a family, such practices as sacrifice to the gods, performance of Taoist or Buddhist rites, and offering of sacred lamps are becoming rare. It was Sun Hsiao-shan, the Chairman of the peasant association, who proposed all this, so the local Taoist priests bear him quite a grudge. In the Lungfeng Nunnery in the North Third district, the peasants and school teachers chopped up the wooden idols to cook meat. More than thirty idols in the Tungfu Temple in the South district were burnt by the students together with the peasants; only two small idols, generally known as "His Excellency Pao",[23] were rescued by an old peasant who said, "Don't commit a sin!" In places where the power of the peasants is predominant, only the older peasants and the women still believe in gods, while the young and middle-aged peasants no longer do so. Since it is the young and middle-aged peasants who are in control of the peasant association, the movement to overthrow theocratic authority and eradicate superstition is going on everywhere.

As to the authority of the husband, it has always been comparatively weak among the poor peasants, because the poor peasant women, compelled for financial reasons to take more part in manual work than women of the wealthier classes, have obtained more right to speak and more power to make decisions in family affairs. In recent years rural economy has become even more bankrupt and the basic condition for men's domination over women has already been undermined. And now, with the rise of the peasant movement, women in many places have set out immediately to organise the rural women's association; the opportunity has come for them to lift up their heads, and the authority of the husband is tottering more and more every day. In a word, all feudal and patriarchal ideologies and institutions are tottering as the power of the peasants rises. In the present period, however, the peasants' efforts are concentrated on the destruction of the landlords' political authority. Where the political authority of the landlords is already completely destroyed, the peasants are beginning their attacks in the other three spheres, namely, the clan, the gods and the relationship between men and women. At present, however, such attacks have only just "begun" and there can be no complete overthrow of the three until after the complete victory of the peasants' economic struggle. Hence at present our task is to guide the peasants to wage political struggles with their utmost strength, so that the authority of the landlords may be thoroughly uprooted. An economic struggle should also be started immediately in order that the land problem and other economic problems of the poor peasants can be completely solved.

The abolition of the clan system, of superstitions and of inequality between men and women will follow as a natural consequence of victory in political and economic struggles. If we crudely and arbitrarily devote excessive efforts to the abolition of such things, we shall give the local bullies and bad gentry a pretext for undermining the peasant movement by raising such slogans of counter-revolutionary propaganda as "The peasant association does not show piety towards ancestors", "The peasant association abuses the gods and destroys religion" and "The peasant association advocates the community of women". Clear proof has been forthcoming recently at both Siangsiang in Hunan and Yangsin in Hupeh, where the landlords were able to take advantage of peasant opposition to the smashing of idols. The idols were set up by the peasants, and in time they will pull them down with their own hands;

there is no need for anybody else prematurely to pull down the idols for them. The agitational line of the Communist Party in such matters should be: "Draw the bow to the full without letting go the arrow, and be on the alert."[24] The idols should be removed by the peasants themselves, and the temples for martyred virgins and the arches for chaste and filial widowed daughters-in-law should likewise be demolished by the peasants themselves; it is wrong for anyone else to do these things for them.

In the countryside I, too, agitated among the peasants for abolishing superstitions. What I said was:

"One who believes in the Eight Characters[25] hopes for good luck; one who believes in geomancy hopes for the beneficial influence of the burial ground.[26] This year the local bullies, bad gentry and corrupt officials all collapsed within a few months. Is it possible that till a few months ago they were all in good luck and all under the beneficial influence of their burial grounds, while in the last few months they have all of a sudden been in bad luck and their burial grounds all ceased to exert any beneficial influence on them?

"The local bullies and bad gentry jeer at your peasant association, and say: 'How strange! It has become a world of committeemen; look, you can't even go to the latrines without meeting one of them!' Quite true, in the towns and in the villages, the trade unions, the peasant association, the Kuomintang and the Communist Party all have their committee members—it is indeed a world of committeemen. But is this due to the Eight Characters and the burial grounds? What a strange thing! The Eight Characters of all the poor wretches in the countryside have suddenly changed for the better! And their burial grounds have suddenly started to exert a beneficial influence!

"The gods? They may quite deserve our worship. But if we had no peasant association but only the Emperor Kuan[27] and the Goddess of Mercy, could we have knocked down the local bullies and bad gentry? The gods and goddesses are indeed pitiful; worshipped for hundreds of years, they have not knocked down for you a single local bully or a single one of the bad gentry!

"Now you want to have your rent reduced. I would like to ask: How will you go about it? Believe in the gods, or believe in the peasant association?"

These words of mine made the peasants roar with laughter.

8. EXTENDING POLITICAL AGITATION

If ten thousand schools of law and political science had been opened, could they have achieved in such a short time so much political education among men and women, young and old, all the way into the remote corners of the country, as the peasant associations have now done? I think not. "Down with imperialism!" "Down with the warlords!" "Down with the corrupt officials!" and "Down with the local bullies and bad gentry!"—these political slogans are flying about everywhere, entering into the heads of adults, youngsters, old men, children and women in countless villages, and coming out from their mouths. If a group of children is at play and if you see one of them get angry at another, opening his eyes wide, stamping his foot and shaking his fist, you will instantly hear the shrill cry, "Down with imperialism!"

In Siangtan, when two children pasturing cattle stage a fight, one will act as T'ang Sheng-chih and the other as Yeh K'ai-hsin;[28] after a while one will be defeated and the other pursue him, the pursuer being T'ang Sheng-chih and the pursued, Yeh K'ai-hsin. Of course, almost every child in the towns can sing the song, "Down with the Imperialist Powers", but now many children in the villages can sing it.

Some of the peasants in the countryside can even read the Testament of Dr. Sun Yat-sen. They pick up from it terms like "freedom", "equality", "the Three People's Principles" and "unequal treaties" and apply them rather crudely in their daily life. When a peasant meets a gentry-like person on a path who for prestige's sake will not make way, he will say angrily, "Hey, you local bully, you bad landlord, don't you know the Three People's Principles?" The peasants from the suburbs of Changsha used to be harried by the police when entering the city to sell vegetables. But now the peasants have got a weapon—the Three People's Principles. Whenever a

4

policeman strikes or swears at a peasant selling vegetables, the peasant will silence him by invoking the Three People's Principles. Once in Siangtan there was a dispute between a district peasant association and a township peasant association, and the chairman of the township association declared, "Oppose the unequal treaties imposed by the district peasant association!"

The extension of political agitation throughout the rural areas is entirely an achievement of the Communist Party and the peasant association. Simple slogans, cartoons and speeches have achieved unusually great and quick results, exercising such an influence on the peasants that every one of them seems to have attended a political school for some time. Comrades engaged in rural work report that political agitation has been extensively carried out in the course of three great mass rallies, namely, the anti-British demonstrations, the anniversary celebrations of the October Revolution and the grand celebrations of the victory of the Northern Expedition. On such occasions, wherever peasant associations existed, political agitation was extensively carried out and the whole countryside was aroused; the effect was tremendous. From now on we should utilise every opportunity gradually to enrich the content and clarify the meaning of those simple slogans.

9. THE PEASANTS' PROHIBITIONS

When, under Communist leadership, the peasant association has established its authority in the countryside, the peasants begin to place prohibitions or restrictions on things they dislike. The most strictly prohibited are three things: gambling games, professional gambling and opium-smoking.

Gambling games: In places where the peasant association is powerful, mahjong, dominoes and card games are completely banned. The peasant association in the Fourteenth district of Siangsiang burnt two basketfuls of mahjong sets.

If you go to the countryside, you will find none of these games being played; he who violates the ban is immediately punished without the least leniency.

Professional gambling: People who were once "gamblers" are now themselves suppressing professional gambling; it has disappeared together with gambling games in places where the peasant association is powerful.

Opium-smoking: Very strictly prohibited. When the peasant association ordered the surrender of opium pipes no one dared raise the least objection. In Liling one of the bad gentry did not surrender his pipes and was arrested and paraded through the villages.

This movement for "disarming the opium-smokers of their 'guns'" compares favourably in its impressiveness with the disarming of the troops of Wu P'ei-fu and Sun Ch'uan-fang[29] by the Northern Expedition Army. Quite a few venerable fathers in the families of the officers of the revolutionary army, so addicted to opium-smoking that they depended on the "gun" for their very life, were all disarmed by the "emperors"[30] (as the peasants are called derisively by the bad gentry). The "emperors" have not only prohibited the growing and smoking of opium, but also its traffic. Large quantities of opium which were being transported from Kweichow to Kiangsi via the counties of Paoking, Siangsiang, Yu and Liling were intercepted on the way and burnt. This affected the government finance. Finally the provincial peasant association, out of consideration for military expenditure in the Northern Expedition, ordered the peasant associations at the lower levels "to postpone temporarily the ban on opium traffic". This, however, upset and displeased the peasants.

Besides these three, there are many other things the peasants have prohibited or restricted, among which are the following:

The flower drum. A minor theatrical entertainment forbidden in many places.

Sedan-chairs. In many counties, and especially in Siangsiang, there have been cases of smashing sedan-chairs. The peasants, heartily detesting the people sitting in the chairs, are always anxious to smash them, but the peasant association has forbidden them to do so. The officials of the peasant association say to the peasants: "If you smash the chairs, you only save the rich money, and the carriers will lose their jobs; isn't that just hurting our own people?" The peasants, having thought the matter over and seen the point, have worked out a new tactic—

to increase considerably the charges of the sedan-chair bearers as a penalty for the rich people.

Wine-making and sugar-refining. The use of rice for making wine and refining sugar is prohibited everywhere and consequently the wine-makers and sugar-refiners have made endless complaints. Wine-making is not banned in Futienpu, Hengshan, but the price of wine is fixed very low; the vintners, deprived of any profit, have had to stop making wine.

Pigs. The number of pigs a family can keep is limited, for pigs consume grain.

Chickens and ducks. In Siangsiang the raising of chickens and ducks is prohibited, but the women object to this prohibition. In Hengshan county, each family is allowed to keep only three fowls at Yangstang and five at Futienpu. In many places the raising of ducks is completely banned, for ducks, which not only consume grain but also ruin the rice plants, are of even less use than chickens.

Feasts. Sumptuous feasts are generally forbidden. In Shaoshan, Siangtan, it has been decided that only three kinds of animal food, namely, chicken, fish and pork, are to be served to guests. It is forbidden to serve bamboo shoots, seaweeds and lentil noodles. In Hengshan it was resolved that only eight dishes can be served,[31] not a single one more. Only five dishes are allowed in the East Third district in Liling, and only three meat and three vegetable dishes in the North Second district, while new-year feasts are forbidden in the West Third district. In Siangsiang, there is a ban on the "sponge-cake feast", which is by no means sumptuous. When a family in the Second district of Siangsiang gave it at a son's wedding, the peasants, considering the host to have violated the prohibition, swarmed into the house and smashed up the feast. In the town of Kiamo, Siangsiang, the people have decided to give up all delicacies and use only fruit when sacrificing to their ancestors.

Draught-oxen. They are a treasure to the peasants. As it is practically a religious tenet that "those who slaughter cattle in this life will become cattle themselves in the next", draughtoxen must never be killed. Before rising to power, the peasants had no means of stopping the slaughter of cattle except the religious taboo. Since the rise of the peasant association they have extended their jurisdiction even over the cattle and have prohibited their slaughter in the cities. Of the six butchers' shops in the county town of Siangtan, five are now closed, and the remaining one sells only the meat of sick or disabled cattle. Cattle-slaughter is prohibited throughout the county of Hengshan. A peasant whose cow stumbled and broke a leg had to consult the peasant association before he dared to kill it. When the Chamber of Commerce of Chu-chow rashly slaughtered a cow, the peasants went to the town to protest and the Chamber, besides paying a fine, had to let off firecrackers by way of apology.

Vagabondage. A resolution has been passed in Liling prohibiting such things as chanting New Year greetings to the accompaniment of castanets, praising the local deities and singing lotus rhymes.[32] In various other counties they have either been prohibited or have disappeared, simply because nobody cares to practise them any more. There are a number of "beggar-bullies" or "vagabonds" who used to be extremely aggressive, but now they have no alternative but to bow to the peasant association. Dare-devil vagabonds who had made a haunt of the temple of the Rain God at Shaoshan, Siangtan, left quietly after the rise of the peasant association. The peasant association in Huti township in the same county caught three such vagabonds and made them carry clay for the brick kilns. A resolution has been passed prohibiting the foolish custom of paying New Year calls.

Besides the above-mentioned, many other minor prohibitions have been introduced in various places, such as the prohibition in Liling of festival processions in honour of the god of pestilence, of buying pastry and fruit for ritual presents, of burning paper clothing during the Festival of Spirits,[33] and of pasting up posters for good luck in the New Year. In Kushi of Siangsiang, there are prohibitions on smoking water-pipes. In the Second district, letting off firecrackers and firing shotguns are forbidden; those who let off firecrackers are fined $1.20 and those who fire shotguns, $2.40. In the Seventh and Twentieth districts Taoist or Buddhist services for the dead are prohibited. And in the Eighteenth district, gifts of money offered at funerals are

forbidden. Things like these are too many to enumerate and
may be generally called the peasants' prohibitions.

These prohibitions are of great significance in two respects:
First, they represent a revolt against bad social customs, such
as gambling games, professional gambling and opium-smoking.
These customs arose together with the corrupt régime of the
landlord class; once the landlords' authority is overthrown,
these things are also swept away in its wake. Secondly, they
are a form of peasants' self-protection against exploitation by
the city merchants, e.g. the prohibition of sumptuous feasts and
of pastry and fruit for ritual presents. As the prices of industrial goods are extremely high and those of farm produce
extremely low, the peasants are impoverished by the ruthless
exploitation of the merchants; thus they have to cultivate
frugality as a means of self-protection. As to the peasants' ban
on sending grain outside the area, this was imposed because
the poor peasants, not having enough grain to feed themselves,
had to buy grain on the market and consequently to prevent
the price from going up. All these things are due to the
impoverishment of the peasants and the contradictions between
town and country; the peasants are certainly not practising the
so-called doctrine of Oriental Culture[34] by rejecting industrial
goods or trade between town and country. To protect themselves economically, the peasants should organise co-operatives
for collective purchasing as consumers. Furthermore, the
government should give aid to the peasant association so that
it can establish credit (loan) co-operatives. After that, the
peasants would naturally find it unnecessary to place an
embargo on the outflow of grain as a means of keeping down
its price, nor would they, as a means of economic self-protection,
resort to the prohibition of the entry of certain industrial goods
to the countryside.

10. ELIMINATING BANDITRY

From Yu, T'ang, Wen and Wu[35] down to the Manchu
emperors and the presidents of the Republic, no ruler in any
dynasty, I think, has shown such prowess in eliminating banditry as the peasant association today. In places where the

peasant association is powerful, not a trace will be found of bandits of any kind. It is indeed remarkable that in certain places even the petty pilferers of vegetables have vanished. In others, pilferers can still be found. But there was not a trace of banditry in the counties I visited, not even in places formerly bandit-ridden. The reasons are:

First, the members of the peasant association are scattered all over the hills and dales; spears or cudgels in hand, hundreds will go into action when one gives the alarm, and the bandits can find no hiding-place.

Secondly, since the rise of the peasant movement the price of grain has dropped—it was six dollars a picul last spring, but only two dollars last winter—and the problem of food becomes less serious to the people than before.

Thirdly, members of the secret societies have joined the peasant association, in which they can openly and legally play the hero and vent their grievances, and there is no further need for the existence of such secret "mountain", "hall", "shrine" and "river" organisations.[36] Killing the pigs and sheep of the local bullies and bad gentry and imposing on them heavy levies and fines, they have found an adequate outlet for their resentment against their erstwhile oppressors.

Fourthly, the armies are recruiting large numbers of soldiers and many of the "unruly fellows" have joined up.

Thus the evil of banditry has come to an end with the rise of the peasant movement. In this respect, even the gentry and the rich approve of the peasant association. Their comment is: "The peasant association? Well, upon my word, I must say that it has some good points too."

In prohibiting gambling games, professional gambling and opium-smoking, and in eliminating banditry, the peasant association has won the approval of the general public.

11. ABOLISHING EXORBITANT LEVIES

As the whole country is not yet unified and the power of imperialism and the warlords is not yet overthrown, it is still impossible to remove the heavy burden of government taxes and levies on the peasants or, to put it more explicitly, the burden of military expenditures of the revolutionary army. However, with the rise of the peasant movement and the downfall of the local bullies and bad gentry, the exorbitant levies imposed on the peasants when the local bullies and bad gentry dominated the rural administration, *e.g.* the acreage levy, have been abolished or at least reduced. This should be counted also among the achievements of the peasant association.

12. CULTURAL MOVEMENT

In China culture has always been the exclusive possession of the landlords, and the peasants had no access to it. But the culture of the landlords is created by the peasants, for its source is nothing else than the peasants' sweat and blood. In China 90 per cent of the people have no culture or education, and of these the majority are peasants.

With the downfall of the power of the landlords in the rural areas, the peasants' cultural movement has begun. And so the peasants, who hitherto bitterly hated the schools, are now zealously organising evening classes. The "foreign-style schools" were always unpopular with the peasants. In my student days I used to stand up for the "foreign-style schools" when, upon returning to my native place, I found the peasants objecting to them. I was myself identified with the "foreign-style students" and "foreign-style teachers", and always felt that the peasants were somehow wrong. It was during my six months in the countryside in 1925, when I was already a Communist and had adopted the Marxist viewpoint, that I realised I was mistaken and that the peasants' views were right. The teaching materials used in the rural primary schools all dealt with city matters and were in no way adapted to the needs of the rural areas. Besides, the primary school teachers behaved badly towards the peasants, who, far from finding them helpful, grew to dislike them. As a result, the peasants wanted old-style rather than modern schools—"Chinese classes", as they call them, rather than "foreign classes"—and they preferred the masters of the old-style school to the teachers in the primary schools.

Now the peasants are energetically organising evening classes, which they call peasant schools. Many such schools have been opened and others are being established; on the average there is one school to every township. The peasants are very enthusiastic about establishing such schools, and regard only such schools as their own. The funds for evening classes come from the "public revenue from superstitious practices", the funds of ancestral temples and other kinds of public funds or public property that have been lying idle. The county education boards wanted to use these public funds for establishing primary schools, that is, "foreign-style schools" not adapted to the needs of the peasants, while the peasants wanted to use them for peasant schools; as a result of the dispute, both sides got part of the funds, though in certain places the peasants got the whole. As a result of the growth of the peasant movement, the cultural level of the peasants has risen rapidly. Before long there will be tens of thousands of schools sprouting up in the rural areas throughout the whole province, and that will be something quite different from the futile clamour of the intelligentsia and so-called "educators" for "popular education", which for all their hullabaloo has remained an idle phrase.

13. THE CO-OPERATIVE MOVEMENT

Co-operatives, especially consumers', marketing and credit co-operatives, are certainly what the peasants need. Exploited by the merchants when buying goods, getting the worst of the bargain when selling their farm produce, and subject to extortion by usurers when borrowing money or grain, the peasants are demanding an immediate solution for these three problems. During the fighting last winter in the Yangtze valley, when the trade route was cut off and the price of salt was forced up in Hunan, many of the peasants organised co-operatives to purchase salt. And now that the landlords have "stopped lending", the peasants in various places have also attempted to organise credit agencies for obtaining loans. The major problem is the absence of detailed and proper rules of organisation. As the co-operatives organised by the peasants themselves in various places often fail to conform to the principles of co-operation, the comrades working among the peasants are always inquiring eagerly about "rules of organisation". If there is proper guidance, the co-operative movement will develop everywhere, along with the expansion of the peasant association.

14. BUILDING ROADS AND EMBANKMENTS

This is also an achievement of the peasant associations. Before the peasant association, the country roads were exceedingly bad. Roads cannot be repaired without money, and as the wealthy were unwilling to contribute money, the roads could only be left to deteriorate. Minor repairs, if any, were regarded as works of charity: a little money was collected from those families "willing to gain merit in the other world" and a few narrow, thinly paved roads were built. Since the peasant association arose it has issued directives specifying such grades of width—three, five, seven or ten *ch'ih*[37]—as may suit the requirements of the road, and has ordered the landlords living along the roads to repair a section each. Once an order is given, who dares disobey? In a short time many good roads have appeared. This is no work of charity but the result of compulsion, yet a little compulsion of this kind is, after all, quite justified.

The same is true of the embankments. The heartless landlords always tried to get everything out of the tenant-peasants, but grudged a few coppers to repair the embankments; they would let the ponds dry up and the tenant-peasants starve, caring about nothing but the collection of land rent. Now that the peasant association exists, orders can be bluntly given to compel the landlords to repair the embankments. When the landlords refuse to do this, the people from the peasant association will say gently to them, "Very well! If you don't see to the repairs, you can contribute grain. A *tou*[38] a day for each worker." As the landlords think that a bad bargain, they hasten to carry out the repairs themselves. Consequently many embankments in bad condition have been turned into solid constructions.

All the fourteen deeds enumerated above have been accomplished by the peasants under the leadership of the peasant associations. Considering the general spirit in which they have been carried out and the revolutionary significance they possess, I would ask the reader to think them over and say which of them is bad? I think that only the local bullies and bad gentry will say that they are bad. Curiously enough, it is reported from Nanchang[39] that in the opinion of Mr. Chiang Kai-shek, Mr. Chang Ching-chiang[40] and others, the activities of the peasants in Hunan are rather to be disapproved. The opinion of Mr. Chiang and Mr. Chang is shared by Liu Yo-chih[41] and other leaders of the right wing in Hunan, who say, "This is simply going Red". But where would the national revolution be without this little bit of Red? If one shouts every day about "arousing the masses of the people", but is scared to death when the people do rise, what is the difference between that and Lord Sheh's love of dragons?[42]

March 1927.

PERIOD
OF THE SECOND
REVOLUTIONARY CIVIL WAR

WHY CAN CHINA'S RED POLITICAL POWER EXIST?

The following, originally entitled *Political Problems and the Tasks of the Party Organisation in the Border Area*, is part of the resolution drawn up for the Second Party Conference of the Hunan-Kiangsi border area, 1928.

I. THE INTERNAL POLITICAL SITUATION

The present régime of the new Kuomintang warlords is still a régime of the comprador class in the cities and the landed gentry in the countryside, a régime which has in foreign affairs capitulated to imperialism and at home replaced old warlords with new ones, and has subjected the working class and peasantry to an economic exploitation and a political oppression even more ruthless than before. The bourgeois-democratic revolution which started from Kwangtung was only half-way through when the comprador class and the landed gentry usurped its leadership and immediately switched it on to the road of counter-revolution; throughout the country the workers, the peasantry, other sections of the common people, and even the bourgeoisie[1] have remained under the counter-revolutionary rule and obtained not the least particle of political or economic liberation.

Before their capture of Peking and Tientsin, the four cliques of the new Kuomintang warlords—Chiang Kai-shek, the Kwangsi warlords, Feng Yu-hsiang and Yen Hsi-shan[2]—formed a temporary alliance against Chang Tso-lin.[3] After their capture of Peking and Tientsin, this alliance immediately broke up and changed into a bitter struggle, and a war is even brewing between the Chiang and the Kwangsi cliques. The contradictions and struggles among the various cliques of warlords in China reflect the contradictions and struggles among the various imperialist powers. Therefore, as long as China is divided up among the imperialist powers, the various cliques of warlords cannot under any circumstances come to a compromise and whatever compromises there might be would only be temporary. Within the temporary compromise of today an even bigger war is brewing for tomorrow.

China is in urgent need of a bourgeois-democratic revolution, and this revolution can be completed only under the leadership of the proletariat. In the revolution of 1926–7 which started from Kwangtung and spread towards the Yangtze river, because the proletariat was not firm in assuming the leadership, the comprador class and the landed gentry seized hold of it and turned the revolution into a counter-revolution. The bourgeois-democratic revolution thus met with a temporary defeat. The defeat meant a serious blow to the Chinese proletariat and peasantry and also a blow to the Chinese bourgeoisie (not the comprador class and the landed gentry). Yet in the last few months organised strikes by the workers in the cities and insurrections by the peasants in the countryside have developed both in the north and the south under the leadership of the Communist Party. Owing to hunger and cold, soldiers in the armies of the warlords are seething with great discontent. Meanwhile the bourgeoisie, prompted by the clique headed by Wang Ching-wei and Ch'en Kung-po, is pushing forward a reformist movement of considerable proportions[4] in various districts along the sea coast and the Yangtze river. This movement constitutes a new development.

The content of China's democratic revolution, according to the directives of the Third International and the Party centre, includes overthrowing the rule in China of imperialism and its tools, the warlords, so as to complete the national revolution; and carrying out the agrarian revolution so as to eliminate the feudal exploitation of the peasants by the landed gentry. The movement for carrying out such a revolution has been actually developing with every passing day since the Tsinan Massacre[5] in May 1928.

2. REASONS FOR THE EMERGENCE AND EXISTENCE OF CHINA'S RED POLITICAL POWER[6]

The phenomenon that within a country one or several small areas under Red political power should exist for a long time amid the encirclement of White political power is one that has never been found elsewhere in the world. There are peculiar reasons for this unusual phenomenon. It can exist and develop only under certain conditions.

First, it cannot occur in any imperialist country or in any colony under direct imperialist rule,[7] but can occur only in such an economically backward, semi-colonial country as China which is under indirect imperialist rule. For this unusual phenomenon can occur only in conjunction with another unusual phenomenon, namely, the warfare within the White régime. A characteristic of semi-colonial China is that, since the first year of the Republic,[8] the various cliques of old and new warlords, supported by imperialism from abroad and by the comprador class and the landed gentry at home, have waged incessant wars against one another. Such a phenomenon is found neither in any of the imperialist countries of the world, nor in any colony under direct imperialist rule, but only in a country like China which is under indirect imperialist rule.

Two things account for its occurrence, namely, localised agricultural economy (instead of unified capitalist economy) and the imperialist policy of division and exploitation by marking off spheres of influence. The prolonged splits and wars within the White régime provide the condition that one or several small Red areas under the leadership of the Communist Party can emerge and hold out amid the encirclement of the White political power. The Hunan-Kiangsi border area, with its independent régime, is one of many such small areas. In difficult or critical times some comrades often have doubts about the survival of such Red political power and fall into pessimism. This is because they have not found the correct explanation of the emergence and existence of such Red political power. If only we realise that splits and wars are incessant within the White régime in China, we shall have no doubt about the emergence, existence and daily growth of the Red political power.

Secondly, the places where China's Red political power first emerges and can last long are not those unaffected by the democratic revolution, like Szechwan, Kweichow, Yunnan, or the northern provinces, but those like the provinces of Hunan, Kwangtung, Hupeh and Kiangsi where, in the course of the

5

bourgeois-democratic revolution of 1926 and 1927, the masses
of workers, peasants and soldiers rose in great numbers. In
many parts of these provinces vast organisations of trade unions
and peasant associations were formed and many economic and
political struggles were waged by the working class and
peasantry against the landlords, the landed gentry and the
bourgeoisie. That is why a people's city government was set up
in Canton and lasted three days and peasants' independent
régimes once existed in Haifeng and Lufeng, in eastern and
southern Hunan, in the Hunan-Kiangsi border area, and in
Hwangan, Hupeh.[9] As to the present Red Army, it too is a
split-off from the National Revolutionary Army which under-
went democratic political training and imbibed the influence
of the masses of workers and peasants. Such elements as may
make up the Red Army certainly cannot yet come from armies
like those under Yen Hsi-shan and Chang Tso-lin, which have
not in the least undergone democratic political training or
imbibed the influence of the workers and peasants.

Thirdly, whether the people's political power in small areas
can last long depends on whether the nation-wide revolutionary
situation continues to develop. If it does, then not only will the
small Red areas undoubtedly last long, but they will inevitably
become one of the many forces for winning nation-wide political
power. If the nation-wide revolutionary situation does not
continue to develop but remains stagnant for some time, then
it will be impossible for the small Red areas to last long. At
present, the revolutionary situation in China continues to
develop along with the continuous splits and wars within the
comprador class and the landed gentry at home as well as
within the international bourgeoisie. Thus not only can the
small Red areas undoubtedly last long, but they will continue
to develop and approach daily nearer the goal of winning
nation-wide political power.

Fourthly, the existence of a regular Red Army of adequate
strength is a necessary condition for the existence of the Red
political power. If we have only Red guards[10] of a local
character but no regular Red Army, then we can only deal
with the house-to-house militia,[11] but not the regular White
troops. Therefore, unless we have regular armed forces of

adequate strength, even though we have won the mass support of the workers and peasants, we certainly cannot create an independent régime, let alone an independent régime that lasts long and develops daily. Hence "a workers' and peasants' armed independent régime" is an important idea to be fully brought home to the Communist Party and the masses of workers and peasants in areas under the independent régime.

Fifthly, another important condition besides those mentioned above is required for the prolonged existence and development of the Red political power, namely, that the Communist Party is strongly organised and commits no mistakes in policy.

3. THE INDEPENDENT RÉGIME IN THE HUNAN-KIANGSI BORDER AREA AND THE AUGUST FIASCO

Splits and wars among the warlords weaken the power of the White régime. Thus the Red political power is given an opportunity to emerge in small areas. But the warfare among the warlords does not go on every day. When the White régime in one or several provinces enjoys temporary stability, the ruling classes there will inevitably combine to exterminate the Red political power with might and main. In areas where the necessary conditions for its establishment and maintenance are not fully present, the Red political power is in danger of being overthrown by the enemy. This is the reason why many Red régimes that emerged at opportune moments before last April in places like Canton, Haifeng and Lufeng, the Hunan-Kiangsi border area, southern Hunan, Liling and Hwangan were destroyed one after another by the White political power. The establishment of the independent régime in the Hunan-Kiangsi border area after April coincided with the spell of stability enjoyed by the ruling power in the south; the Hunan and Kiangsi provincial governments usually dispatched eight or nine or more regiments, sometimes as many as eighteen, to "annihilate" us. Yet with a force of less than four regiments we fought the enemy for as long as four months, daily expanding the territory under our independent régime, daily deepening the agrarian revolution, daily extending the organisation of the people's political power, and daily strengthening the Red Army and the Red guards: this was precisely because the policies of the Communist Party (the local Party organisation and the Party organisation in the army) in the Hunan-Kiangsi border area were correct. At that time, the policies of the Special Committee and the Army Committee of the Party were as follows: Struggle resolutely against the enemy, set up a régime in the middle section of the Losiao mountain range,[12] and oppose flight-ism; deepen the 'agrarian revolution in areas under the independent régime; promote the development of the local Party organisation through the help of the Party organisation in the army and the development of the local armed forces through the help of the regular army; concentrate the Red Army to fight the enemy confronting it at opportune moments, and oppose the division of forces in order to avoid being smashed separately by the enemy; and adopt the policy of advancing in a series of waves for the expansion of the area under the independent régime and oppose the policy of venturesome advance. Thanks to these appropriate policies, plus a terrain favourable to struggle and the absence of proper co-ordination between the invading troops from Hunan and those from Kiangsi, we were able to win a number of victories in the four months from April to July. Although the enemy was several times stronger, he failed not only to destroy the independent régime but even to prevent its daily expansion, and this independent régime tended to exert a daily increasing influence on Hunan and Kiangsi provinces. The August fiasco was entirely due to the fact that a section of our comrades, not realising that the period was one in which the ruling classes enjoyed temporary stability but adopting on the contrary a strategy applicable in the period of political splits among the ruling classes, divided up the forces for a venturesome advance and courted defeat in both the border area and southern Hunan. Comrade Tu Hsiu-ching, representative of the Hunan Provincial Committee of the Party, who ignored the prevailing situation and disregarded the resolutions of the joint conference of the Special Committee, the Army Committee and the Yungsin County Committee, cared only for carrying out mechanically the Hunan Provincial Committee's order and seconded the proposal of the Twenty-ninth Regiment of the Red Army to escape from the struggle and return home; his mistake was indeed exceedingly grave. This disastrous situation was saved only because after September the Special Committee and the Army Committee took steps to rectify the mistake.

4. THE ROLE OF THE INDEPENDENT RÉGIME OF THE HUNAN-KIANGSI BORDER AREA IN HUNAN, HUPEH AND KIANGSI

The significance of the workers' and peasants' armed inde-dendent régime in the Hunan-Kiangsi border area, with Ning-kang as its centre, is definitely not confined to the counties in the border area; such an independent régime will also be of great significance in the process of seizing political power in Hunan, Hupeh and Kiangsi through the insurrection of the workers and peasants in these three provinces. To extend the influence of the border area's agrarian revolution and the people's political power to the lower valleys of the principal rivers in Hunan and Kiangsi and even to Hupeh; to daily expand the Red Army and enhance its quality through struggle so that it can fulfil its requisite missions in the coming general insurrection of the three provinces; to expand the local armed forces in the counties—the Red guards and the workers' and peasants' insurrection corps—and enhance their quality so that they can fight the house-to-house militia and small armed forces at the present time and safeguard the political power of the border area in the future; and to make local work less and less dependent upon the Red Army for the supply of personnel until the border area can have its own personnel to take charge of the work and even provide personnel for the Red Army and the expanded territory of the independent régime—all these are extremely important tasks for the Party organisation in the border area in developing an insurrection in the three provinces.

5. THE ECONOMIC PROBLEMS

Amid the encirclement of White forces, serious problems have arisen because of shortage of daily necessities for the army and the people and shortage of cash. Since last year, because of the enemy's tight blockade, daily necessities like salt, cloth and medicine have at all times been quite scarce and dear in the area under the independent régime, and this has caused discomfort, sometimes to an extreme degree, to the masses of workers, peasants and the petty bourgeoisie,[13] as well as the soldiers of the Red Army. The Red Army has at one and the same time to fight the enemy and to provision itself. It finds itself even lacking the daily cash allowance for the food subsidy and five cents per head which is provided in addition to grain; many soldiers have fallen ill of malnutrition, and the wounded in the hospitals are suffering even more. Such difficulties are of course unavoidable before the seizure of nation-wide political power, yet it is a pressing need to overcome them to some extent, to improve somewhat our living conditions, and, above all, to secure relatively sufficient supplies for the Red Army. If the Party in the border area cannot find adequate economic measures, then, under the condition that the enemy's rule remains stable for some time, the independent régime will come up against great difficulties. An adequate solution of the economic problems certainly deserves the attention of every Party member.

6. THE PROBLEM OF MILITARY BASES

The Party organisation in the border area has another task, namely, the consolidation of the two military bases at the Five Big and Small Wells[14] at Kiulung. The mountain district of the Five Big and Small Wells at the juncture of the four counties of Yungsin, Ling, Ningkang and Suichwan, and the Kiulung mountain district at the juncture of the counties of Yungsin, Ningkang, Chaling and Lienhwa[15]—both districts being in a commanding position topographically, especially the district of the Five Big and Small Wells where the masses support us and the terrain is highly strategic—are not only important military bases of the border area at the present time, but will remain such in the future development of the insurrection in the three provinces of Hunan, Hupeh and Kiangsi. The ways to consolidate them are: first, to build strong fortifications, second, to store up sufficient foodstuffs, and third, to establish better Red Army hospitals. The Party organisation in the border area must strive to do a really good job along these lines.   *October 5, 1928.*

THE STRUGGLE IN THE CHINGKANG MOUNTAINS

This is a report submitted to the Central Committee of the Chinese Communist Party in November 1928.

THE INDEPENDENT RÉGIME IN THE HUNAN-KIANGSI BORDER AREA AND THE AUGUST FIASCO

The phenomenon that within a country one or several small areas under Red political power came into existence amid the encirclement of White political power is one which, of all the countries in the world today, occurs only in China. Upon analysis we find that one of the reasons for its occurrence lies in the incessant splits and wars within China's comprador class and landed gentry. So long as splits and wars continue within these classes, the workers' and peasants' armed independent régime can also continue to exist and develop. In addition to this, the existence and development of such an armed independent régime require the following conditions: (1) a sound mass basis, (2) a first-rate Party organisation, (3) a Red Army of adequate strength, (4) a terrain favourable to military operations, and (5) economic strength sufficient for self-support.

The independent régime in a given area must adopt a different strategy against the ruling class forces which encircle it according to whether their political power is enjoying temporary stability or is splitting up.

When splits take place within the ruling classes, e.g. the war between Li Tsung-jen and T'ang Sheng-chih in Hunan and Hupeh[1] and that between Chang Fa-k'uei and Li Chi-shen in Kwangtung,[2] we may adopt a strategy of comparatively venturesome advance and expand the independent régime over a comparatively large area by fighting. Yet all the same we must take care to lay a solid foundation in the central districts so that we shall have something to rely upon and nothing to fear when the White terror comes. When the political power of the ruling classes is relatively stable, as in the southern provinces after April this year, our strategy must be one of gradual advance. We must then take the utmost care neither to divide up our forces for venturesome advance in the military field, nor to scatter our personnel and neglect to lay a solid foundation in the central districts in the field of local work (including the distribution of land, the establishment of political power, the expansion of the Party and the organisation of local armed forces).

The failure in various small Red areas has been due either to a lack of favourable objective conditions or to subjective tactical mistakes. The tactics have been mistaken precisely because of the failure to distinguish clearly between the two different periods, the period when the political power of the ruling classes is temporarily stable and the period when it is splitting up. In the period when the political power of the ruling classes was temporarily stable, some comrades, as if oblivious of the fact that the enemy could muster for an attack not only the house-to-house militia, but also regular troops, advocated dividing our own forces for a venturesome advance, and even proposed to leave the defence of an extensive area to the Red guards singlehanded. In local work they utterly neglected to lay a solid foundation in the central districts, but aimed exclusively at unlimited expansion, regardless of whether we were strong enough to achieve this. And anyone who advocated gradual expansion in military work and, in civilian work, concentration of forces to build up a solid foundation in the central districts, thus placing ourselves in an invincible position, was called a "conservative". Precisely such erroneous views were the fundamental cause of the fiasco in August this year in the Hunan-Kiangsi border area and of the simultaneous defeat of the Fourth Army of the Red Army in southern Hunan.

The work in the Hunan-Kiangsi border area was started last October. At first we had absolutely no Party organisations in the counties but two units of local armed forces in the vicinity of the Chingkang mountains, under Yuan Wen-t'sai and Wang Tso respectively, each with sixty rifles in bad repair, while all the rifles of the peasant self-defence corps in the counties of

Yungsin, Lienhwa, Chaling and Ling had been surrendered to the landed gentry; the revolutionary fervour of the masses had been suppressed. By February this year county Party committees were set up in Ningkang, Yungsin, Chaling and Suichwan, and a special district Party committee was set up in Ling; a Party organisation was being set up in Lienhwa and connections established with the County Committee of Wanan. Small units of local armed forces were now to be found in all the counties except Ling. In Ningkang, Chaling, Suichwan and Yungsin, especially in the last two counties, a number of guerrilla uprisings for overthrowing the landed gentry and arousing the masses were carried out, all with fairly good results. At that time the agrarian revolution had not yet deepened. The organ of political power was named the government of workers, peasants and soldiers. Soldiers' committees[3] were organised in the army. Action committees were set up to direct the army when its operations were dispersed. The higher leading body of the Party at that time was the Front Committee (with Mao Tse-tung as secretary), appointed during the Autumn Harvest Uprising by the Hunan Provincial Party Committee. In early March, upon the request of the Special Party Committee of Southern Hunan, the Front Committee was abolished and reorganised as the Divisional Party Committee (with Ho T'ing-ying as secretary), and thus became an organ which was in charge only of the Party organisation in the army but had no authority over the local Party organisations. Meanwhile Mao's troops were dispatched to southern Hunan, upon the request of the Special Party Committee there, and consequently for more than a month the enemy held the Hunan-Kiangsi border area. At the end of March came the defeat in southern Hunan; in April the two forces under Mao Tse-tung and Chu Teh, together with the peasant army of southern Hunan, withdrew to Ningkang and started anew the independent régime in the border area.

The establishment of the independent régime in the Hunan-Kiangsi border area since April coincided with the spell of stability enjoyed by the ruling power in the south, and the reactionary forces for "annihilation" dispatched by the Hunan and Kiangsi provincial governments numbered at least eight or nine regiments, sometimes as many as eighteen. Yet with a force of less than four regiments we fought the enemy for as long as four months, daily expanding the territory under our independent régime, daily deepening the agrarian revolution, daily extending the people's political power and daily strengthening the Red Army and the Red guards; this was precisely because the policies of the Party in the border area (the local and the army Party organisations) were correct. The policies of the Border Area Special Party Committee (with Mao Tse-tung as secretary) and the Army Party Committee (with Ch'en Yi as secretary) were then as follows: struggle resolutely against the enemy, establish a régime in the middle section of the Losiao mountain range and oppose flight-ism; deepen the agrarian revolution in areas under the independent régime; promote the development of the local Party organisation through the help of the army Party organisation, and the development of the local armed forces through the help of the regular army; adopt a defensive strategy for Hunan where the ruling power was comparatively strong and an offensive strategy for Kiangsi where the ruling power was comparatively weak: devote great efforts to the development of Yungsin, set up an independent régime of the masses there and make preparations for a prolonged struggle; concentrate the Red Army to fight at opportune moments the enemy confronting it and oppose the division of the forces in order to avoid their being smashed separately by the enemy; and adopt the policy of advancing in a series of waves for the expansion of the area under the independent régime and oppose the policy of venturesome advance. Thanks to these appropriate policies, plus the terrain in the border area (which is favourable to our struggle) and the absence of perfect co-ordination between the invading troops from Hunan and those from Kiangsi, we were able to win a number of military victories and expand the independent régime of the masses in the four months from April to July.

The enemy, though several times stronger, failed not only to destroy the independent régime but even to check its development. And this independent régime tended to exert a daily increasing influence on the two provinces of Hunan and

Kiangsi. The August fiasco was entirely due to the fact that a section of our comrades, not realising that the period was one in which the ruling classes enjoyed temporary stability but adopting on the contrary a strategy applicable in the period of splits among the ruling classes, divided up the forces for a venturesome advance on southern Hunan and courted defeat in both the border area and southern Hunan. Tu Hsiu-ching, representative of the Hunan Provincial Committee, and Yang K'ai-ming, secretary of the Special Committee of the Border Area appointed by the Provincial Committee, taking advantage of the fact that people firmly dissenting from them like Mao Tsetung and Wan Hsi-hsien happened to be far away at Yungsin, and failing to grasp the situation at the time, disregarded the resolutions of the joint conference of the Army Committee, the Special Committee and the Yungsin County Committee, which disagreed with the views of the Hunan Provincial Committee; they cared only for carrying out mechanically the Hunan Provincial Committee's order to march to southern Hunan, which chimed in with the desire of the Red Army's Twenty-ninth Regiment (composed of peasants from Ichang) to escape from the struggle and return home; and consequently they courted defeat in both the border area and southern Hunan.

Previously, in the middle of July, the Eighth Army of the enemy forces in Hunan under Wy Shang had invaded Ningkang and proceeded farther to Yungsin; as it had sought battle with us in vain (our men missed them when seeking to attack them through one of the smaller passes) and was afraid of the masses who supported us, it hurriedly retreated to Chaling via Lienhwa. In the meantime, the major detachment of the Red Army advancing from Ningkang to attack Ling and Chaling changed their plan in Ling and turned towards southern Hunan, while the enemy forces from Kiangsi, five regiments of the Third Army under Wang Chun and Chin Han-ting and six regiments of the Sixth Army under Hu Wen-tou, again made a joint assault on Yungsin. At that time we had only one regiment in Yungsin, which, shielded by the broad masses, carried out guerrilla fighting in all directions, and kept these eleven enemy regiments cornered within thirty *li* of the county town of Yungsin, for as long as twenty-five days. We lost Yungsin in the end because of the enemy's fierce assault, and also lost Lienhwa and Ningkang shortly afterwards. Then a quarrel suddenly broke out among the enemy forces in Kiangsi; the Sixth Army under Hu Wen-tou withdrew in a flurry and presently engaged Wang Chun's Third Army at Changhu. The five regiments from Kiangsi that were left behind also withdrew helter-skelter to the county town of Yungsin. Had our major detachment not gone to southern Hunan, it would have been fully possible to rout this enemy force and to extend the area under the independent régime to Kian, Anfu and Ping-siang and make it contiguous to Pingkiang and Liuyang. But as the major detachment was away and as, furthermore, the men in the one regiment we had were much too fatigued, it was decided that one part of the regiment should be left to defend the Chingkang mountains together with the two units under Yuan Wen-ts'ai and Wang Tso respectively and the other part should be led by Mao Tse-tung to meet and escort the major detachment on its way back by going in the direction of Kweitung. By that time the major detachment had retreated from southern Hunan to Kweitung and on August 23 we joined forces there.

No sooner had the Red Army's major detachment arrived in Ling in the middle of July, than both officers and men of the Twenty-ninth Regiment became unruly because of their political vacillation and their desire to return to their homes in southern Hunan, while the Twenty-eighth Regiment, though opposed to going to southern Hunan, would not return to Yungsin because it wanted to go to southern Kiangsi. As Tu Hsiu-ching encouraged the Twenty-ninth Regiment in its erroneous view and the Army Party Committee failed to stop this, our major detachment set out from Ling for Chen on July 17. On July 24 we engaged the enemy forces under Fan Shih-sheng in Chen; we were victorious at first but defeated afterwards, whereupon we withdrew from the battle. The Twenty-ninth Regiment immediately acted on its own and hurried homeward to Ichang, with the result that a number of its men were annihilated at Lokchong by bandits under Hu Feng-chang, others were dispersed in places like Chen and

Ichang and met an unknown fate, and not more than a hundred were re-assembled on that day. Fortunately our main force, the Twenty-eighth Regiment, which had suffered only slight losses, occupied Kweitung on August 18. On August 23 the Regiment was joined by the troops from the Chingkang mountains, and it was decided that the forces were to return to the Chingkang mountains via Tsungyi and Shangyiu. When they reached Tsungyi, battalion commander Yuan Ch'ung-ch'uan mutinied with one infantry and one artillery company under his command; although we pursued and brought back the two companies, regimental commander Wang Erh-cho lost his life. Seizing their opportunity when our men, though homeward bound, had not yet arrived, detachments from enemy forces in both Hunan and Kiangsi attacked the Chingkang mountains on August 30. Entrenching itself in strategic positions, our defence force of less than one battalion resisted and routed the enemy and thus saved the base.

The causes of the defeat were: (1) Some of our officers and men, vacillating and home-sick, lost their fighting capacity, while others, reluctant to go to southern Hunan, were not very active. (2) Long marches in sweltering summer tired out our men. (3) Having ventured several hundred *li* away from Ling, our men lost contact with the border area and became an isolated force. (4) The masses in southern Hunan not yet having risen, the campaign proved to be a sheer military adventure. (5) We were uninformed about the enemy situation. (6) The preparations being inadequate, officers and men did not understand the significance of the operation.

THE CURRENT SITUATION IN THE AREA UNDER THE INDEPENDENT RÉGIME

Since April this year the Red areas have gradually expanded. After the battle of Lungyuankow (on the borders of Yungsin and Ningkang) on June 23, in which we defeated the enemy forces from Kiangsi for the fourth time, the border area reached its peak of development, extending over the three entire counties of Ningkang, Yungsin and Lienhwa, small sections of Kian and Anfu, the northern section of Suichwan, and the

south-eastern section of Ling. In the Red areas the greater part
of the land had been redistributed, and the redistribution of the
remainder was in progress. District and township governments
were established everywhere. County governments were set up
in Ningkang, Yungsin, Lienhwa and Suichwan, and the border
area government was also formed. In the villages the workers'
and peasants' insurrection corps were extensively organised,
and there were Red guards in the districts and counties.
In July the enemy forces from Kiangsi launched an attack
and in August the enemy forces from both Hunan and Kiangsi
jointly attacked the Chingkang mountains; all the county
towns and the entire flat country of the counties in the border
area were occupied by the enemy. The peace preservation
corps and the house-to-house militia, both tools of the enemy,
ran amuck, and White terror reigned throughout the towns and
the countryside. Most of the Party organisations and organs of
political power collapsed. The rich peasants and opportunists
within the Party became turncoats one after another. After the
battle in the Chingkang mountains on August 30, the enemy
forces from Hunan retreated to Ling, but those from Kiangsi
still held all the county towns and most of the villages. However, it has always been beyond the power of the enemy to
capture the mountain areas, which include the western and
northern districts in Ningkang; the Tienlung, Siaosikiang and
Wannienshan districts in the northern, western and southern
sections of Yungsin respectively; the Shangsi district in Lienhwa;
the Chingkang mountain district in Suichwan; and the districts
of Tsingshihkang and Tayuan in Ling. In July and August one
regiment of the Red Army, in co-ordination with the Red
guards of the counties, fought scores of big and small battles
with a loss of only thirty rifles, but finally withdrew to the
mountains.

As our men were marching back to the Chingkang mountains
via Tsungyi and Shangyiu, the enemy forces in southern
Kiangsi, the Independent Seventh Division under Liu Shih-yi,
pursued us as far as Suichwan. On September 13 we defeated
Liu Shih-yi, captured several hundred rifles and took Suichwan.
On September 26 our men returned to the Chingkang mountains. On October 1 we engaged in Ningkang Chou Hunyuan's

brigade under Hsiung Shih-hui, winning the battle and recovering the entire county. Meanwhile 126 men of the enemy forces from Hunan under Yen Chung-ju, which had been stationed at Kweitung, came over to us and were organised into a special task battalion with Pi Chan-yun as commander. On November 9 we again routed one regiment of Chou's brigade at the county town of Ningkang and Lungyuankow. Next day we advanced to Yungsin and occupied the town, but withdrew to Ningkang shortly afterwards. At present our area, extending from the southern slope of the Chingkang mountains in Suichwan in the south to the border of Lienhwa in the north, embraces the whole county of Ningkang and sections of Suichwan, Ling and Yungsin, and forms a narrow unbroken strip stretching from the north to the south. The Shangsi district in Lienhwa and the Tienlung and Wannienshan districts in Yungsin, however, are not quite connected with this unbroken strip. The enemy is attempting to destroy our base area by military attacks and economic blockade and we are making preparations to defeat his attacks.

THE MILITARY PROBLEM

Since the struggle in the border area is exclusively military, both the Party and the masses have to be placed on a war footing. How to deal with the enemy and how to fight have become the central problems in our daily life. An independent régime must be an armed one. Wherever there are no armed forces, or the armed forces are inadequate, or the tactics for dealing with the enemy are wrong, the enemy will immediately come into occupation. As the struggle is getting fiercer every day, our problems have also become extremely complicated and serious.

Origins of the Red Army men in the border area: (1) troops formerly under Yeh T'ing and Ho Lung in Chaochow and Swatow;[4] (2) the Guards Regiment of the former Wuchang National Government;[5] (3) peasants from Pingkiang and Liu-yang;[6] (4) peasants from southern Hunan[7] and workers from Shuikowshan;[8] (5) men captured from the forces under Hsu K'e-hsiang, T'ang Sheng-chih, Pai Ch'ung-shi, Chu P'ei-teh,

Wu Shang and Hsiung Shih-hui; and (6) peasants from the counties in the border area. But after fighting for more than a year, the troops formerly under Yeh and Ho, the Guards Regiment, and the peasants from Pingkiang and Liuyang have been reduced to only one-third of their original strength. The peasants from southern Hunan have also suffered heavy casualties. Thus although the first four sections have remained to this day the backbone of the Fourth Army of the Red Army, they are far outnumbered by the last two. Furthermore, of the last two sections the captured soldiers are more numerous; without replacement from this section, man-power would have become a serious problem. For all this, however, enlistment still cannot keep up with the increase in rifles; we seldom lose rifles, though we often lose soldiers, *e.g.* when they are wounded or killed, fall ill or desert. The Hunan Provincial Party Committee has promised to send workers here from Anyuan[9] and we hope it will do this at once.

As to the composition of the Red Army, one part consists of workers and peasants and the other of *lumpen*-proletarians. It is of course inadvisable to have too large a proportion of *lumpen*-proletarians. But as fighting is going on every day and casualties mounting, it is already no easy matter to get for replacements the *lumpen*-proletarians, who are good fighters. In these circumstances the only thing to do is to intensify political training.

The majority of the Red Army soldiers came from mercenary armies; but once in the Red Army, they change their character. First of all the Red Army has abolished the mercenary system, making the soldiers feel that they are not fighting for somebody else but for themselves and for the people. The Red Army has not to this day instituted a system of regular pay, but issues only rice, an allowance for oil, salt, firewood and vegetables, and a little pocket money. Land has been allotted to all Red Army officers and men who are natives of the border area, but it is rather hard to allot land to those from distant areas.

After receiving some political education, the Red Army soldiers have all become class-conscious and acquired a general knowledge about redistributing land, establishing political power, arming the workers and peasants, etc.; and they all know that they are fighting for themselves and for the working class and the peasantry. Hence they can endure the bitter struggle without complaint. Each company, battalion or regiment has its soldiers' council which represents the interests of the soldiers and carries out political and mass work.

Experience has proved that the system of Party representatives[10] must not be abolished. As the Party branch is organised on the company basis, the Party representative at the company level is particularly important. He has to supervise the soldiers' committee in carrying out political training, to direct the work of the mass movement, and to act at the same time as the secretary of the Party branch. Facts have proved that the better the company Party representative is, the better is the company, while the company commander can hardly play such an effective political role. As the casualties among the lower cadres are heavy, soldiers captured from the enemy a short time ago have often been made platoon or company commanders and some of those captured only last February or March are now battalion commanders. Superficially it might seem that, since our army is called the Red Army, it could do without Party representatives; actually the reverse is the case. The Twenty-eighth Regiment in southern Hunan once abolished this system only to restore it later. To rename Party representatives "directors" would be to confuse them with the directors of the Kuomintang, who are detested by the captured soldiers. Moreover, changes in title do not affect the nature of a system. Hence we have decided against the change. To make up for the heavy casualties in Party representatives we hope that, besides starting training classes ourselves, the Party centre and the two provincial Party Committees will send us at least thirty comrades eligible as Party representatives.

The average soldier needs six months' or a year's training before he can fight, but our soldiers, though recruited only yesterday, have to fight today with practically no training to speak of. Exceedingly poor in military technique, they fight by courage alone. As a long period for rest and training is impossible, we shall see whether we can find ways to avoid certain battles in order to gain time for training. For the training of lower officers we have formed a training corps of 150 men and intend to make it a permanent institution. We hope that the Party centre and the two provincial committees will send us more officers from the rank of platoon and company commanders upwards.

The Hunan Provincial Committee has asked us to attend to the material life of the soldiers and to make it at least a little better than that of the average worker or peasant. At present the very reverse is the case, for, besides rice, each man gets only five cents a day for cooking oil, salt, firewood and vegetables, and it is hard even to keep this up. The monthly cost of these items alone amounts to more than ten thousand silver dollars, which are obtained exclusively through expropriating the local bullies.[11] We have now obtained cotton for the winter clothing of the whole army of five thousand men but are still short of cloth. Cold as the weather is, many of our men are still wearing two suits of clothes of single thickness. Fortunately we are inured to hardships. Furthermore all alike share the same hardships: everybody from the army commander down to the cook lives on a daily fare worth five cents, apart from grain. In the matter of pocket money, if two dimes are allotted, it is two dimes for everybody; if four dimes are allotted, it is four dimes for everybody.[12] Thus the soldiers harbour no resentment against anyone.

After each engagement there are a number of wounded soldiers. And a great many officers and men have fallen ill from malnutrition, exposure to cold and other causes. The hospital up in the mountains gives both Chinese and Western treatments, but is short of doctors as well as medicine. At present there are over eight hundred patients in the hospital. The Hunan Provincial Committee promised to procure medicine for us but so far we have not received any. We still have to ask the Party centre and the two provincial committees to send us some iodine and a few doctors with Western training.

Apart from the role played by the Party, the reason why the Red Army can sustain itself without collapse in spite of such a poor standard of material life and such incessant engagements, is its practice of democracy. The officers do not beat the men; officers and men receive equal treatment; soldiers enjoy freedom of assembly and speech; cumbersome formalities and ceremonies are done away with; and the account books are open to the inspection of all. The soldiers handle the messing arrangements and, out of the daily five cents for oil, salt, firewood and vegetables, can even save a little sum for pocket money (called "mess savings") of approximately sixty or seventy cash[13] for each person every day. All these measures are very satisfactory to the soldiers. The newly captured soldiers in particular feel that our army and the Kuomintang's army are worlds apart. They feel that, though in material life they are worse off in the Red Army than in the White army, spiritually they are liberated. The fact that the same soldier who was not brave in the enemy army yesterday becomes very brave in the Red Army today shows precisely the impact of democracy. The Red Army is like a furnace in which all captured soldiers are melted down and transformed the moment they come over. In China not only the people need democracy but the army needs it too. The democratic system in an army[14] is an important weapon for destroying the feudal mercenary army.

The Party organisations are now divided into four levels: the company branch, the battalion committee, the regimental committee and the army committee. In a company there is the branch, and in a squad, the group. An important reason why the Red Army has been able to undertake such severe struggle without falling apart is that the *Party branch is organised on the company basis*. Two years ago our organisations in the Kuomintang army did not have any hold on the soldiers, and even among Yeh T'ing's troops[15] there was only one Party branch in a regiment; this is why they could not stand up to any crucial test. In the Red Army today the ratio of Party members to non-Party men is approximately one to three, *i.e.* on the average there is one Party member among every four men. Recently we have decided to recruit more Party members among the combat soldiers, so as to attain a fifty-fifty ratio between Party members and non-Party men.[16] At present the company branches are short of good secretaries and we ask the Party centre to send us for this purpose a large number of the activists from among those who can no longer stay where they are. The working personnel from southern Hunan are almost all doing Party work in the army. In August some of them left us during the flight in southern Hunan, and therefore we have no personnel to spare now.

The local armed forces are the Red guards and the workers' and peasants' insurrection corps. The insurrection corps is armed with spears and fowling-pieces and organised on a township basis with a contingent in every township, the strength of which is proportional to the township population. Its job is to suppress counter-revolution, to protect the township government, and, when the enemy comes, to assist the Red Army and the Red Guards in war. The insurrection corps was started in Yungsin as an underground force; it has come out in the open since we captured the entire county. The organisation has now been expanded in other counties of the border area and the name remains unchanged. The arms of the Red guards are mainly five-round rifles but also include some nine-round and single-round ones. There are: 140 rifles in Ningkang, 220 in Yungsin, 43 in Lienhwa, 50 in Chaling, 90 in Ling, 130 in Suichwan and 10 in Wanan, making a total of 683. While most of the rifles were supplied by the Red Army, a small number were captured from the enemy by the Red guards themselves. Fighting regularly against the peace preservation corps and the house-to-house militia of the landed gentry, most of the Red guards in the counties are daily increasing their fighting capacity.

Before the Incident of May 21,[17] there were peasant self-defence corps in all counties. They had 300 rifles in Yu, 300 in Chaling, 60 in Ling, 50 in Suichwan, 80 in Yungsin, 60 in Lienhwa, 60 in Ningkang (Yuan Wen-ts'ai's men) and 60 in the Chingkang mountains (Wang Tso's men), totalling 970. After the incident, apart from the rifles of Yuan's and Wang's men in which no losses were incurred, only six in Suichwan and one in Lienhwa were saved while all the rest were seized by the landed gentry. Such inability on the part of the peasant self-defence corps to hold on to their rifles is the result of the opportunist line. At present the rifles of the Red guards in the counties are still far from being sufficient and are fewer than those of the landed gentry; the Red Army should continue to help the Red guards with arms. In so far as its own fighting capacity is not reduced the Red Army should do its best to help the people to arm themselves.

We have laid it down that each battalion of the Red Army is to be made up of four companies, with seventy-five rifles to each company; when these are added to the rifles of the special task company, the machine-gun company, the trench-mortar company and the headquarters detachments of the three battalions and of the regiment itself, each regiment will have 1,075 rifles. Rifles captured in action should be used as far as possible for arming the local forces. The commanders of the Red guards should be people who have been sent from the counties to the training corps instituted by the Red Army and have finished the course. The Red Army should send fewer and fewer people from distant areas to be captains of local forces. Chu P'ei-teh is also arming his peace preservation corps and house-to-house militia and the landed gentry's armed forces in the counties in the border area are considerable in size and fighting capacity. All the more reason why there must not be a moment's delay in expanding our Red local forces.

The principle for the Red Army is concentration and that for the Red guards, dispersion. In the present period of the temporary stability of the reactionary régime the enemy can mass huge forces to attack the Red Army, and it is disadvantageous for the Red Army to disperse itself. In our experience, the dispersion of forces has almost always led to defeat, while the concentration of forces to fight an enemy whose strength was inferior, equal or slightly superior to ours often led to victory. The area in which the Party's Central Committee has instructed us to develop guerrilla warfare is too extensive, covering several thousands of *li* in length and breadth; this is probably due to an over-estimation of our strength. For the Red guards, dispersion is advantageous and at present the Red guards in the counties have all resorted to dispersed operations.

In the propaganda directed to the enemy forces, the most effective means are releasing the captured soldiers and giving medical treatment to their wounded. Whenever soldiers or platoon, company or battalion commanders of the enemy forces are captured, propaganda is immediately carried on among them; they are divided into those who wish to stay and those who wish to leave, and the latter are given travelling expenses and set free. This immediately shatters the enemy's calumny that "the Communist bandits kill every one on sight". Concerning this measure, Yang Ch'ih-sheng's *Ten-Day Review of the Ninth Division* once exclaimed in astonishment: "Deadly indeed!" The comfort given by Red Army soldiers to the captured soldiers and the farewell made to them are extremely warm-hearted, and at every "Farewell Party to New Brothers" the captured soldiers make speeches to express in return their heartfelt gratitude. Medical treatment for the enemy wounded is also a very effective means. Recently, in imitation of us, clever persons on the enemy side, *e.g.* Li Wen-pin, kill no prisoners and give medical attention to the wounded ones. Despite this, it has twice happened that at the next engagement some of our men have rejoined us with their arms. In addition, we have done as much written propaganda, *e.g.* slogan painting, as possible. Wherever we go, we write slogans all over the walls. But we are short of people skilled in drawing pictures, and hope that the Party centre and the two provincial committees will send us a few.

Military bases: The first base is the Chingkang mountains, situated at the juncture of the four counties of Ningkang, Ling, Suichwan and Yungsin. Its northern slope is at Maoping in Ningkang and its southern slope at Hwangao in Suichwan, the two being 90 *li* apart. Its eastern slope is at Nashan in Yungsin and its western slope at Shuikow in Ling, the two being 80 *li* apart. The circumference measures 550 *li* altogether, running from Nashan all the way through Lungyuankow (both in Yungsin), Sincheng, Maoping, Talung (all in Ningkang), Shihtu, Shuikow, Siatsun (all in Ling), Yingpanyu, Taikiapu, Tafen, Tuitzechien, Hwangao, Wutowkiang and Cheso (all in Suichwan) and back to Nashan. There are both paddy-fields and villages in the mountains, at places like Big Well, Small Well, Upper Well, Middle Well, Lower Well, Tzeping, Siachwang, Singchow, Tsaoping, Painihu and Lofu—places which used to be nests of bandits and stragglers but have now turned into one of our bases. But the population there is less than two thousand, and the yield of unhusked rice less than ten thousand piculs, and so all the food for the army has to be sent from the counties of Ningkang, Yungsin and Suichwan. All the strategic passes in the mountains are fortified. The hospital, the bedding and clothing factory, the ordnance department and the rear offices of the regiments are all here. Foodstuffs are now being sent to the mountains from Ningkang. Provided there are adequate supplies, the enemy will never be able to break in. The second base is the Kiulung mountains, situated at the juncture of the four counties of Ningkang, Yungsin, Lienhwa and Chaling; less important than the Chingkang mountains, it is the last base for the local armed forces of the four counties and has also been fortified. For a Red independent régime encircled by White political power, it is necessary to make use of the strategic advantages of the mountains.

THE AGRARIAN PROBLEM

The agrarian situation in the border area: Roughly speaking, more than 60 per cent of the land used to belong to the landlords and less than 40 per cent to the peasants. In the Kiangsi section, land ownership was most concentrated in Suichwan where about 80 per cent of it belonged to the landlords. The next was Yungsin, where about 70 per cent of the land belonged to the landlords. In Wanan, Ningkang and Lienhwa there were more owner-peasants, but the land of the landlords still formed a larger proportion—about 60 per cent of the total, while the peasants owned only 40 per cent. In the Hunan section, in both Chaling and Ling, about 70 per cent of the land was in the hands of the landlords.

The problem of the intermediate class: The agrarian situation being such, the confiscation and redistribution of all the land[18] can win the support of the majority of the population. But people in the rural areas are generally divided into three classes: the class of big and middle landlords, the intermediate class of small landlords and rich peasants, and the class of middle and poor peasants. The interests of the rich peasants are often interwoven with those of the small landlords. The land of the rich peasants makes up but a small percentage of the total acreage, yet with the land of the small landlords counted in, the amount is considerable. Perhaps this is more or less the

case throughout the country. The agrarian policy adopted in
the border area is complete confiscation and thorough redistribution; thus in the Red area the landed gentry and the
intermediate class are both under attack. Such being the policy,
in actual execution we nevertheless meet with considerable
obstruction from the intermediate class. In the early period of
the revolution the intermediate class apparently capitulated
to the poor peasantry, but in reality they took advantage of the
former social position of the poor peasants as well as of their
clannishness, in order to threaten them and delay land
redistribution. When no further delay was possible they
withheld information about the actual acreage of their land,
or kept the good land for themselves and left the poor land
to other people. In this period the poor peasants, having
long been ill-treated and feeling uncertain about the victory of
the revolution, often accepted the proposals of the intermediate
class and dared not take positive action. Positive action is
taken in the villages against the intermediate class only at a
time of real revolutionary upsurge, when, for instance, political
power has been seized in one or several counties, the reactionary
army has been defeated a number of times, and the prowess of
the Red Army has been repeatedly demonstrated. The most
serious instances of delaying land redistribution and withhold-
ing information about land acreage were found, for example, in
the southern section of Yungsin, where the intermediate class
was the largest. We actually went ahead with redistribution
only after the Red Army had won a great victory at Lungyuankow on June 23 and the district government had dealt with
several people for delaying land redistribution. But the feudal
patriarchal organisations are widespread in every county, and
in most cases one clan inhabits a whole village or several villages;
thus it will be quite a long time before the process of class
differentiation is completed and the clan sentiment overcome
in the villages.

The volte-face of the intermediate class under White terror: The
intermediate class, having suffered blows during the revolutionary upsurge, immediately goes over to the other side when
the White terror comes. It was precisely the small landlords
and rich peasants in Yungsin and Ningkang who incited the

reactionary troops to set fire to large numbers of houses of revolutionary peasants there. Acting on the directions of the reactionaries, they burnt down houses and arrested people, and quite boldly too. When the Red Army returned to the area of Ningkang, Sincheng, Kucheng and Lungshih, thousands of the peasants there, deceived by the reactionary propaganda that the Communists would kill them, fled with the reactionaries to Yungsin. It was only as a result of our propaganda—"Do not kill peasants who have become turncoats" and "Peasants who have become turncoats are welcome home to reap their crops" —that some of the peasants eventually came back.

When the revolution in the country as a whole is at a low ebb, the most difficult problem in areas under the independent régime is our lack of a firm hold on the intermediate class. The intermediate class turns traitor to the revolution mainly because it has received too heavy a blow. But when the country as a whole is in a revolutionary upsurge, the poor peasantry gains courage because it has something to rely upon while the intermediate class dares not get out of hand because it also has something to fear. When the war between Li-Tsung-jen and T'ang Sheng-chih spread to Hunan, the small landlords in Chaling tried to placate the peasants; some of them sent pork to the peasants as a New Year gift (by then the Red Army had retreated from Chaling and gone to Suichwan). But after that war was over, no one heard of such things any more. At present when the tide of counter-revolution is rising high in the country as a whole, the intermediate class in the White areas, having been subjected to heavy attack, has attached itself almost entirely to the landed gentry, and the poor peasantry has become an isolated force. This is indeed a very serious problem.[19]

The pressure of daily life as a cause of the volte-face of the inter-mediate class: Opposed to each other, the Red areas and the White areas have become two enemy countries. Owing to both the enemy's tight blockade and our improper treatment of the petty bourgeoisie, trade between the two areas has almost entirely ceased; since daily necessaries like salt, cloth and medicine are scarce and costly and agricultural products like timber, tea and cooking oil cannot be marketed in the White areas, the peasants' source of income is cut off and all the people are affected. The poor peasantry is, comparatively speaking, able to bear such hardships, but the intermediate class will capitulate to the landed gentry the moment it finds them past bearing. If splits and wars among the landed gentry and the warlords in China do not continue, and if the revolutionary situation throughout the country does not develop, then the Red independent régime in small areas will come under great economic pressure and its prolonged existence will become doubtful. For such economic pressure is not only intolerable to the intermediate class, but will some day prove so even to the workers, poor peasants and Red Army soldiers. In the counties of Yungsin and Ningkang there was at one time no salt for cooking and supplies of cloth and medicine were entirely cut off, not to mention other things. Salt is now obtainable there but the price is very high. Cloth and medicine are still totally lacking. Timber, tea and cooking oil, all abundantly produced in Ningkang, western Yungsin and northern Suichwan (all under our independent régime at present) cannot yet be transported to the White areas. [20]

The criterion in land redistribution: The township is taken as the basis of land redistribution. In regions where there are more hills and less farm land, *e.g.* the Siaokiang district in Yungsin, three or four townships were sometimes taken as one unit, but such cases were extremely rare. All the country people, male or female, old or young, received equal shares. In accordance with the Party centre's plan, a change is now made whereby ability to work is taken as the criterion: a person with ability to work is allotted twice as much as one without. [21]

The problem of making concessions to the owner-peasants: This has not yet been discussed in detail. The rich owner-peasants have themselves requested that productive power be taken as the criterion, *i.e.* those who have more labour power and capital (such as farm implements) should be allotted more land. The rich peasants feel that neither equal redistribution nor redistribution according to ability to work is to their advantage. They have indicated that they are willing to put in more labour power which, coupled with the power of their capital, would enable them to raise bigger crops. They will be unsatisfied if, with their special efforts and extra capital neglected (*i.e.* left idle), they are only allotted the same amount of land as the people in general. Here the redistribution is still being carried out according to the Party centre's plan. But this problem deserves further discussion, and another report will be submitted when a conclusion is reached.

The Land Tax: In Ningkang it is being collected at the rate of 20 per cent of the crop, exceeding by 5 per cent the rate specified by the Party centre; as the collection is already under way, the rate should not be altered just now but will be reduced next year. Besides, the sections of Suichwan, Ling and Yungsin under our independent régime are all hilly areas, and the peasants are so poverty-stricken that taxation is inadvisable. For the maintenance of the government and the Red guards we rely on expropriating the local bullies in the White areas. As to provisions for the Red Army, rice can be obtained temporarily through collecting the land tax in Ningkang, while cash is also obtained entirely through expropriating the local bullies. During our guerrilla operations in Suichwan in October we collected more than ten thousand dollars, which will last for a while, and we shall see what can be done when the sum is spent.

THE PROBLEM OF POLITICAL POWER

The people's political power at county, district and township levels has been universally established, but the reality belies its name. In many places there is no council of workers, peasants and soldiers to speak of. The executive committee of the township, district or even county government is invariably elected at some sort of mass meeting. But mass meetings called on the spur of the moment can neither thrash out questions nor give political education to the masses; furthermore they are very apt to be manipulated by intellectuals and careerists. At some places a council is established, but it is regarded merely as a temporary organ for electing the executive committee; once the election is over, absolute authority is vested in the committee and the council is never heard of any more. Not that there are no councils of workers, peasants and soldiers worthy of the name but that there are very few of them. This is due to the lack of propaganda and education concerning this new political system. The evil practice of arbitrary dictation in feudal times, deeply rooted in the minds of the masses and even of the Party members in general, cannot be swept away at once; when anything comes up, people seek the easy way out and do not like the elaborate democratic system. In mass organisations democratic centralism can be widely and effectively put into practice only when its efficacy is demonstrated in revolutionary struggle and the masses are made to understand that it can best mobilise their forces and help their struggle. We are drafting a detailed organic law of the councils at all levels (on the basis of the Party centre's outline) in order gradually to correct the previous mistakes. The councils of soldiers' representatives at all levels in the Red Army are now being established on a permanent basis so as to correct the previous mistake of having only soldiers' committees but no councils of soldiers' representatives.

At present what the masses of the people generally know as the "workers', peasants', and soldiers' government" is the executive committee, because, still unaware of the power of the council, they regard the executive committee as the organ of supreme power. An executive committee without a council behind it often neglects the sentiment of the masses in its actions and, as is seen everywhere, hesitates and makes compromises in the confiscation and redistribution of land, wastes and embezzles funds, and gives way before the White forces or struggles only irresolutely against them. Furthermore, the committee seldom meets in full session and all affairs are handled by its standing committee. In both the district and township governments even the standing committee rarely meets and matters are handled separately by its chairman, secretary, treasurer and the captain of the Red guards (or the captain of the insurrection corps), who attend the office regularly. Thus not even in government work is democratic centralism regularly practised.

In the early days the small landlords and rich peasants scrambled to get on to government committees, especially those at the township level. Wearing red ribbons and simulating enthusiasm, they wormed themselves into the government committees by deceitful means and proceeded to manipulate them, leaving only a minor role to the poor-peasant members. They can be cleared out only after they are unmasked and the poor peasantry rises to its feet in the course of struggle. Such a state of affairs, though not universal, has been found in many places.

The Party enjoys great prestige and authority among the masses, while the government falls far behind in this respect. This is because the Party for convenience' sake handles many things directly and brushes aside the organ of political power. There are many instances of this. In some places there are no Party factions in the organs of political power and in other places, where they do exist, they are not fully utilised. From now on the Party must carry out its task of giving leadership to the government; the Party's recommendations and measures must, apart from the agitation undertaken for them, be carried out through government organisations. The Kuomintang's erroneous practice of issuing orders direct to the government should be avoided.

THE PROBLEM OF PARTY ORGANISATION

The struggle against opportunism: About the time of the Incident of May 21, the Party organisations of the counties in the border area may be said to have been controlled by opportunists. When the counter-revolution set in, we scarcely waged any resolute struggle. Last October when the Red Army (the First Regiment of the First Division of the First Army of the Workers' and Peasants' Revolutionary Army) arrived in the counties in the border area, only a few Party members who had gone into hiding were found and the Party organisations had been entirely destroyed by the enemy. The period from last November to April was one of rebuilding the Party, and the period since May has been one of the Party's great expansion. During the past year opportunism within the Party was still found everywhere. A section of Party members, for example, lacking the determination to fight, fled to the remote hills when the enemy came; they called this "lying in ambush". Another section of Party members, though fully active, resorted to adventurist uprisings. All these were manifestations of petty-bourgeois ideas. After a long period of steeling in struggle and of inner-Party education, such things have become less frequent. Meanwhile similar petty-bourgeois ideas have also been found in the Red Army. Upon the advance of the enemy either a desperate fight or flight would be proposed. Both ideas were often put forward by the same person during discussions on military operations. They were gradually rectified only after prolonged inner-Party struggle and through the lessons learnt from objective facts—for example, the losses incurred in a desperate fight and the reverses suffered in a flight.

Localism: The economy in the border area is agricultural, with some places remaining in the stage of the hand-pestle (*e.g.* while foot-pestles made of stone are frequently used on the plains, in the hilly regions rice is generally polished with wooden hand-pestles). The basis of social organisation everywhere is the clan, consisting of persons bearing the same surname. In the Party organisations in the villages, it often happens that since many Party branches are formed for residential reasons by Party members of the same surname, a Party branch meeting becomes virtually a clan meeting. In these circumstances it is very hard indeed to build a "fighting Bolshevik Party". Such members do not quite understand that the Communist Party does not discriminate between nations and provinces, nor do they understand that it does not discriminate between counties, districts or townships. Localism affects strongly the relation between counties and the relation between districts and even townships in the same county. In eliminating localism arguments can at best produce certain limited results, but the oppression of the White forces, which are not localised, counts for much. For instance, only when the counter-revolutionary "joint expedition" of the two provinces gives the people a sense of their common lot in the struggle, can their localism be gradually broken. Localism is declining as a result of many such lessons.

The problem of the native inhabitants and the settlers: There is another peculiar thing in the counties in the border area, namely, the cleft between the native inhabitants and the settlers. A very wide cleft has existed between the native inhabitants and the settlers whose forefathers moved here from the north several hundred years ago; their traditional hatred of each other is so deep-rooted that it sometimes leads to bitter conflict. Numbering several millions, these settlers are found in the region extending from the border between Fukien and Kwangtung all the way along the border of Hunan and Kiangsi to southern Hupeh. The settlers who occupy the hilly regions have been oppressed by the native inhabitants who occupy the plains, and have never had any political rights. They welcomed the national revolution of the two previous years, thinking that the day had come for them to hold their heads high. But unfortunately the revolution failed and they remain oppressed by the native inhabitants.

Within our own area the problem of the native inhabitants and settlers exists in Ningkang, Suichwan, Ling and Chaling, and is most serious in Ningkang. Allying themselves with the settlers and led by the Communist Party, the native revolutionaries in Ningkang in the two previous years overthrew the political power of the native landed gentry and gained control of the whole county. In June last year the Chu P'ei-teh government in Kiangsi turned counter-revolutionary; in September the landed gentry led Chu's troops for "annihilation" to Ningkang and stirred up once again the conflict between the native inhabitants and the settlers. Theoretically, such a cleft between the native inhabitants and the settlers ought not to find its way into the exploited classes of workers and peasants, still less into the Communist Party. But in reality it does exist as the hang-over of a tradition of many years. During the August fiasco in the border area, for instance, the native landed gentry led the reactionary troops to return to Ningkang and carried on the propaganda that the settlers were going to massacre the native inhabitants, whereupon the native peasants mostly became turncoats, put on white ribbons and led the White troops to set fire to houses and search the hills. When the Red Army routed the White troops in October and November, the native peasants fled with the reactionaries, and the settler-peasants seized the belongings of the native inhabitants in turn. This situation, duplicated in the Party, often leads to senseless conflicts. Our policy is, on the one hand, to propagate the slogans, "kill no peasants who have become turncoats" and "peasants who have become turncoats are also given land when they return", so that they may shake off the influence of the landed gentry and return home without misgivings; and on the other hand, to give orders through our county governments that the settler-peasants should return to the owners what they have seized, and to post notices that the native peasants will be protected. Education must be intensified in the Party so that unity is ensured between the two sections of Party members.

The volte-face of the careerists: Seizing the occasion of the open recruitment of Party members during the revolutionary up-surge (in June), many careerists sneaked into the Party, with the result that the Party's membership in the border area rose at once to more than ten thousand. As those in charge of the branches and district committees were mostly new members, good inner-Party education was out of the question. As soon as the White terror came, the careerists became turncoats and led the counter-revolutionaries to arrest our comrades, and the Party organisations in the White areas mostly collapsed. After September a drastic purge of the Party was carried out and strict restrictions were placed on membership qualifications. All the Party organisations in the counties of Yungsin and Ningkang were dissolved and a re-registration was undertaken. Though greatly reduced in number, the membership has increased its fighting capacity. In the past the Party organisa-tions were all in the open, but since September underground organisations have been built so that activities can be continued should the reactionaries come. At the same time, we have been making every effort to penetrate into the White areas and operate inside the enemy camp. But there is as yet no founda-tion for Party organisations in the neighbouring towns. This is because, first, the enemy is generally stronger in the cities, and secondly, since our army during its occupation of the cities damaged the interests of the bourgeoisie too much, it is difficult for Party members to keep a foothold there. At present we are rectifying our mistakes and trying our best to build up our organisations in the cities, but so far the result has not been notable.

The leading bodies of the Party: The branch board has been renamed the branch committee. Above the branch there is the district committee, and above the district committee, the county committee. In special cases district committees may be formed as intermediate organisations between the district and the county committees, as in the Special District of the Northern Section and the South-eastern Special District in Yungsin. In the border area there are altogether five county committees in Ningkang, Yungsin, Lienhwa, Suichwan and Ling. In Chaling there used to be a county committee, but as our work could make no headway, most of the organisations built up there last winter and this spring have been destroyed by the White forces; for the last half-year we have been able to work only in its hilly regions near Ningkang and Yungsin, and its county committee has therefore been reorganised as a special district committee. People were sent to the counties of Yu and Anjen, which can be reached only via Chaling, but they returned without accomplishing anything. The Wanan County Committee held a joint meeting with us in Suichwan in January; then it was cut off from us by the White forces for more than half a year and fresh contact was made only in September, when the Red Army reached Wanan in a guerrilla operation. Eighty revolutionary peasants followed our men to the Chingkang mountains and were organised as the Wanan Red Guards. There is no Party organisation in Anfu. The county committee of Kian, which borders on Yungsin, has got in touch with us only twice, and strange to say, it has not given us any help. In March and in August land was twice redistributed in the Shatien area in Kweitung county, where Party organisations have been built up and placed under the jurisdiction of the Southern Hunan Special Committee with its centre at Shiherhtung, Lungki. Above the county committees there is the Special Committee of the Hunan-Kiangsi Border Area. On May 20 the first congress of the Party organisation in the border area was held at Maoping in Ningkang, and elected the First Special Committee[22] of twenty-three members with Mao Tse-tung as secretary. In July the Hunan Provincial Committee sent Yang K'ai-ming over and he became acting secretary. In September Yang fell ill and T'an Chen-lin took his place. In August when the major detachment of the Red Army had gone to southern Hunan and the White forces were bringing full pressure on the border area, we held an emergency meeting at Yungsin. In October, as the Red Army had returned to Ningkang, we convened at Maoping the second congress of the Party organisation in the border area. The congress, which met for three days beginning from October 14, adopted resolutions including "Political Problems and the Tasks of the Border Area Party Organisation" and elected the Second Special Committee[23] of nineteen members: T'an Chen-lin, Chu Teh, Ch'en Yi, Lung Ch'ao-ch'ing, Chu Ch'ang-chieh, Liu T'ien-ch'ien, Yuan P'an-chu, T'an Szu-ts'ung, T'an Ping, Li Chueh-fei, Sung Yi-yo, Yuan Wen-ts'ai, Wang Tso-nung, Ch'en Cheng-jen, Mao Tse-tung, Wan Hsi-hsien, Wang Tso, Yang K'ai-ming and Ho T'ing-ying. Five of them became members of the standing committee, with T'an Chen-lin (a worker) as secretary and Ch'en Cheng-jen (an intellectual) as deputy secretary. The Sixth General Assembly of the Red Army held on November 14 elected an army committee of twenty-three members, five of them forming a standing committee with Chu Teh as secretary. Both the Special Committee and the Army Committee are subordinate to the Front Committee. The Front Committee was reorganised on November 6, with five members designated by the Party centre: Mao Tse-tung, Chu Teh, the secretary of the local Party headquarters (T'an Chen-lin), a worker comrade (Sung Ch'iao-sheng), and a peasant comrade (Mao K'o-wen), with Mao Tse-tung as secretary. For the time being the Front Committee has set up a secretariat, a propaganda department, an organisation department, a trade union commission and a military commission. The Front Committee is in charge of the local Party. It is still necessary to keep the Special Committee because sometimes the Front Committee has to move with the troops.

We feel that the problem of proletarian ideological leadership is a very important one. The Party organisations in the counties in the border area are composed almost entirely of peasants, who will go astray without proletarian ideological leadership. Besides paying close attention to the trade union movement in the county towns and other bigger towns, we should increase the number of workers' representatives in the organs of political power. In the Party's leading bodies at all levels the proportion of workers and poor peasants should also be increased.

THE PROBLEM OF THE CHARACTER OF THE REVOLUTION

We fully agree with the Communist International's resolutions concerning China. At present China certainly remains in the stage of the bourgeois-democratic revolution. A programme for a thorough democratic revolution in China includes, externally, the overthrow of imperialism so as to achieve complete national liberation, and, internally, the clean-up of the influence of the comprador class in the cities, the completion of the agrarian revolution, the elimination of feudal relations in the villages, and the overthrow of the government of the warlords. We must go through such a democratic revolution before we can lay a real foundation for passing on to socialism. Having fought in various places in the past year, we are keenly aware that the revolutionary upsurge in the country as a whole is subsiding. While Red political power has been established in a few small areas, the people of the country as a whole still do not possess basic democratic rights; the workers and the peasants and even the bourgeois democrats have no rights of speech and assembly, and joining the Communist Party constitutes the greatest crime. Wherever the Red Army goes, it finds the masses cold and reserved; only after propaganda and agitation do they slowly rouse themselves. We have to fight the enemy forces hard whoever they are, and scarcely any mutiny or uprising has taken place within the enemy forces. The same is true even of the Sixth Army, which recruited the greatest number of "rebels" after the Incident of May 21. We have an acute sense of loneliness and are every moment longing for the end of such a lonely life. To turn the revolution into a seething, surging tide all over the country, it is necessary to launch a political and economic struggle for democracy involving also the urban petty bourgeoisie.

We carried out our policy towards the petty bourgeoisie fairly well before February this year. In March the representative of the Southern Hunan Special Committee arrived in Ningkang and criticised us for leaning to the Right, for having not done enough burning and killing, and for having failed to carry out the policy of "turning the petty bourgeois into proletarians and then forcing them into the revolution"; whereupon the leadership of the Front Committee was changed and there was a shift in our policy. In April when our entire army had arrived in the border area, though we still did not do much burning and killing, yet we quite rigorously confiscated the property of the middle merchants in the cities and assessed contributions from the small landlords and rich peasants in the countryside. The slogan of "all factories to the workers" put forward by the Southern Hunan Special Committee was also widely propagated. This ultra-Left policy of attacking the petty bourgeois drove most of them to the side of the landed gentry; they put on white ribbons and opposed us. Since this policy has been gradually changed of late, the situation has also gradually improved. Good results have been achieved in Suichwan in particular, for the merchants in the county towns and market places no longer shun us and quite a few of them speak well of the Red Army. The fair in Tsaolin (a midday fair held once in every three days) is attended by twenty thousand people, which is something unprecedented. This is a proof that our policy is now correct. The landed gentry imposed very heavy taxes and assessments on the people, while the pacification guards[24] of Suichwan levied five toll charges along the seventy-*li* road from Hwangao to Tsaolin, no agricultural produce being exempt. We crushed the pacification guards and abolished these tolls, thus winning the support of all the peasants as well as the small and middle merchants.

As the Party centre has requested us to announce a political programme which also takes into account the interests of the petty bourgeoisie, we on our part propose that the Party centre work out, as a guidance for various places, a programme for the whole democratic revolution which takes into account the interests of the workers, the agrarian revolution and national liberation.

In the revolution in China, a country dominated by agricultural economy, the development of armed insurrections is a special feature. We suggest to the Party centre that it should devote great attention to military affairs.

THE PROBLEM OF THE LOCATION OF THE INDEPENDENT RÉGIME

The area that stretches from northern Kwangtung, along the border between the Hunan and Kiangsi provinces to southern Hupeh, falls entirely within the region of the Losiao mountain range. We have traversed the entire range and a comparison of its different sections shows that the middle section, with Ningkang as its centre, is the most favourable for our armed independent régime. The terrain in the northern section is not so favourable as that in the middle section, where we can advance or defend ourselves at will; furthermore it is too close to the big political centre of the enemy and, unless we have plans for the speedy seizure of Changsha or Wuhan, it will be dangerous to station large forces in the area of Liuyang, Liling, Pingsiang and Tungku. The terrain in the southern section is better than that in the northern section, but the mass base is not so good as in the middle section—politically it cannot exert so much influence on Hunan and Kiangsi as the middle section, where any single action may affect the lower river valleys of the two provinces. The advantages of the middle section are: (1) A mass base which we have been building for more than a year. (2) A fairly firm basis for the Party organisations. (3) Over more than a year, we have built up local armed forces that are well experienced in struggle—a very rare achievement, and the strength of these local forces, coupled with that of the Red Fourth Army, is indestructible by any enemy force. (4) An excellent military base—the Chingkang mountains, with bases for our local armed forces in all the counties. (5) It can exert influence on two provinces and even on the lower valleys of their principal rivers; compared with southern Hunan or southern Kiangsi, which can exert influence only on one province, or even only the upper river valley and the hinterland of one province, this section has a quite different political significance. The disadvantage of the middle section is that, having long been under the independent régime, it is confronted by the enemy's large forces of "encirclement and annihilation" and the economic problem, especially that of cash, is an extremely difficult one.

As regards the plan for our action here, the Hunan Provincial
Party Committee changed its mind three times within a few
weeks in June and July. At first Yuan Te-sheng came and
approved of the plan for establishing our political power in the
middle section of the Losiao mountain range. Then Tu Hsiu-
ching and Yang K'ai-ming arrived, and proposed that the Red
Army should drive ahead to Southern Hunan "without the
least hesitation", leaving only a force of two hundred rifles to
defend the border area together with the Red guards; they said
that this was an "absolutely correct" policy. The third time,
barely ten days later, Yuan Te-sheng came again, bringing us a
letter which contained, besides much admonition, a proposal
that the Red Army should set out for eastern Hunan; this was
again said to be an "absolutely correct" policy and we were
again asked to act "without the least hesitation". When
we received such rigid directives we indeed found ourselves
in a dilemma, because failure to comply with them would
be tantamount to disobedience while compliance with them
would mean certain defeat. When the second letter came, the
Army Committee, the Special Committee and the Yungsin
County Committee held a joint conference, which considered
it dangerous to go to southern Hunan and decided not to carry
out the proposals of the Provincial Committee.

But a few days later Tu Hsiu-ching and Yang K'ai-ming,
insisting on the proposals of the Provincial Committee and
taking advantage of the Twenty-ninth Regiment's provincial-
ism, dragged off the whole Red Army to attack the county town
of Chen and thus courted disaster for both the border area and
the Red Army. The Red Army lost about half its men, while
in the border area countless houses were burnt down and people
massacred; counties fell one after another and some of them
remain in the enemy hands to this minute.

As for an advance on eastern Hunan, unless there is a split
within the régime of the landed gentry in the provinces of
Hunan, Hupeh and Kiangsi, it is certainly inadvisable for the
main forces of the Red Army to undertake it. If we had not
advanced on southern Hunan in July, we would not only
have averted the August fiasco in the border area but would
have taken advantage of the war in Changshu, Kiangsi,

between the Kuomintang's Sixth Army and Wang Chun's forces to crush the enemy forces in Yungsin, and would have swept over Kian and Anfu and sent our vanguard to Pingsiang to effect a junction with the Red Fifth Army in the northern section. Even then we should have set up our general headquarters in Ningkang, and dispatched only the guerrilla forces to eastern Hunan. As war had not broken out between sections of the landed gentry and formidable enemy forces were still in Pingsiang, Chaling and Yu on the Hunan border, it would have been giving the enemy his chance if we had moved our main forces towards the north. The Party centre asked us to consider an advance on eastern or southern Hunan, but in practice it is very dangerous either way; though the proposal for an advance on eastern Hunan has not been carried out, that on southern Hunan has already proved disastrous. It is worth our while to remember always this painful experience.

Up to the present no split has occurred within the régime of the landed gentry, and the enemy's forces for "annihilation" that are deployed round the border area still number more than ten regiments. But if we can continue to find some way out in the matter of cash (food and clothing are not much of a problem now), then, basing ourselves on the foundation in the border area, we shall be able to cope with the enemy force at its present strength, or even at a greater strength. As far as the border area is concerned, once the Red Army moves away a devastation like that of August would befall it. Though not all of our Red guards would be wiped out, the whole basis of the Party and of the masses would be heavily damaged, and although the independent régime in some of the mountain areas might hold out, all of us in the plains would have to go underground as we did in August and September. If the Red Army does not move away, then with our present base we can gradually expand to all the surrounding areas and our prospects are very bright. And for the Red Army to expand, it must engage the enemy in a long struggle in the area round the Chingkang mountains, i.e. the four counties of Ningkang, Yungsin, Ling and Suichwan, where we have a mass base, taking advantage of the clash of interests between the enemy forces of Hunan and Kiangsi and of the enemy's need to man the defences on all sides and consequently his inability to concentrate his forces. We must use correct tactics and fight no battle unless we can win victory and capture the enemy's arms and men, so as to expand the Red Army gradually. With the mass base well laid in the border area in the period from April to July, the Red Army's major detachment could undoubtedly have expanded itself in August, if it had not made an expedition to southern Hunan. Although a mistake was made, the Red Army has returned to the border area where the terrain is favourable and the people friendly, and the prospects are still not bad. In a place like the border area the Red Army must be fully determined for the struggle and have the stamina for fighting, for only thus can it increase its arms and train good men.

For a whole year the Red flag has been kept flying in the border area; though it has incurred the hatred of the landed gentry of Hunan, Hupeh and Kiangsi provinces and even of the whole country, it has gradually aroused the hopes of the masses of workers, peasants and soldiers in the nearby provinces. Regarding the "bandit-annihilation" campaign against the border area as a major task and issuing statements like "a million dollars were consumed in a year's campaign to annihilate the bandits" (Lu Ti-p'ing), and the Communists "number 20,000 armed with 5,000 rifles" (Wang Chun), the warlords have gradually directed the attention of their soldiers and disheartened lower-rank officers to us and thereby supplied another source for the expansion of the Red Army, because more and more of such officers and men will come over to us. Furthermore, the fact that the Red flag has never been struck in the border area shows not only the strength of the Communist Party but the bankruptcy of the ruling classes; this is of great significance in national politics. That is why we have always held that it is entirely necessary and correct to build up and expand the Red political power in the middle section of the Losiao mountain range.

November 25, 1928.

ON THE RECTIFICATION OF INCORRECT IDEAS IN THE PARTY

This is a resolution written for the Ninth Conference of the Party organisation of the Fourth Army of the Red Army in December 1929. The building of the Chinese people's armed forces has gone through a difficult course. The Chinese Red Army (which became the Eighth Route Army and New Fourth Army during the Anti-Japanese War and is now the People's Liberation Army), created on August 1, 1927, at the time of the Nanchang Uprising, had by December 1929 been in existence for more than two years. During these years the Communist Party in the Red Army, in combating various incorrect ideas, had learnt a great deal and accumulated considerable experience, which was summed up in this resolution. The resolution placed the building of the Red Army entirely on a Marxist-Leninist basis and eliminated all the influences of the old-type armies. It was not only carried out in the Fourth Army of the Red Army but was also followed sooner or later by all other units of the Red Army; in this manner the whole Red Army was completely transformed into a genuine army of the people. In the last twenty and more years the Chinese people's armed forces have made tremendous developments and innovations in their Party activities and political work, and conferred on them a totally new aspect, but the basic line in such activities and work remains the same as that laid down in this resolution.

In the Communist Party organisation in the Fourth Army of the Red Army, there are various non-proletarian ideas which greatly hinder the carrying out of the Party's correct line. If they are not thoroughly rectified, then the Fourth Army of the Red Army will certainly be unable to shoulder the tasks which China's great revolutionary struggle has assigned to it. The source of various incorrect ideas in the Party organisation in the Fourth Army lies, of course, in the fact that the Party's organisational basis is largely made up of peasants and other elements of petty-bourgeois origin; yet the failure of the Party's leading bodies to wage a concerted and determined struggle against these incorrect ideas and to educate the members along the correct line is also an important cause of the existence and growth of such incorrect ideas. This conference, basing itself on the spirit of the September letter of the Party centre, herewith points out the manifestations of various non-proletarian ideas in the Party organisation in the Fourth Army, their sources, and the methods of rectifying them, and calls upon all comrades to eliminate them thoroughly.

ON THE PURELY MILITARY VIEWPOINT

The purely military viewpoint is unusually widespread among a number of comrades in the Red Army. It manifests itself as follows:

1. To regard military work and political work as opposed to each other; to fail to recognise military work as only one of the means for accomplishing political tasks. Even to declare, "When military work is well done, political work will naturally be well done; when military work is not well done, political work cannot be well done either"—this is to go a step farther and to regard military work as leading political work.

2. To regard the task of the Red Army as similar to that of the White army—merely fighting. To ignore the fact that the Chinese Red Army is an armed force for carrying out the political tasks of the revolution. Especially at the present time, certainly the Red Army exists not merely to fight; besides fighting to destroy the enemy's military strength, it should also shoulder such important tasks as agitating the masses, organising them, arming them, and helping them to set up revolutionary political power, and even establishing organisations of the Communist Party. When the Red Army fights, it fights not merely for the sake of fighting but to agitate the masses, to organise them, to arm them, and to help them to establish revolutionary political power; apart from such objectives, fighting loses its meaning and the Red Army the reason for its existence.

3. Organisationally, therefore, to subordinate the organs of the Red Army's political work to those of its military work, and to put forward the slogan, "Army HQ deals with the public". If such an idea continues to develop, it may lead to estrangement from the masses, to domination of the government by the army, and to a departure from proletarian leadership—in a word, to the same path of warlordism as that followed by the Kuomintang army.

4. At the same time, in agitational work, to overlook the importance of the agitation teams. In organising the masses, to overlook the organisation of the soldiers' councils in the army and the organisation of the local masses of workers and peasants. As a result, both agitational and organisational work are abandoned.

5. To be conceited when a battle is won and to be dejected when it is lost.

6. Group egoism, *i.e.* to approach everything only in the interests of the Fourth Army without understanding that to arm the local masses is one of the Red Army's important tasks. This is an enlarged form of cliquism.

7. Limited by the immediate environment of the Fourth Army, a small number of comrades think that no other revolutionary forces exist. Hence the extremely deep-rooted idea of conserving its strength by avoiding action. This is a remnant of opportunism.

8. To disregard the subjective and objective conditions, to be seized with revolutionary impetuosity, to hate to take pains over any minor, detailed work among the masses, but to wish only to do big things and to be chock-full of illusions. This is a remnant of adventurism. [1]

The source of the purely military viewpoint:

1. The low political level. Hence the failure to recognise the role of political leadership in the army or to recognise the fact that the Red Army and the White army are basically different.

2. The ideology of the mercenary troops. As soldiers captured from the enemy in battles are very numerous, such elements, when taken into the Red Army, have brought with them their deep-rooted ideology of the mercenary troops, thereby providing a rank-and-file basis for the purely military viewpoint.

3. From the two preceding causes arises a third, namely, over-confidence in military strength and lack of confidence in the strength of the masses of the people.

4. The Party's failure to actively attend to and discuss military work is also a cause for the emergence of the purely military viewpoint among a number of comrades.

The methods of rectification:

1. To raise the political level in the Party by means of

education, to eradicate the theoretical roots of the purely military viewpoint, to recognise clearly the basic difference between the Red Army and the White army. At the same time, to eliminate also the remnants of opportunism and adventurism and to break down the group egoism of the Fourth Army.

2. To intensify the political education of both officers and men, especially the education of soldiers captured from the enemy. At the same time, let the local governments select, by all possible means, workers and peasants experienced in struggle to join the Red Army, thus organisationally weakening and even eradicating the root of the purely military viewpoint.

3. To arouse the local Party organisations to make criticism of the Party organisations in the Red Army, and the organs of mass political power to make criticism of the Red Army in order to influence the Party organisations in the Red Army and officers and men of the Red Army.

4. The Party must actively pay attention to military work and hold discussions on it. After being discussed and decided upon by the Party, all work is to be carried out through the masses.

5. To draw up rules and regulations which clearly define the tasks of the Red Army, the relationship between the organs for military work and those for political work, the relationship between the Red Army and the masses of the people, and the powers and functions of the soldiers' council and its relationship with the military and political organs.

ON EXTREME DEMOCRATISATION

Since the Fourth Army of the Red Army followed the directives of the Party centre, extreme democratisation has diminished considerably. For example, the decisions of the Party can now be carried out fairly well; and no longer does anyone bring up such erroneous proposals as to carry out in the Red Army "democratic centralism from the bottom to the top" or "ask the lower levels to discuss first, then let the higher levels decide". Actually, however, this diminution is only temporary and superficial and does not yet mean the elimination of the idea of extreme democratisation. In other words, the roots of exteme democratisation still lie deep in the minds of many comrades. Witness all sorts of reluctance to carry out the decisions of the Party.

The methods of rectification:

1. To eradicate ideologically the roots of extreme democratisation. First of all, it should be pointed out that the danger of extreme democratisation lies in the tendency to damage and even completely destroy the Party organisation, to weaken and even completely destroy the Party's fighting capacity, and to incapacitate the Party from shouldering its fighting tasks, thereby causing the defeat of the revolution. Next it should be pointed out that the source of extreme democratisation lies in the nature of the petty bourgeoisie, which is easy-going and averse to discipline. Such a nature, having found its way into the Party, manifests itself politically and organisationally as the idea of extreme democratisation. This idea is basically incompatible with the fighting tasks of the proletariat.

2. Organisationally, to enforce strictly the democratic way of life under centralised guidance. The line for this is as follows:

(1) The leading body of the Party must give a correct line of guidance and find solutions when problems arise, in order to establish itself as a leading centre.

(2) The higher body must clearly understand the conditions of the lower bodies and of the life of the rank and file, so as to secure an objective basis for correct leadership.

(3) Party organisations at all levels should not make decisions without due deliberation. Once a decision is reached, it must be firmly carried out.

(4) All decisions of any importance made by the Party's higher bodies must be promptly transmitted to the lower bodies and the rank-and-file Party members. The method for doing this is to call a meeting of activists or a general membership meeting of the Party branch or (when circumstances permit) even of the column[2] and to assign people to make reports at such meetings.

(5) The lower bodies of the Party and the rank-and-file Party members must discuss in detail directives from the higher bodies in order to understand their significance thoroughly and decide on the methods to carry them out.

ON THE NON-ORGANISATIONAL VIEWPOINT

The non-organisational viewpoint existing in the Party organisation in the Fourth Army manifests itself as follows:

(*a*) The insubordination of the minority to the majority. For example, after a minority find their motion voted down, they do not sincerely carry out the decisions of the Party organisation.

The methods of rectification:

1. At a meeting, all people should be made to voice their opinions fully. The right and wrong sides over a controversial issue should be clearly established without compromise or equivocation. Anything that cannot be settled at one meeting may be discussed at another (provided no work is affected) in order to reach a clear-cut conclusion.

2. Party discipline requires, among other things, that the minority should obey the majority. The minority, after their suggestion has been rejected, must support the decision adopted by the majority. If necessary, they can bring up the matter again for discussion at the next meeting, but they must not show any opposition in their activities.

(*b*) Non-organisational criticism:

1. Inner-Party criticism is a weapon to fortify the Party's organisation and increase its fighting capacity. In the Party organisation of the Red Army, however, criticism is sometimes not of this character, but develops into personal attacks. As a result, it damages not only individuals but also the Party's organisation. This is a manifestation of petty-bourgeois individualism. The method of rectification is to make it clear to Party members that criticism aims at increasing the Party's fighting capacity in order to achieve victory in the class struggles and that it should never be used as a means of personal attack.

2. Many Party members make their criticisms not inside the Party but outside it. This is because in general the members have not yet grasped the importance of the Party's organisation (its meetings, etc.), seeing no difference between criticism inside the organisation and that outside it. The method of rectification is to educate Party members so as to make them understand that the Party's organisation is important and that any

criticism of Party committees or comrades ought to be made at Party meetings.

ON ABSOLUTE EQUALITARIANISM

Absolute equalitarianism in the Red Army once developed to a very serious extent. For example: To object to granting different allowances to the wounded soldiers according to the seriousness of the wound but to advocate equal allowances. To deny the necessity for officers to ride horses in performing their duties but to regard horse-riding as denoting inequality. To demand absolutely equal distribution of supplies and to object to a larger allotment to special cases. To demand equal assignment for all persons in carrying rice, irrespective of age or physical condition. To demand equal space in allotting billets and even to condemn the HQ for occupying a larger house. To demand equal assignment of fatigue duties and to refuse to do any extra work. Even when there are two wounded men but only one stretcher, to prefer to abandon both rather than to carry either. All these prove that absolute equalitarianism among officers and men of the Red Army is still serious.

Like extreme democratisation in political matters, absolute equalitarianism can be traced back to an economy of handicrafts and small peasant farming as its source, the only difference being that the one manifests itself in political life and the other in material life.

Method of rectification: It should be pointed out that not only is absolute equalitarianism merely an illusion of the peasants and small proprietors in the days when capitalism has not been abolished, but even in the days of socialism, material things will be distributed on the principle of "from each according to his ability and to each according to his work" as well as to the needs of his work, and there is definitely no such thing as absolute equalisation. The distribution of material things among the personnel of the Red Army must on the whole be equal, such as equal allowances for officers and men, because this is required by the present circumstances of the struggle. But absolute equalitarianism beyond reason must be opposed because it is not needed in our struggle; on the contrary, it hinders the struggle.

ON SUBJECTIVISM

Subjectivism exists to a serious extent among certain Party members and this is very harmful in analytically studying a political situation and in guiding the work. Subjective analysis of a political situation and subjective guidance of work inevitably result either in opportunism or in adventurism. As to subjective criticism inside the Party, random talk not based on facts, or mutual suspicion, it often foments unprincipled conflicts and disrupts the Party's organisation.

Another point should be mentioned in connection with inner-Party criticism, namely, that some comrades in their criticism do not pay attention to the major issues, but only to the minor ones. They do not understand that the main purpose of criticism is to point out political and organisational mistakes. As to personal defects, unless they are related to political and organisational errors, one need not be so censorious as to place the comrades concerned in a quandary. Moreover, there is a great danger that, once such criticism develops, the attention of the Party may be entirely concentrated on trivial defects, and everybody may become timorous, punctiliously well-mannered and forget the Party's political tasks.

The method of rectification: Chiefly to educate Party members so as to raise their thought and their inner-Party life to a political and scientific level. To achieve this end we must: (1) Teach Party members to apply the Marxist-Leninist method in analysing a political situation and appraising class forces in place of subjective analysis and appraisal. (2) Direct the Party members' attention to social and economic investigations and studies, to determine thereby the tactics of struggle and the methods of work, and make comrades understand that without the investigation of actual conditions they will fall into the abyss of fantasy and adventurism. (3) In inner-Party criticism, guard against subjective, dogmatic and vulgar tendencies: statements must be based on facts and criticisms must centre round politics.

ON INDIVIDUALISM

The individualist tendency in the Party in the Red Army assumes the following manifestations:

1. Vindictiveness. After being criticised inside the Party by a soldier comrade, to seek chances to retaliate on him outside the Party—beating or scolding is one way of retaliation. Retaliation is also sought inside the Party: you attack me at this meeting, so I shall retaliate by finding fault with you at the next. Such vindictiveness proceeds solely from placing personal considerations above the interests of the class and of the Party as a whole. Its target is not the enemy class but individuals in our own ranks. It is a corrosive which weakens the organisation and its fighting capacity.

2. Cliquism. To care only about the interests of one's own small group and ignore general interests—although apparently not concerned with personal interests, this contains in reality individualism of an extremely narrow kind and likewise has an exceedingly corrosive and centrifugal effect. In the Red Army, cliquism has all along been rampant; although it has now become less serious as a result of criticism, its remnants still exist and further effort is needed to overcome it.

3. The mercenary view. Not to appreciate that one is a member of the Party and the Red Army, both of which are instruments for carrying out revolutionary tasks. Not to appreciate that one fulfils a responsible role in the revolution, but to think oneself only responsible to individual officers and not to the revolution. This passive mercenary view of revolution is also a manifestation of individualism. The mercenary view of revolution explains why there are so few people who are enthusiastic and active, and exert themselves unreservedly. If the mercenary view is not eliminated, the number of such people cannot be increased and the heavy burden of the revolution will always rest on the shoulders of a few, much to the detriment of the struggle.

4. Hedonism. In the Red Army there are also quite a few whose individualism finds expression in seeking pleasure. They constantly hope that the troops will march to the big cities. They want to go there not to work but to enjoy themselves.

What they dislike most is to work in the Red areas where life is hard.

5. Passivity and inactivity. To become passive and stop working whenever things go against one's wishes. This is mainly due to lack of education, though sometimes it is also due to the leadership's incorrect ways of handling matters, assigning work or enforcing discipline.

6. The desire to leave the army. The number of people who ask for transfer from work in the Red Army to local work is on the increase. This not entirely due to personal reasons but also to: (1) the material hardships of life in the Red Army; (2) the feeling of exhaustion after a long struggle; and (3) the leadership's incorrect ways of handling matters, assigning work or enforcing discipline.

The methods of rectification: Chiefly to intensify education in order to rectify individualism ideologically. Next, to handle matters, assign work and enforce discipline correctly. Furthermore, to take measures to improve the material life in the Red Army and utilise every available opportunity for rest and rehabilitation in order to ameliorate the material conditions. We must explain clearly in carrying out education that individualism is in its social source a reflection in the Party of petty-bourgeois and bourgeois ideologies.

ON THE IDEA OF THE ROVING INSURGENTS

The political idea of the roving insurgents arises in the Red Army because the vagabond elements form a very large proportion of it and because there are enormous numbers of vagabonds in the country, especially in the southern provinces. This idea manifests itself as follows: (1) To be unwilling to expand our political influence by strenuous work in founding base areas and establishing the political power of the masses of the people, but to try to expand it by applying only mobile guerrilla methods. (2) In expanding the Red Army, to follow not the line of first expanding the local detachments of the Red guards, then the local units of the Red Army, and finally the main forces of the Red Army, but the line of "hiring men and buying horses" and "recruiting deserters and taking in mutineers".[3] (3) To be impatient in carrying on hard struggles together with the masses, and to hope only to go to the big cities and indulge in eating and drinking. All such manifestations of the idea of the roving insurgents seriously hamper the Red Army in accomplishing its proper tasks; thus the elimination of this idea is indeed one of the important aims of the ideological struggle of the Party organisation in the Red Army. It must be recognised that the idea of the roving insurgents of the Huang Ch'ao[4] or Li Ch'uang[5] type is no longer permissible under present-day conditions.

The methods of rectification:

1. To intensify education, criticise incorrect ideas, and eliminate the idea of the roving insurgents.

2. To intensify education against the vagabond outlook among the basic sections of the Red Army and the newly captured soldiers.

3. To strive to draw into the ranks of the Red Army active workers and peasants experienced in struggle in order to change the composition of the Red Army.

4. To create new units of the Red Army from among the masses of workers and peasants who are in the midst of struggle.

ON THE REMNANTS OF ADVENTURISM

The Party organisation in the Red Army has already waged struggles against adventurism, but not yet to a full extent. Therefore remnants of the adventurist idea still exist in the Red Army. Their manifestations are: (1) To act blindly regardless of subjective and objective conditions. (2) To carry out inadequately and irresolutely the policy for the cities. (3) Slack military discipline, especially in moments of defeat. (4) The misdemeanour committed by some units of setting fire to houses. (5) The practice of shooting deserters and of corporal punishment—these are also in the nature of adventurism. Adventurism, in its social source, is a combination of the ideology of the *lumpen*-proletariat with that of the petty bourgeoisie.

The methods of rectification:

1. To eliminate adventurism ideologically.

2. To rectify adventurist action by laying down proper rules and regulations and adopting correct policies.

December 1929.

A SINGLE SPARK CAN START A PRAIRIE FIRE

This is a letter written in January 1930 to a comrade in criticism of a pessimistic view then existing in the Party.

On the question of the appraisal of the current situation and our actions ensuing from it, comrades in our Party still lack a correct understanding. Though convinced that a revolutionary upsurge will inevitably arise, they do not believe that it may arise soon. Thus they disapprove of the plan to seize Kiangsi and favour only mobile guerrilla-like activities in the three border areas between Fukien and Kwantung and Kiangsi; and as they have no profound notion about establishing the Red political power in the guerrilla areas, so they have no profound notion about accelerating the nation-wide revolutionary upsurge by consolidating and expanding such Red political power. They seem to think that, since the revolutionary upsurge is still far away, it will be labour lost to attempt to build up our political power by hard work; they want instead to extend our political influence in the unhampered and mobile manner of the guerrillas and, once the masses throughout the country have been won over, or more or less won over, to launch an armed uprising which, with the forces of the Red Army thrown in, would become a great nation-wide revolution.

Their theory that we should, on a nation-wide scale and in all regions, win over the masses first and establish political power afterwards, does not fit in with the actual situation of the Chinese revolution. It stems in the main from the failure to understand clearly that China is a semi-colony contended for by many imperialist powers. If one clearly understands this, then first, one can understand why in China alone in the world there is such an unusual thing as a prolonged strife within the ruling classes, why the fight intensifies and expands day by day, and why no unified political power has ever come into being. Secondly, one can understand how important the peasant problem is, and consequently why rural uprisings have developed on such a nation-wide scale as at present. Thirdly, one can understand the correctness of the slogan about a workers' and peasants' democratic political power. Fourthly, one can understand another unusual thing which corresponds to and arises out of the unusual thing that in China alone in the world there is a prolonged strife within the ruling classes, and that is the existence and development of the Red Army and guerrilla troops, and, together with them, the existence and development of small Red areas that have grown amid the encirclement of the White political power (no such unusual thing is found anywhere except in China). Fifthly, one can also understand that the formation and development of the Red Army, the guerrilla units and the Red areas are the highest form of the peasant struggle under the leadership of the pro- letariat in semi-colonial China, the inevitable outcome of the growth of the peasant struggle in a semi-colony, and are undoubtedly the most important factors in accelerating the revolutionary upsurge throughout the country. And sixthly, one can also understand that the policy of purely mobile guerrilla-like activities cannot accomplish the task of accelerat- ing the nation-wide revolutionary upsurge, while the kind of policies adopted by Chu Teh and Mao Tse-tung and by Fang Chih-min [1] are undoubtedly correct—policies such as establish- ing base areas; building up political power according to plan; deepening the agrarian revolution; and expanding the people's armed forces by developing in due order first the township Red guards, then the district Red guards, then the county Red guards, then the local Red Army, and then a regular Red Army; and expanding political power by advancing in a series of waves, etc., etc. Only thus can we win the confidence of the revolutionary masses throughout the country, just as the Soviet Union has done throughout the world. Only thus can we create tremendous difficulties for the reactionary ruling classes, shake their very foundations, and precipitate their internal disintegration. And only thus can we really create a Red Army that will be our chief weapon in the coming great revolution. In short, only thus can we accelerate the revolu- tionary upsurge.

Comrades who suffer from revolutionary impetuosity unduly

over-estimate the subjective forces of the revolution[2] and under-estimate the forces of the counter-revolution. Such an appraisal largely stems from subjectivism. In the end, it will doubtless lead to the path of adventurism. On the other hand, if one under-estimates the subjective forces of the revolution and over-estimates the forces of the counter-revolution, that will also be an inappropriate appraisal and will inevitably produce another kind of bad result. Therefore, in sizing up the political situation in China it is necessary to understand the following features:

1. Although the subjective forces of the revolution in China at present are still weak, yet so are all the organs (government, armed forces, parties, etc.) of the reactionary ruling classes with their foothold on the backward and fragile social and economic structure of China. This explains why revolution cannot break out at present in the countries of Western Europe where, although the subjective forces of the revolution are perhaps stronger than those in China, the forces of the reactionary ruling classes are many times stronger than those in our country. Although the subjective forces of the revolution in China at present are weak, yet because the forces of the counter-revolution are correspondingly weak, the revolution will certainly move towards an upsurge more quickly in China than in Western Europe.

2. Since the defeat of the revolution in 1927, the subjective forces of revolution have indeed been greatly weakened. The force that remains is to all appearances very small and this naturally makes some comrades (who judge by appearances) feel pessimistic. But it is a quite different thing if we look into the essence of the matter. Here the old Chinese proverb, "A single spark can start a prairie fire", is applicable. In other words, although the force is only a small one at present, it will rapidly develop. In China, as things stand, its development is not merely a possibility but a necessity; this was fully proved in the May 30 Movement and the Great Revolutionary Movement which followed. When we study an event, we must examine its essence and treat its appearance merely as a guide to the threshold of the essence; and once we cross the threshold, we must grasp the essence—this alone is the reliable and scientific method of analysis.

3. Similarly, in estimating the counter-revolutionary forces, we should never look merely at their appearance, but must study their essence. In the early period of our independent régime on the Hunan-Kiangsi border, some comrades seriously believed in the incorrect appraisal made by the Hunan Provincial Party Committee of that time, and regarded our class enemy as not worth a rap; the two phrases, "extremely shaky" and "exceedingly panicky", which have been passed on as standing jokes even to this day, were precisely the description used at that time (from May to June 1928) by the Hunan Provincial Party Committee in sizing up Lu Ti-p'ing,[3] the ruler of Hunan. Political adventurism necessarily ensued from such an appraisal. But during the four months from November 1928 to February 1929 (before the war between Chiang Kai-shek and the Kwangsi warlords[4] broke out), when the enemy's third "joint expedition"[5] pressed forward to the Chingkang mountains, a section of comrades raised the question, "How long can the red flag be kept flying?" As a matter of fact, the struggle in China between Britain, the United States and Japan had by then become quite open, and the situation was taking shape for a fight between Chiang Kai-shek, Feng Yu-hsiang and the Kwangsi warlords; hence in reality it was just the time when the counter-revolutionary tide began to ebb and the revolutionary tide to rise again. But during this very period not only was a pessimistic view found in the Red Army and local Party organisations, but the Party centre was also more or less perplexed by surface conditions and became pessimistic in its tone. The February letter from the Party centre furnished a proof of the pessimism shown by the Party in its political analysis at that time.

4. The present objective situation may still easily perplex those comrades who observe only the appearance of the existing conditions but not its essence. Those of us working in the Red Army, especially when defeated in battle, encircled on all sides or pursued by strong enemy forces, often unwittingly universalise and magnify what are after all only momentary, particular and local conditions, as if the whole situation in China and throughout the world was dark and gloomy, and the prospect of victory of the revolution dim and remote. They

cling to the appearance and neglect the essence because they have not made a scientific analysis of the essence of the general situation. If it is asked whether the revolutionary upsurge will arise soon in China, we can give a definite answer only after studying carefully whether the contradictions leading to the revolutionary upsurge are really developing. Since contradictions are developing internationally between the imperialist countries, between the imperialist countries and their colonies, and between imperialism and the proletariat in these countries, the imperialists feel all the more urgently the need to contend for China. As the imperialists' contention for China intensifies, both the contradiction between the imperialist powers and the whole Chinese nation and the contradiction among the imperialists themselves develop simultaneously in China, a daily expanding and intensifying strife thus ensues between the various cliques of the reactionary rulers in China and the contradictions between them develop daily. From these contradictions between the various cliques of the reactionary rulers—the strife between the warlords—ensues an increase of taxation; thus the development of the contradiction between the broad masses of taxpayers and the reactionary rulers is accelerated with every passing day.

From the contradiction between imperialism and China's native industry ensues the failure on the latter's part to obtain concessions from the former; this intensifies the contradiction between China's bourgeoisie and China's working class, with the Chinese capitalists trying to find a way out through the desperate exploitation of the workers and with the Chinese workers putting up resistance. From the dumping of commodities by imperialism, the inroads of Chinese merchant capital, and the increase of taxation by the government, ensues the sharpening of the contradiction between the landlords and the peasants; the exploitation through rent and usury becomes heavier and the peasants nurse a greater hatred for the landlords. Because of the pressure of foreign goods, the exhaustion of the purchasing power of the broad masses of the workers and peasants, and the increase of taxation by the government, dealers in domestic products and independent producers are forced daily further on the road to bankruptcy. Because the reactionary government endlessly expands its troops without sufficient provisions and funds to support them, wars multiply every day and the masses of soldiers constantly find themselves in straitened circumstances. Because of the increase of taxation by the government, the mounting burden of rent and interest demanded by the landlords, and the daily extension of the horrors of war, famine and banditry have spread all over the country and the broad masses of the peasantry and the city poor are brought to such a pass that they can hardly survive. Because funds are lacking for keeping schools open, many students are worried about the interruption of their education; because China is backward in her production, many graduates are deprived of the hope of obtaining employment.

Once we understand all these contradictions, we shall see how desperately precarious is the situation, and how chaotic the state in which China finds herself. We shall see also how inevitably the revolutionary upsurge against the imperialists, the warlords and the landlords will arise, and very speedily at that. China is littered all over with dry firewood which will soon be kindled into a conflagration. The proverb "A single spark can start a prairie fire" appropriately describes how the current situation will develop. We need only look at the development of the workers' strikes, peasant uprisings, soldiers' mutinies and students' strikes in many places, to see that it will undoubtedly not take long for these "sparks" to become "a prairie fire".

The gist of what is said above was given in the letter from the Front Committee to the Party centre, dated April 5, 1929. It reads in part:

"The letter of the Party centre (dated February 9 last year) gives too pessimistic an appraisal of the objective situation and our subjective forces. The Kuomintang's three campaigns of 'annihilation' against the Chingkang mountains marked the height of the counter-revolutionary tide. But there it stopped, and since then the counter-revolutionary tide has gradually receded while the revolutionary tide has been gradually rising. Although our Party's

fighting capacity and organisational strength have been
weakened even to the extent described by the Party centre,
yet, with the gradual ebbing of the counter-revolutionary
tide, they will recover speedily, and passivity among cadres
in the Party will also soon disappear. The masses will
certainly come over to us. For not only has the policy of
massacre[6] been 'sending fish to the water' but even reformism no longer appeals to the masses. It is certain that the
illusions of the masses about the Kuomintang will quickly
evaporate. In the situation that will arise, no party can
compete with the Communist Party in winning over the
masses. The political line and the organisational line laid
down by the Party's Sixth National Congress[7] are correct: the
revolution at the present stage is democratic and not socialist;
the immediate task of the Party [here I should have added the
words "in the big cities"][8] is to win over the masses and not to
stage immediate uprisings. But the revolution will rapidly
develop, and in making propaganda and preparations for
armed uprisings, a positive attitude should be adopted. In
the great chaos of the current situation, only by putting
forward positive slogans and by taking a positive attitude
can we lead the masses. It is also certain that only by adopting such a positive attitude can the Party recover its fighting
capacity. . . . Proletarian leadership is the sole key to the victory of the revolution. The laying of the Party's proletarian
basis and the establishment of the Party branches in industrial
enterprises in key districts are the important organisational
tasks of the Party at present; but at the same time the development of struggles in the countryside, the establishment of the
Red political power in small areas, and the creation and
expansion of the Red Army, are in particular the main conditions for helping the struggle in the cities and accelerating the
revolutionary upsurge. It is therefore a mistake to abandon
the struggle in the cities, and in our opinion it is also a mistake
for any of our Party members to fear the development of the
power of the peasants lest it become stronger than that of
the workers and hence detrimental to the revolution. For the
revolution in semi-colonial China will fail only if the peasant
struggle is deprived of the leadership of the workers, and it

will never suffer just because the peasants, through their struggle, become more powerful than the workers."

The letter also contains the following reply to the question of the Red Army's line of action:

"To preserve the Red Army and arouse the masses, the Party centre directs that we divide up our forces into very small units and disperse them widely over the countryside, and that Chu Teh and Mao Tse-tung leave the ranks so that the major targets will be hidden from the enemy. This is an unpractical way of thinking. To divide up our forces into units of companies or battalions, each operating on its own: to disperse them widely over the countryside; to arouse the masses through guerrilla-like activities; and to avoid becoming the enemy's target— all these we planned and tried on numerous occasions ever since the winter of 1927, but they all proved failures. The reasons are: (1) Most of the soldiers in the main force of the Red Army came from the outside and are different from the local Red guardsmen in their origin. (2) With small dispersed units, the leadership will become so weak as to be unable to cope with adverse circumstances, hence we will be liable to suffer defeat. (3) Small units are easy for the enemy to crush separately. (4) The more adverse the circumstances, the greater becomes the need for the forces to be concentrated and for the leadership to conduct a resolute struggle, for only thus can we achieve internal unity against the enemy. Only in favourable circumstances can the forces be divided for guerrilla operations, and it is only then that the leaders need not stay with the ranks all the time, as they must do in adverse circumstances."

The defect of this passage is that the reasons given against the division of forces are of a negative character; that is far from adequate. The positive reason for concentrating our troops is this: only concentration will enable us to wipe out comparatively large enemy units and occupy the cities. Only after wiping out comparatively large enemy units and occupying the cities can we arouse the masses on a large scale and build up a unified political power over a number of adjoining counties. Only thus can we arouse the attention of the people far and near (*i.e.* "expanding our political influence"), and make a material contribution towards accelerating the revolutionary upsurge. For instance, both the régime we created on the Hunan-Kiangsi border in the year before last and the régime created in western Fukien last year[9] were the results of our policy of concentrating the troops. This is the general principle. Are there, however, not times when the forces should be divided up? Yes, there are. The letter to the Party centre from the Front Committee speaks of the Red Army's guerrilla tactics, including the division of forces within a short radius:

"The tactics we have worked out during the last three years in the course of the struggle are indeed different from any employed in ancient or modern times, in China or elsewhere. With our tactics, the struggles of the masses are daily expanding and no enemy, however powerful, can cope with us. Ours are guerrilla tactics. They consist mainly of the following points:

"Disperse the forces among the masses to arouse them, and concentrate the forces to deal with the enemy.

"The enemy advances, we retreat: the enemy halts, we harass; the enemy tires, we attack; the enemy retreats, we pursue.

"In an independent régime with stabilised territory,[10] we adopt the policy of advancing in a series of waves. When pursued by a powerful enemy, we adopt the policy of circling around in a whirling motion.

"Arouse the largest numbers of the masses in the shortest possible time and by the best possible methods.

"These tactics are just like casting a net; we should be able to cast the net wide or draw it in at any moment. We cast it wide to win over the masses and draw it in to deal with the enemy. Such are the tactics we have applied in the past three years."

Here, "to cast the net wide" means to divide up our forces for a short term. For example, when we captured for the first time the county town of Yungsin on the Hunan-Kiangsi border, we divided up the Twenty-ninth and Thirty-first Regiments within the boundaries of Yungsin. Again, when we captured for the third time the county town of Yungsin, we divided our forces by dispatching the Twenty-eighth Regiment to the border of Anfu, the Twenty-ninth to Lienhwa, and the Thirty-first to the border of Kian county. And again, in April and May last year, our troops were divided up in the counties of southern Kiangsi, and in July they were divided up in the counties of western Fukien. As to the dispersion of forces over a wide area, it is possible only under two conditions: when circumstances are comparatively favourable and when the leading body is comparatively sound. For the aim of dividing up our forces is to render ourselves more capable of winning over the masses, of deepening the agrarian revolution and establishing political power, and of expanding the Red Army and the local armed forces. It is better not to divide up the forces if it is impossible to attain these aims, or if division of forces could only lead to defeat and a weakening of the Red Army, as in August of the year before last when our forces were divided up on the Hunan-Kiangsi border for an attack on Chenchow.[11] If the two above-mentioned conditions are present, we should undoubtedly divide up the forces, because then division is more advantageous than concentration.

The February letter from the Party centre was not written in the right spirit, and has exerted a bad influence upon a number of comrades in the Party in the Fourth Army. The Party centre also issued at that time a circular stating that war between Chiang Kai-shek and the Kwangsi warlords might not break out. Since then, however, its appraisals and directives have in the main been correct. It has already issued another circular to correct the one containing the inadequate appraisal. Although it did not make any correction as to the letter to the Red Army, its subsequent directives were not tainted with such pessimism and its views on the Red Army's movements now agree with ours. Yet that letter remains a bad influence on a section of comrades. Thus I feel that even now it is still necessary to give some explanation on the question.

The plan to seize Kiangsi within a year was also proposed by the Front Committee to the Party centre in April last year, and a resolution was subsequently passed at Yutu. The reason given then in the letter to the Party centre was as follows:

"The troops of Chiang Kai-shek and of the Kwangsi war-lords are drawing near each other in the environs of Kiu-kiang, and big battles will take place presently. The resumption of mass struggle, coupled with the intensification of contradictions within the reactionary ruling camp, makes it possible for the revolutionary upsurge to arise soon. In preparing our work in these circumstances, we feel that, so far as the southern provinces are concerned, the military forces of the compradors and landlords in Kwangtung and Hunan are too strong, while in Hunan, because of the Party's adventurist mistake, we have lost almost all our mass following outside as well as inside the Party. In the three provinces of Fukien, Kiangsi and Chekiang, however, the situation is different. First, the enemy's military strength there is at its feeblest. In Chekiang, there are only a small number of provincial guards under Chiang Poch'eng.[12] In Fukien, though there are altogether fourteen regiments under five commands, Kuo Feng-ming's brigade[13] has already been smashed; the troops under the respective command of Ch'en Kuo-hui and Lu Hsing-pang[14] are bandit forces of small fighting capacity; the two brigades of marines stationed along the coast have never seen action and certainly cannot have great fighting capacity; Chang Chen[15] alone is comparatively able to fight, but even he, according to an analysis made by the Provincial Committee of Fukien, has under his command only two regiments of some fighting capacity. In addition, Fukien is now entirely in a state of confusion and disunity. In Kiangsi there are altogether sixteen regiments under two commands— that of Chu P'ei-teh[16] and that of Hsiung Shih-hui;[17] the military strength there is superior to that of either Fukien or Chekiang, but still far inferior to that of Hunan. Secondly, we have committed fewer adventurist mistakes in these three provinces. In both Fukien and Kiangsi the Party's organisations and mass following is not very clear to us. So far as Kiangsi is concerned, we still retain a fairly adequate basis in Teian, Siushui and Tungku in northern Kiangsi; in Ningkang, Yungsin, Lienhwa and Suichwan in western Kiangsi the Party and the Red guards are still powerful; and in southern Kiangsi the situation is all the more hopeful, as the Second and Fourth Regiments of the Red Army tend to grow every day in counties like Kian, Yungsin and Hsingkuo, and the Red Army under Fang Chih-min is by no means wiped out. All this places us in a position to close in on Nanchang.

"We hereby propose to the Party centre that during the period of prolonged warfare between the Kuomintang war-lords, we contend with both Chiang Kai-shek and the Kwangsi clique for Kiangsi while including also western Fukien and western Chekiang as the objectives of our endeavour. In these three provinces the Red Army should be expanded, and an independent régime of the masses created; we set the time-limit at one year for accomplishing this plan."

The above proposal about seizing Kiangsi erred in setting the time-limit at one year. As to the proposal about the seizure of Kiangsi, it was based, apart from the conditions in the province itself, on the consideration that the nation-wide revolutionary upsurge would arise soon. For if we had not been convinced of this, we could not possibly have arrived at the conclusion about the seizure of Kiangsi in a year. The only defect in the proposal was setting the time-limit at one year, affecting thereby the meaning of the word "soon" in the statement that "a revolutionary upsurge will arise soon" and making the work smack more or less of impetuosity.

As to the subjective and objective conditions in Kiangsi, they well deserve our attention. Besides the subjective conditions stated in the letter to the Party centre, three things concerning the objective conditions can now be clearly pointed out:

First, the economy in Kiangsi is chiefly feudalistic; the power of merchant capital is relatively weak, and the armed forces of the landlords are weaker than in any other southern province.

Secondly, Kiangsi has no troops of its own; it has always been garrisoned by troops from other provinces. Sent there for the "annihilation of Communists" or "annihilation of bandits", these troops are not very enthusiastic because they are un-familiar with local conditions and cannot feel such personal concern as native troops do.

And thirdly, Kiangsi, unlike Kwantung which is close to Hongkong, and where almost all things are under British control, is comparatively free from the influence of imperialism.

Once we have grasped these three points, we can explain why rural uprisings have been more widespread and the Red Army and guerrilla units more numerous in Kiangsi than in any other province.

How to interpret the two words "arise soon" in the phrase "a revolutionary upsurge will arise soon" is a common question among many comrades. A Marxist is not a fortune-teller: of future developments and changes he should and can only point out the general direction; he should not and cannot mechani-cally fix the day and the hour. My statement that the revo-lutionary upsurge in China will arise soon emphatically does not refer to something utterly devoid of significance for action, to a tantalising phantom, which, in the words of some people, "may arise".

It is like a ship on the sea whose mast-head is already seen at a distance by people standing on the shore; it is like the morning sun which, rising with radiant beams in the east, is already seen from afar by people standing on the top of a mountain; it is like an almost fully formed child stirring in its mother's womb.

January 5, 1930.

WE MUST ATTEND TO ECONOMIC WORK

The following is a speech delivered at the economic construction conference of seventeen counties of southern Kiangsi, August 1933.

The intensification of the revolutionary war makes it imperative that we mobilise the masses to extend immediately the campaign on the economic front and carry out various kinds of necessary and possible economic construction. Why? Because all our work at present should aim at winning victory in the revolutionary war, first and foremost a complete victory in smashing the enemy's fifth campaign of "encirclement and annihilation";[1] at securing material conditions to guarantee provisions and supplies for the Red Army; at improving the living conditions of the masses of the people in order to further induce their active participation in the revolutionary war; at organising the broad masses of the people on the economic front and educating them so that we shall be provided with fresh mass strength in the war; and at consolidating, through economic construction, the alliance of the workers and peasants and their joint democratic dictatorship as well as strengthening the leadership of the proletariat. For all this, it is necessary to carry out economic construction. This is what everyone engaged in revolutionary work must clearly understand.

In the past, some comrades thought that as the revolutionary war already kept people ceaselessly busy, no time could possibly be spared for economic construction; so when they found anyone discussing economic construction, they would condemn him as a "Rightist". They held that economic construction cannot be carried out in the midst of a revolutionary war but can be carried out only when the war is finally won and peaceful and tranquil circumstances prevail. Comrades, such views are incorrect. Comrades who hold such views do not realise that without economic construction the material conditions for the revolutionary war cannot be secured and that the people will be worn out in a prolonged war. Just look, the enemy is

9

enforcing an economic blockade, the unscrupulous traders and the reactionaries are disrupting our finance and commerce, and the trade between our Red areas and outside is under a great handicap. If we do not overcome these difficulties, will not the revolutionary war be seriously affected? Salt is very dear, sometimes even unobtainable. Unhusked rice is cheap in autumn and winter, but becomes terribly dear in spring and summer. All this immediately affects the living conditions of the workers and peasants, and renders their betterment impossible. Will that not affect the basic line—the workers' and peasants' alliance? If the masses of workers and peasants become dissatisfied with their living conditions, will that not affect the expansion of our Red Army and the mobilisation of our masses to take part in the revolutionary war?

Therefore, it is an utterly mistaken view that there should be no economic construction in the midst of a revolutionary war. Adherents to this view also often say that everything should be subordinated to the war effort, without knowing that in giving up economic construction, they are not subordinating everything to the war effort but weakening it. It is only by extending the work on the economic front and developing the economy in the Red areas that we can provide a certain material basis for the revolutionary war, proceed smoothly with our military offensive, and deal an effective blow to the enemy's campaign of "encirclement and annihilation"; that we can become strong enough to expand the Red Army, move our war front to regions thousands of *li* away, enable the Red Army, unharassed by worries, to attack Nanchang and Kiukiang when circumstances become favourable, *i.e.* relieve it of the task of provisioning itself so that it can focus its attention on fighting the enemy; and that we can make the broad masses more or less satisfied with their living conditions so that they will join the Red Army or take up more enthusiastically various kinds of revolutionary work. Only in so doing can we talk of subordinating everything to the war effort.

Among those engaged in revolutionary work in various places, many still do not understand the importance of economic construction in a revolutionary war, and many local governments have not attached importance to the discussion of the

problems of economic construction. The departments of
national economy in the government bodies in various places
are as yet not well organised; some departments are still without directors, while others have taken on rather incompetent
people just to fill the vacancies. The development of the
co-operatives is still in the initial stage, and the regulation of
food supplies has only been started in some places. In many
places no propaganda has been made among the broad masses
for the tasks of economic construction (though this is absolutely
urgent), and no fervent atmosphere has been created for the
fight for economic construction. All this is due to the neglect
of the importance of economic construction.

We must, through your discussions at this conference and
through your reports after it, create a fervent atmosphere for
economic construction among all government personnel as well
as among the broad masses of workers and peasants. We must
make clear to all of them the importance of economic construction in the revolutionary war and endeavour to promote
the subscription to Economic Construction Bonds, develop the
co-operative movement, and set up everywhere public granaries
and famine relief granaries. A sub-bureau for the regulation
of food supplies must be set up in every county, with branch
offices in important districts and market places. On the one
hand, within the Red areas our grain should flow from places
with a surplus to the needy sections, so that it will not pile up
in some places and become unobtainable in others, and its price
will not be too low in one place and too high in another; on the
other hand, the surplus grain of our areas should be sent out
according to plan (not without limit), and necessaries should be
purchased from the White areas, without exploitation by
unscrupulous merchants acting as middlemen. We must all
strive to develop agricultural and handicraft production and to
manufacture more farm implements and produce larger quantities of lime in order to ensure a bigger crop next year, and to
restore to their former levels the output of such special products
as tungsten ore, timber, camphor, paper, tobacco, linen, dried
mushrooms and peppermint oil, and market these products to
the White areas in large quantities.

To judge by the volume of our external trade, grain ranks

first among our principal outgoing articles. About three million piculs of unhusked rice are sent out every year, averaging one picul per person in a population of three million, in exchange for necessaries; this is certainly no small amount. But who is handling this business? The merchants are handling it entirely and carrying on ruthless exploitation in it. Last year peasants in the counties of Wanan and Taiho sold unhusked rice at five dimes a picul to the merchants, who shipped it to Kanchow and resold it for four dollars, making a sevenfold profit. Look again at the fact that every year our three million people consume about nine million dollars' worth of salt and need about six million dollars' worth of cotton cloth. In the past the merchants, needless to say, handled exclusively this business of bringing in fifteen million dollars' worth of salt and cotton cloth, and we did nothing about it. The exploitation by the merchants as middlemen has really been enormous. For instance, they went to Mei county and bought salt at one dollar for seven catties, and shipped it to our areas to sell it at one dollar for twelve liang.[2] Isn't such a rate of exploitation shocking? We can no longer leave these matters as they are and from now on we must take them up. Our bureau of trade with outside areas must make very great efforts in this connection.

How shall we make use of three million dollars' worth of Economic Construction Bonds? We plan to make use of them in the following way: One million to be allotted to the Red Army for its war expenses, and two million to be loaned as capital funds to the co-operatives, the bureaux for the regulation of food supplies and the bureaux of external trade. Of the latter amount, a smaller portion will be used for developing production and the rest for expanding our external trade. Our objective is not only to develop production but also to sell our products at adequate prices to the White areas and then purchase salt and cloth at lower prices from them for distribution among the masses of our people so as to break the enemy's blockade and counteract the merchants' exploitation. We must daily accelerate the development of the people's economy, greatly improve the living conditions of the masses, substantially increase public revenue and firmly lay a material foundation for the revolutionary war and for economic construction.

This is a great task, a great class struggle. But let us ask, can this task be accomplished in the midst of a fierce war? I think it can. We are not talking about building a railway to Lungyen, nor, for the time being, about building a motor road to Kanchow. We are not talking about a complete monopoly on the sale of grain, nor are we talking about letting the government handle all the salt and cloth business valued at fifteen million dollars to the exclusion of the merchants. This is not what we are talking about, nor is this what we are doing. What we are talking about and doing is to start temporarily with a fund of two million plus the shares invested by the masses, to develop agricultural and handicraft production, to send out grain and tungsten ore and to bring in salt and cloth. Is this a thing that should not be taken up, cannot be taken up, or cannot be accomplished? We have already started doing such work and have already achieved some results. This year's autumn harvest is 20–25 per cent bigger than last year's, exceeding the 20 per cent increase anticipated. In the handicraft industries the production of farm implements and lime is looking up and that of tungsten ore is beginning to look up. The production of tobacco, paper and timber is also becoming somewhat brisk. In the regulation of food supplies considerable results have been achieved this year. Some start has been made in bringing in salt. These achievements form the basis of our firm belief that it is possible to make further developments in the future. Is it not clearly a mistaken view to say that economic construction is possible only after the war and not at present?

It is thus clear that, at the present stage, economic construction must revolve round the central task—the revolutionary war. The revolutionary war is now the central task and economic construction work is undertaken for its sake, revolves round it, and is subordinated to it. It is likewise a mistake to regard economic construction as already the pivot of all our present tasks and to neglect the revolutionary war and wish to undertake economic construction apart from the revolutionary war. It is only when the civil war is over that economic construction can and should be regarded as the centre of all our tasks. It is a mere delusion to wish to carry out, in the midst of a civil war, peace-time economic construction which ought to be undertaken in the future but not now, and which is permissible in future circumstances but not in present circumstances. The present tasks are those urgently demanded by the war. Every one of these serves the war and none is a peace-time undertaking separate from the war. If any comrade still entertains the ideas of carrying out economic construction apart from the war, he should rectify his error at once.

Without a correct method of leadership and of work, it is impossible to extend rapidly the campaign on the economic front. This is also an important problem to be solved at this conference. For, upon your return, you will not only have to take up immediately many kinds of work yourselves, but also have to direct a great number of personnel to work along the same line. In particular, comrades working at the town or township level, and comrades in such organisations as the co-operatives, the food bureaux, the trade bureaux and the supply offices, are practical workers who personally mobilise the masses to organise co-operatives, regulate and transport food supplies, and supervise our trade with outside areas; if their method of leadership is not right or if they do not adopt correct and effective methods of work, our work will be immediately affected and we shall fail to win the support of the broad masses for our various kinds of work and to carry out, in the autumn and winter of this year and in the spring and summer of the coming year, the central government's plan of economic construction as a whole.

Hence I want to point out to comrades the following:

Firstly, mobilise the masses through their organisations. The foremost thing is that comrades in the presidiums, in departments of national economy and in finance departments of government bodies at all levels must regularly put on their agenda the discussion, supervision and check-up of such work as the sale of bonds, the development of co-operatives, the regulation of food supplies and the promotion of production and trade. Next, mass organisations, chiefly the trade unions and poor peasant leagues, are to be set in motion. The trade unions should be called upon to mobilise the masses of their membership to join the economic front. The poor peasant leagues provide a strong basis for mobilising the masses to develop the co-operatives and to subscribe to the bonds; and the district and township governments should exert great efforts to lead them.

Furthermore, we must agitate for economic construction at mass meetings called on the basis of a village or house, explaining clearly the relationship between the revolutionary war and economic construction and discussing in the most practical terms the improvement of the living conditions of the masses and the increase of our fighting capacity. Call upon the masses to subscribe to the bonds, develop the co-operatives, regulate food supplies, consolidate the finances and develop trade; call upon them to fight for these slogans and heighten their enthusiasm. Our objective cannot be obtained if we do not mobilise the masses and agitate them in such an organised way, that is to say, if the presidiums, departments of national economy and finance departments of government bodies at all levels do not vigorously take up economic construction and discuss it and check up on it, if they neglect to set the mass organisations in motion and hold mass meeting for agitation.

Secondly, we must not be bureaucratic in our methods of mobilising the masses. Bureaucratic leadership will not be tolerated in economic construction any more than in any other branch of revolutionary work. This great evil, bureaucracy, must be thrown into the cesspool, because no comrade likes it. What every comrade ought to like is the method of a mass character, *i.e.* a method welcomed by every worker and peasant. One of the manifestations of bureaucracy is slackness in work due to indifference or perfunctoriness. We must wage a sharp struggle against this phenomenon. Another manifestation is authoritarianism. Superficially, authoritarians are not slack in their work and seem to be hard working. Actually, to develop co-operatives in an authoritarian way will bring no success; even if they are apparently developed for the time being, they cannot be consolidated, and in the end they will be discredited and their development hindered. To promote the subscription to the bonds in an authoritarian way regardless of whether people understand it or how much they can afford to subscribe, and to impose arbitrary quotas in a dictatorial manner will finally incur the displeasure of the masses and render a good subscription impossible. We certainly must reject authoritarianism; what we need is energetic agitation to convince the masses and, according to specific circumstances and the real feelings of the masses, to develop the co-operatives, promote the subscription to the bonds and do all kinds of work for economic mobilisation.

Thirdly, to extend the campaign of economic construction, large numbers of cadres are needed. This is not a matter for some tens or hundreds of people, but for thousands and tens of thousands whom we must organise, train and dispatch to the front of economic construction. They are the commanders on the economic front, while the broad masses are the soldiers. People often sigh over the shortage of cadres. Comrades, is there really a shortage of cadres? From the masses who have been steeled in the agrarian and economic struggles and in the revolutionary war, innumerable cadres have sprung up. How can we say there is a shortage of cadres? Give up your erroneous viewpoint and you will find cadres standing right in front of you.

Fourthly, economic construction is, at present, inseparable not only from the general task of the war, but from other tasks as well. It is only through a thorough-going land-investigation campaign[3] that the feudal and semi-feudal ownership of land can be completely abolished, that the peasants' activity in production can be enhanced, and that the broad masses of peasants can be induced to join quickly the front of economic construction. It is only through the resolute enforcement of the labour law that the living conditions of the masses of workers can be improved, that they can participate actively and speedily in economic construction and strengthen their leadership over the peasants. It is only through correct guidance in the election campaign and in the campaign of popular prosecution,[4] which develops along with the land-investigation campaign, that our government organisations can be strengthened and our government can even more vigorously lead the revolutionary war and various other kinds of work, including economic work.

To raise the political and cultural level of the masses through cultural and educational work is also very important in developing the national economy. It goes without saying that the expansion of the Red Army must not be neglected

for a single day. Everybody understands that without the
Red Army's victories the enemy's economic blockade will
be further tightened. On the other hand, the development
of national economy and the improvement in the living
conditions of the masses will undoubtedly be of great help
to the expansion of the Red Army and induce the broad
masses to march eagerly to the front. To sum up, if we have
secured all the conditions mentioned above, including the
very important new condition of economic construction, and
have placed all of them at the service of the revolutionary war,
then victory in the revolutionary war will undoubtedly be ours.

August 20, 1933.

HOW TO ANALYSE THE CLASSES IN THE RURAL AREAS

This document, written in October 1933 to rectify deviations that had occurred in the work of agrarian reform and to give a correct solution to the agrarian problem, was adopted by the Workers' and Peasants' Democratic Central Government as providing the criterion in determining class status in the rural areas.

I. THE LANDLORD

A landlord is a person who possesses land, who does not engage in labour himself or merely takes part in labour as a supplementary source of income, and who lives by exploiting the peasants. The landlord's exploitation chiefly assumes the form of collecting land rent; besides that, he may also lend money, hire labour, or engage in industrial or commercial enterprise. But his exaction of land rent from the peasants is the principal form of his exploitation. Administering communal properties and collecting school rent[1] also belong to the category of exploitation by land rent.

Those landlords shall still be considered landlords who, although having gone bankrupt, still do not engage in labour but live by swindling and plundering or on the assistance of relatives or friends, and are better off than the average middle peasant.

The warlords, the bureaucrats, the local bullies and the bad gentry politically represent the landlord class and are its most ferocious members. Often there are also lesser local bullies and bad gentry among the rich peasants.

Those people who assist the landlords in collecting land rent and in managing their households, who rely on the landlords' exploitation of the peasants as the main source of their income, and who are better off than the average middle peasant, shall be treated in the same way as the landlords.

A person who relies upon exploitation by usury as the main source of his income and who is better off than the average middle peasant, is a usurer and shall be treated in the same way as the landlord.

2. THE RICH PEASANT

The rich peasant as a rule possesses land. But there are some who possess only a part of the land they farm and rent the remainder. There are still others who possess no land at all and rent all the land they farm. The rich peasant as a rule possesses comparatively abundant means of production and liquid capital, engages in labour himself, but regularly relies upon exploitation for a part or the major part of his income. The exploitation the rich peasant practises is chiefly that of hired labour (hiring long-term labourers). In addition, he may also let a part of his land for exploitation by rent, lend money or engage in industrial and commercial enterprises. Most of the rich peasants also administer communal properties. Some of them possess a considerable amount of good land and engage in labour themselves without hiring labourers, but exploit other peasants by means of land rent, interest on loans, and so on; these people shall also be treated as rich peasants. A rich peasant engages regularly in exploitation and, in many cases, his income from exploitation forms the major part of his total income.

3. THE MIDDLE PEASANT

In many cases the middle peasant possesses land. In some cases he possesses only a part of the land he farms and rents the remainder. In other cases he possesses no land at all and rents all the land he farms. In all cases he has adequate implements of his own. The middle peasant relies wholly or mainly on his own labour as the source of his income. As a rule he does not exploit other people; in many cases he is even exploited by other people and has to pay a small amount of land rent and interest on loans. But the middle peasant as a rule does not sell his labour power. A section of the middle peasants (the well-to-do middle peasants) subjects other people to some slight exploitation, but this is not its regular or principal occupation.

4. THE POOR PEASANT

In some cases the poor peasant possesses a part of the land he farms and an incomplete set of implements; in other cases he possesses no land at all, but only an incomplete set of implements. As a rule the poor peasant has to rent land for cultivation and, exploited by others, has to pay land rent and interest on loans and hire out a small part of his labour.

As a rule, while the middle peasant need not sell his labour power, the poor peasant has to sell a small part of his—this is the principal criterion for distinguishing the middle peasant from the poor peasant.

5. THE WORKER

The worker (including the farm labourer) as a rule does not possess any land or implements, and only in some cases possesses a very small amount of land and a few implements. A worker makes his living wholly or mainly by selling his labour power.

October 1933.

OUR ECONOMIC POLICY

This is a report delivered at the Second National Congress of the Soviet Republic of China, held in January 1934 in Juikin, Kiangsi.

Only the most shameless Kuomintang warlords, after practically impoverishing the people in the areas under their rule and exhausting their financial resources, will go on spreading rumours about how utterly devastated the Red areas are. The aim of imperialism and the Kuomintang is to wreck the Red areas, to undermine the economic construction now in progress there, and to destroy the welfare of the tens of millions of the liberated workers and peasants. Therefore they have not only organised armed forces to carry out a military campaign of "encirclement and annihilation", but have also carried out a ruthless policy of economic blockade. But with the broad masses and the Red Army under our leadership, we have not only repeatedly smashed the enemy's campaigns of "encirclement and annihilation" but are also engaging in all kinds of economic construction possible as well as essential in order to break down the enemy's vicious scheme of economic blockade. This step has now also brought about one victory after another.

The principle governing our economic policy is to proceed with all kinds of economic construction possible as well as essential, to concentrate our economic strength to provide for the war, and, at the same time, to do our best to improve the people's living conditions, to consolidate the economic alliance of the workers and peasants, to ensure the hegemony of the proletariat over the peasantry, and to strive for the hegemony of state enterprises over private enterprises so as to create the prerequisites for the future development into socialism.

Our economic construction centres round the development of agricultural and industrial production, trade with the White areas, and the co-operatives.

Agriculture in the Red areas is now obviously making progress. In the area of southern Kiangsi and western Fukien the agricultural output of 1933 was increased by 15 per cent over that of 1932, and in the Fukien-Chekiang-Kiangsi border area, by 20 per cent. The harvest in the Szechwan-Shensi border area was good. In the Red areas, during the first year or two after their establishment, agricultural output often declines.[1] But as land ownership is stabilised after land redistribution and production is promoted, the labour enthusiasm of the peasant masses has increased and production is looking up. Today in some places the output has not only been restored to the pre-revolutionary level but has even surpassed it. In other places people have not only reclaimed land lying waste during the revolutionary uprisings, but have brought new land under cultivation. In many places mutual-aid working groups and ploughing teams[2] have been organised to adjust the utilisation of labour power in the villages, and draught-oxen co-operatives have been organised to relieve the shortage of draught-oxen. At the same time, the broad masses of women have taken part in production.

All this certainly could not have been done in the Kuomintang period. At that time, as land belonged to the landlords, the peasants were neither willing nor able to improve it by their own efforts. It is only after we distributed land to the peasants and promoted and encouraged the peasants' production that the labour enthusiasm of the peasant masses has burst forth and great victories in production have been achieved. It should be pointed out here that under present conditions agricultural production occupies the first place in our economic construction, and must solve not only the most important problem of grain, but also the problem of supplying raw materials like cotton, hemp, sugar-cane, bamboo, etc., for daily necessaries such as clothes, sugar and paper. Afforestation and stock-raising also form an important part of agriculture. It is permissible as well as necessary to draw up suitable plans on the basis of small peasant farming for certain important agricultural products and to mobilise the peasants to strive to carry out such plans. We should pay closer attention and devote even greater efforts to this.

We must vigorously lead the peasants to solve those difficult problems concerning the conditions necessary for agricultural production, like labour power, draught oxen, fertiliser, seeds and irrigation. To adjust the utilisation of labour power in an organised manner and encourage women to join in production is our most basic task in the sphere of agricultural production. To organise mutual-aid working groups and ploughing teams as well as to mobilise and supervise all the people in the villages during the important ploughing seasons of spring and summer, are the necessary means for solving the problem of labour power. Another big problem is that quite a large proportion of the peasants (about 25 per cent) are short of draught oxen. We must attend to the organisation of draught-oxen co-operatives by encouraging households without oxen to take out shares on a voluntary basis in order to buy oxen for common use. Irrigation is the lifeline of agriculture and also deserves our close attention. Of course we cannot as yet raise the question of state farming and collective farming, but for the sake of speeding up agricultural development, it is an urgent need to organise small-scale agricultural experimental stations and establish agricultural research schools, and set up exhibition halls for farm produce at various places.

The enemy's blockade has created difficulties for marketing our goods in outside areas. The production of many handicraft trades in the Red areas has declined, notably that of tobacco and paper. But such difficulties in the trade with the White areas are not entirely insurmountable. Because of the demand of the broad masses we have an extensive market of our own. Primarily for self-support and secondarily for trade with the White areas, we should restore and develop the handicraft trades and certain industries according to plan. During the last two years, especially since the first half of 1933, many handicraft trades and a few industries have begun to look up because producers' co-operatives have gradually developed among the masses. The most important among them are tobacco, paper, tungsten, camphor, farm implements and fertilisers (like lime). Moreover, under the present circumstances we should not neglect to weave our own cotton cloth, make our own medicines, and refine our own sugar. In the Fukien-Chekiang-Kiangsi border area, some industries which were previously lacking, such as paper-making, cotton-weaving and sugar-refining, have, however, been developed and have achieved success. In order to relieve the shortage of table salt, the refining of salt from saltpetre has also been started.

It requires proper planning to keep the industries going. Detailed and comprehensive planning is of course impossible on the basis of scattered handicraft trades. Yet in certain main enterprises, first and foremost the state enterprises or the co-operatives, fairly detailed plans of production are absolutely necessary. Each of our state or co-operative industrial enterprises must, from the very beginning, make accurate calculations of the production of raw materials and estimate the prospects of marketing both in enemy areas and in our own.

It is particularly necessary at present to organise according to plan the people's trade with the White areas and let the state handle directly the circulation of certain essential commodities, for example, bringing in table salt and cotton cloth, sending out grain and tungsten, and adjusting food supplies inside our own areas. Such work was first undertaken in the Fukien-Chekiang-Kiangsi border area, and started in the Central area in the spring of 1933. Initial successes have been achieved since the establishment of the Bureau of Trade with Outside Areas and other agencies.

At present our national economy is made up of three sectors: state enterprises, co-operative enterprises and private enterprises.

State enterprises are confined at present to what is possible and essential. The state-operated industrial and commercial enterprises have already started to grow; their future is unlimited.

As regards private enterprises, so long as they do not transgress the legal limits set by our government, we shall not only refrain from prohibiting them, but shall promote and encourage them. The development of private enterprise is necessary at present in the interests of the state and the people. Private enterprise, needless to say, is now in an absolutely preponderant position and will continue to be so for a considerable length of time. In the Red areas now private enterprises remain as small-scale operations.

Co-operative enterprises are developing at great speed. According to the statistics of September 1933 from seventeen counties in Kiangsi and Fukien provinces, there are altogether 1,423 co-operatives of various kinds with a capital of over 300,000 dollars. Consumers' co-operatives and grain co-operatives have flourished most, with producers' co-operatives coming next. The activities of credit co-operatives have just been started. When they have been co-ordinated and have passed through a considerable period of development, co-operatives and state enterprises will become a tremendous force in the economic sphere and will gradually gain pre-ponderance and assume leadership over private enterprises. Therefore, the development of state enterprises in every possible way and the development of co-operatives on a large scale should proceed simultaneously with the encouragement and development of private enterprises.

In order to develop state enterprises and render aid to the co-operatives, we have issued, with the support of the masses, Economic Construction Bonds to the value of three million dollars. To rely in such a way on the strength of the masses for solving the problem of funds for economic construction is the only possible means at this moment.

To increase our revenue through the development of the national economy is the basic line in our fiscal policy, whose effect has been clearly manifest in the Fukien-Chekiang-Kiangsi border area and is beginning to become manifest in the Central area. To carry out this line seriously is the duty of our financial and economic organisations. What requires our full attention here is that the state bank should issue notes basically according to the requirements of the development of national economy; purely fiscal needs can only be given secondary con-sideration.

Financial expenditure must be governed by the principle of economy. We should make it clear to all government personnel that corruption and waste are the greatest crimes. In the past the fight against corruption and waste achieved some results and further efforts are required. The principle in our account-ing system is that every single copper coin should be saved for the war, for the revolutionary cause and for our economic construction. There should be a sharp distinction between our way and the Kuomingtang's way of expending state revenue.

At a time when China has been plunged into economic disaster and hundreds of millions of people are in straitened circumstances, pressed by hunger and cold, our people's government is earnestly carrying out, regardless of all difficulties, economic construction for the revolutionary war and for the interests of the nation. The whole matter is perfectly clear: Only when we have defeated imperialism and the Kuomintang, only when we have carried out planned and organised economic construction, can we deliver the people of the whole country from such an unprecedented disaster.

January 23, 1934.

TAKE CARE OF THE LIVING CONDITIONS OF THE MASSES AND ATTEND TO THE METHODS OF WORK

This is part of the concluding statement made at the Second National Congress of the Soviet Republic of China, held in January 1934 in Juikin, Kiangsi.

There are two problems which comrades have failed to stress during the discussions and which, I feel, should be brought up for some explanation.

The first problem concerns the living conditions of the masses.

Our central task at present is to mobilise the broad masses to take part in the revolutionary war, thereby overthrowing imperialism and the Kuomintang, spreading the revolution throughout the country, and driving imperialism out of China. Whoever takes this central task lightly is not a good revolutionary worker. If our comrades really grasp this central task and understand that the revolution must at all costs be spread throughout the country, then they cannot in the least neglect or take lightly the problem of the immediate interests of the broad masses, the problem of their living conditions. As the revolutionary war is a war of the masses, we can carry out the war only by mobilising the masses and relying on them.

If we do no other work than simply mobilising the people to carry out the war, can we achieve the aim of defeating the enemy? Of course not. If we want to win, we still have to do a great deal of work. Leading the peasants in agrarian struggles and distributing land to them; arousing their labour enthusiasm so as to increase agricultural production; safeguarding the interests of the workers; establishing co-operatives; developing trade with outside areas; solving the problems that face the masses, problems of clothing, food and shelter, of fuel, rice, cooking oil and salt, of health and hygiene, and of marriage. In short, all problems facing the masses in their actual life should

claim our attention. If we have these problems at heart and
solve them to the satisfaction of the masses, we shall really
become the organisers of the life of the masses and they will
really rally round us and warmly support us. Comrades, can
we then call upon the masses to take part in the revolutionary
war? We can, absolutely.

We have found the following state of affairs among our personnel. They talk only about expanding the Red Army,
enlarging the transport teams, collecting land taxes and
promoting subscription to the bonds; as to all other matters,
these people neither talk about them nor attend to them, and
even ignore them altogether.

For instance, there was a time when the Tingchow City
Government, bent on the expansion of the Red Army and the
mobilisation for the transport teams, paid not the least attention
to the problems of the living conditions of the masses. The
problems facing the masses of Tingchow city were that they had
no firewood; that salt was not available on the market because
the capitalists had hoarded it; that some people had no houses
to live in; and that there was a shortage of rice and its price
was high. These were the practical problems facing the masses
of the people of Tingchow city, who eagerly expected us to
help them to find a solution. But the Tingchow City Government discussed none of these matters. Thus after several
meetings at which only the expansion of the Red Army and
the mobilisation for the transport teams were discussed, while
the living conditions of the masses were completely ignored, the
one hundred or more newly elected delegates of the workers'
and peasants' congress of Tingchow city showed no interest
in attending the congress any longer or in holding further
sessions. As a result, very little was achieved in the expansion
of the Red Army and the mobilisation for the transport teams.
This is one kind of situation.

Comrades, you have probably read the pamphlets given you
on the two model townships. There the situation is the reverse.
How greatly has the Red Army been expanded in Changkang
township[1] in Kiangsi and Tsaiki township[2] in Fukien! In
Changkang township eighty out of every hundred young and
middle-aged men and women have joined the Red Army; in

Tsaiki township eighty-eight out of every hundred have joined the Red Army. Subscriptions to the bonds are also remarkable: Changkang township with a population of only 1,500 has subscribed to the value of 4,500 silver dollars. Great achievements have likewise been made in other spheres of work. What is the reason? A few examples will make this clear. In Changkang township a fire burnt out one room and about a half of another in a poor peasant's house, and the township government appealed to the masses to contribute money to help him. Three persons were starving and the township government and the mutual-aid society immediately started collecting rice for their relief. In the famine of last summer, the township government obtained rice from Kunglueh county,[3] more than two hundred *li* away, for the relief of the masses. In Tsaiki township very good work was also done along these lines. Such township governments are really models of their kind. They are absolutely different from the Tingchow City Government with its bureaucratic method of leadership. We should learn from the Changkang and Tsaiki townships and oppose bureaucratic leaders like those in Tingchow city.

I earnestly suggest to this congress that we take a deep interest in problems of the living conditions of the masses, from their land and labour to their fuel, rice, cooking oil and salt. The masses of women want to learn ploughing and hoeing. Whom can we get to teach them? Children want to go to school. Has any primary school been set up? The wooden bridge over there is too narrow and people may fall off. Should not repairs be made? Many people have boils or other complaints. What measures can we take? All such problems concerning the living conditions of the masses should be placed on our agenda. Discussions should be held, decisions reached, actions taken and results checked up. We should make the broad masses realise that we represent their interests, that our life and theirs are intimately interwoven.

We should make them understand on the basis of these matters the tasks of a higher order which we propose, namely, the tasks of the revolutionary war, so that they will support the revolution and spread it throughout the country, and respond to our political appeals and struggle to the last for the victory of the revolution. The masses in Changkang township say: "The Communist Party is really good—it has thought of everything for us." The personnel in Changkang township are an example to all of us. What splendid people they are! They have won the genuine affection of the broad masses; their call for war mobilisation has won the support of the broad masses. Do we want to win the support of the masses? Do we want to devote all their efforts to the war front? If we do, we must go among the masses; arouse them to activity; concern ourselves with their weal and woe; and work earnestly and sincerely in their interests and solve their problems of production and of living conditions, their problems of salt, rice, shelter, clothing and childbirth, in short, all their problems. If we do so, the broad masses will certainly give us support and regard the revolution as their very life and their most glorious banner. Should the Kuomintang launch attacks on the Red areas, the broad masses will stake their lives to fight. There can be no doubt about this, for haven't we actually smashed the enemy's first, second, third and fourth campaigns of "encirclement and annihilation"?

The Kuomintang is now carrying out its policy of building blockhouses,[4] erecting any number of "tortoise-shells"[5] as if they were walls of bronze and iron. Comrades, are they really walls of bronze and iron? Not in the least! Just think: for thousands of years, didn't the feudal emperors' fortresses and palaces stand firm enough? But they crumbled one after another the moment the masses rose. The Czar of Russia was one of the fiercest rulers in the world, but what was left of him when the revolution of the proletariat and the peasantry broke out? Nothing was left. His walls of bronze and iron? All crumbled. Comrades, what is really a wall of bronze and iron? The masses, the millions upon millions of the masses who sincerely and earnestly support the revolution. They really are a wall of bronze and iron which no force can break down, absolutely none. The counter-revolutionary forces can never break us, but we shall break them. By rallying millions upon millions of the masses round the revolutionary government and by expanding the revolutionary war, we shall be able to wipe out any counter-revolution and take over the whole of China.

The second problem concerns methods of work.

We are the leaders and organisers of the revolutionary war as well as the leaders and organisers of the life of the masses. To organise a revolutionary war and to improve the living conditions of the masses are our two major tasks. Here we are confronted with the serious problem of methods of work. We should not only propose tasks, but also solve the problem of the methods of accomplishing them. Our task may be the crossing of a river, but we cannot cross it without a bridge or a boat. Without solving the problem of bridge or boat, all talk about crossing the river would be idle. Without solving the problem of methods, it is sheer blether to talk about tasks. Without paying attention to leadership in expanding the Red Army, or attaching importance to the methods of expanding it, we can achieve no success in the end, even though we repeat a thousand times the phrase "expanding the Red Army". What is more, in land investigation,[6] economic construction, culture and education, and the work in the newly liberated areas and the outlying districts of our areas, in fact, in all sorts of work, we cannot accomplish any of the tasks if we only propose them but do not attend to methods for carrying them out, if we do not oppose bureaucratic methods of work and adopt instead practical and specific methods of work, and if we do not discard the authoritarian method of work and adopt instead the method of patient persuasion.

Comrades in Hsingkuo have done first-rate work and deserve our praise as model workers. Likewise, comrades in north-eastern Kiangsi have done excellent work and are also model workers. As the comrades in Hsingkuo and in north-eastern Kiangsi have linked the life of the masses with the revolutionary war, they have solved the problem of revolutionary methods of work together with the problem of revolutionary tasks. They are working conscientiously and solving problems with minute care; they have taken up their responsibilities in earnest in face of the revolution; they are good organisers and leaders of the revolutionary war as well as good organisers and leaders of the life of the masses. Besides, in some places in the counties of Shanghang, Changting and Yungting in Fukien; in Sikiang and other places in southern Kiangsi; in some places in the counties of Chaling, Yungsin and Kian in the Hunan-Kiangsi border area; in some places in Yangsin county in the Hunan-Hupeh-Kiangsi border area; in districts and townships in many other counties of Kiangsi; and in Juikin, the county directly administered by the central government—in these places comrades have made progress in their work and likewise deserve our praise.

There is no doubt that in all the places under our leadership, many active cadres, comrades who can do excellent work, have sprung from the masses. These comrades carry upon their shoulders a responsibility, *i.e.* to help to improve the work in those places where it is not well done and to help those comrades who are not yet competent. We are face to face with a great revolutionary war; we must break through the enemy's large-scale "encirclement and annihilation", and we must spread the revolution throughout the country. All revolutionary workers carry on their shoulders a tremendous responsibility. After this congress we must introduce practical measures to improve our work; the advanced areas should advance even farther, and the backward areas should catch up with the advanced. We must bring into being thousands of Changkang townships and scores of Hsingkuo counties. These will be our firm bases. Once we possess them, we shall be able to proceed to shatter the enemy's campaign of "encirclement and annihilation" and overthrow the rule of imperialism and the Kuomintang in the whole country.

January 27, 1934.

ON THE TACTICS OF FIGHTING JAPANESE IMPERIALISM

This is a report delivered at a conference of Party activists held at Wayaopao, northern Shensi, after the meeting of the Political Bureau of the Central Committee of the Chinese Communist Party at the same place in December 1935. The Political Bureau meeting, one of the most important ever held by the Party centre, refuted the mistaken view in the Party that it was impossible for the Chinese national bourgeoisie to join forces with the Chinese workers and peasants to resist Japan, and decided on the tactics of building up a national united front. On the basis of the decisions of the Party centre, Comrade Mao Tse-tung fully elucidated how under the conditions of the Anti-Japanese War it was possible as well as important to re-establish a united front with the national bourgeoisie. He emphatically pointed out the decisive significance of the leading role to be played by the Communist Party and the Red Army in this united front. He pointed out the protracted character of the Chinese revolution. And he criticised the narrow closed-door sectarianism and revolutionary impetuosity which, for a long time prevalent in the Party, had been the basic cause of the severe setbacks of the Party and the Red Army during the Second Revolutionary Civil War. Meanwhile he called the Party's attention to the historical lesson of how Ch'en Tu-hsiu's "Right" opportunism led the revolution to defeat in 1927 and pointed out that Chiang Kai-shek would inevitably seek to destroy the forces of the revolution. Thus he enabled the Party to remain clear-headed in the new situation and save the forces of the revolution from losses in spite of Chiang Kai-shek's endless deceit and innumerable armed assaults.

At the enlarged meeting of the Political Bureau of the Central Committee in January 1935 held in Tsunyi, Kweichow, a new leadership of the Central Committee headed by Comrade Mao Tse-tung had been established in place of the former leadership of the "Left" opportunists. However, as this meeting was held in the course of the Red Army's Long March, decisions could be made only on the most urgent military problems of the moment and on the organisation of the Secretariat and the Revolutionary Military Commission of the Central Committee. It was only when the Red Army had reached northern Shensi after the Long March that the Party centre found it possible to elucidate systematically the various problems of political strategy, of which the fullest analysis is given in this report.

THE CHARACTERISTICS OF THE PRESENT POLITICAL SITUATION

Comrades, a very great change has now taken place in the political situation. Our Party has defined its tasks on the basis of this change.

What is the present situation?

The main characteristic of the present situation is that Japanese imperialism wants to reduce China to its colony.

As everybody knows, China has for nearly a hundred years been a semi-colonial country under the joint control of several imperialist powers. Thanks to the Chinese people's fight against imperialism and the conflicts among the imperialist powers, China can yet retain her semi-independent status. The First World War had for a time given Japanese imperialism an opportunity to dominate China exclusively. But as a result of the Chinese people's fight against Japanese imperialism and the intervention of other imperialist powers, the Twenty-one Demands[1] signed by the then arch traitor Yuan Shih-k'ai[2] for surrendering China to Japan, could not but become null and void. At the Nine-Power conference called by the United States at Washington in 1922, a pact[3] was concluded which again brought China back under the joint control of several imperialist powers. Before long, however, the situation changed again. With the Incident of September 18, 1931,[4] began the stage of Japan's colonisation of China. But Japanese aggression was for a time confined to the four north-eastern provinces[5] and this made some people feel that the Japanese imperialists probably would not advance farther. Things are now different: there are unmistakable signs that the Japanese imperialists want to advance into China Proper[6] and occupy the whole of China. Now they want to change the whole of China from a semi-colony shared among several imperialist powers into a colony monopolised by Japan. The recent Eastern Hopeh Incident[7] and diplomatic parleys[8] are clear indications of a trend of events that threatens the existence of the people throughout the country. In such circumstances all classes and all political groups in China are faced with the following question: What is to be done? Resist? Surrender? Or vacillate between the two?

Now, let us see how the various classes in China answer this question.

Both the workers and peasants in China are demanding resistance. The revolution of 1924–7, the agrarian revolution from 1927 up to the present, and the anti-Japanese upsurge since the Incident of September 18, 1931, all prove that the Chinese working class and peasantry are the most resolute forces in the Chinese revolution.

The Chinese petty bourgeoisie also demands resistance. Have not the young students and the urban petty bourgeoisie already started a broad anti-Japanese movement?[9] The petty bourgeois elements in China took part in the revolution of 1924-7. Their economic status, like that of the peasants, is one of small-scale production, which is incompatible with imperialism. Imperialism and the forces of the counter-revolution in China have done them great harm, reducing many of them to unemployment, bankruptcy or semi-bankruptcy. Now, seeing that they may soon becomes slaves of a foreign nation, they find no way out but resistance.

But what of the national bourgeoisie, the comprador and landlord classes, what of the Kuomintang, when they are confronted with the question?

The big local bullies and bad gentry, the big warlords, the big bureaucrats and the big compradors have long made up their minds. They have said and are still saying that revolution (of whatever kind) is after all worse than imperialism. They have formed a camp of traitors; for them such a question as whether or not they are to become slaves of a foreign nation does not exist, because they have already obliterated national demarcations and their interests are inseparable from those of imperialism; and their chief of chiefs is none other than Chiang Kai-shek.[10] The traitors of this camp are the sworn enemies of the Chinese people. Were there not such a pack of traitors, Japanese imperialism could not have been so outrageous. They are the jackals of imperialism.

The national bourgeoisie presents a complicated problem. This class took part in the revolution of 1924-7, but badly frightened by the flames of that revolution, it subsequently went over to the side of the people's enemies, i.e. the Chiang Kai-shek bloc. The question is whether, under the present circumstances, the national bourgeoisie can change. We believe it can. This is because the national bourgeoisie is not the same as the landlord and comprador classes and there is a difference between them. The national bourgeoisie has not so much of the feudal character as the landlord class; nor has it so much of the comprador character as the comprador class. Within the national bourgeoisie there is a section of people who have more affiliations with foreign capital and Chinese landed interests, people who constitute its right wing, and we shall not for the time being speculate whether they can change or not. The problem lies with the sections which have no or comparatively little affiliation of this kind. We believe that in the new situation, when China is threatened with being reduced to a colony, the attitude of these sections of the national bourgeoisie can change. And the change is marked by their vacillation. They dislike imperialism on the one hand and fear the thoroughness of the revolution on the other, and thus vacillate between the two. This explains why during the revolution of 1924–7 they took part in the revolution and why, at the end of that period, they went over to the side of Chiang Kai-shek.

What is the difference between the situation at present and that of 1927 when Chiang Kai-shek betrayed the revolution? China at that time was still a semi-colony but now she is heading for the status of a colony. In the past nine years the national bourgeoisie forsook their ally, the working class, and made friends with the landlord and comprador classes, but have they gained any advantage? None at all; what they have got is the bankruptcy or semi-bankruptcy of native industry and commerce. Hence we believe that in the present situation the attitude of the national bourgeoisie can change. What will be the extent of the change? Its general feature will be vacillation. But at certain stages of our struggle, one section of it (the left wing) can take part in the struggle. And the other section can pass from vacillation to neutrality.

What class interests does the Nineteenth Route Army led by Ts'ai T'ing-k'ai[11] and others represent? It represents those of the national bourgeoisie, the upper stratum of the petty bourgeoisie, and the rich peasants and small landlords in the countryside. Did not Ts'ai T'ing-k'ai and his associates once fight desperate battles against the Red Army? But later on they concluded an anti-Japanese and anti-Chiang alliance with this Red Army. They attacked the Red Army in Kiangsi, but later resisted Japanese imperialism in Shanghai; and after they went

to Fukien, they came to terms with the Red Army and opened
fire on Chiang Kai-shek. Regardless of the course Ts'ai
T'ing-k'ai and his associates may take in the future and
regardless of the fact that during the time of their Fukien
People's Government they adhered to their old practices
without rallying the people for the struggle, it must be considered an act beneficial to the revolution that they turned the
fire originally trained on the Red Army against Japanese
imperialism and Chiang Kai-shek. This marked a split within
the Kuomintang camp. If this section of people could split
away from the Kuomintang camp under the circumstances
following the Incident of September 18, 1931, why then cannot
there be another split within the Kuomintang under today's
circumstances? Those in our Party are wrong who hold the view
that the whole camp of the landlord class and the bourgeoisie
is united and consolidated, and that under no circumstances
can it be made to change. Such people not only fail to realise
the grave situation of today, but have also forgotten history.

Let me speak a little more about history. In 1926 and 1927,
from the time when the revolutionary army was advancing on
Wuhan to the time when it captured Wuhan and penetrated
into Honan, T'ang Sheng-chih and Feng Yu'hsiang[12] joined
the revolution. Even in 1933, Feng Yu-hsiang and the Communists joined forces to form the Anti-Japanese Allied Armies
in Chahar.

To take another striking example: Didn't the Kuomintang's
Twenty-sixth Route Army, which had once attacked the Red
Army in Kiangsi in conjunction with the Nineteenth Route
Army, stage the Ningtu Uprising[13] in December 1931, and
transform itself into a Red army? The leaders of the Ningtu
Uprising, Chao Po-sheng, Tung Chen-t'ang and others have
become steadfast comrades in the revolution.

The anti-Japanese activities of Ma Chan-shan[14] in the three
north-eastern provinces constitute another split in the camp
of the ruling classes.

All these instances indicate that when the range of the
Japanese bombers extends to the whole of China, when the
struggle changes its normal pace and suddenly surges forward,
there will be a split in the enemy camp.

Now, comrades, let us turn to another aspect of the subject.

Is it correct to object to our views on the ground of the political and economic flabbiness of the national bourgeoisie and to hold that China's national bourgeoisie cannot change its attitude even though circumstances change? Again I think not. If the national bourgeoisie cannot change its attitude because of its flabbiness, why then did it change its normal attitude in 1924-7, not merely vacillating but even joining the revolution? Can it be that the flabbiness of the national bourgeoisie is an ailment contracted after its birth and not a congenital one brought along from its mother's womb? Can it be that this class is flabby today, but was not so at an earlier date? One of the chief characteristics of the politics and economy of a semi-colony is exactly the flabbiness of its national bourgeoisie. This is exactly why imperialism dares to bully this class, and this determines one of the features of this class, its dislike of imperialism. Of course we will fully admit rather than deny that again because of this feature, the imperialists and the landlords and compradors can easily draw this class over by using temporarily some sort of bribe as a bait, hence its lack of thoroughness towards the revolution. But for all this, we cannot say that in the present circumstances there is no difference between the national bourgeoisie and the landlord and comprador classes.

We have therefore pointed out with emphasis that the Kuomintang camp will split up when the national crisis reaches its critical point. Such a split has become manifest in the vacillation of the national bourgeoisie and in the activities of such anti-Japanese figures as Feng Yu-hsiang, Ts'ai T'ing-k'ai and Ma Chan-shan, who are enjoying a spell of popularity. This state of affairs is, basically speaking, unfavourable to the counter-revolution and favourable to the revolution. The possibility of such a split is increased because of the unevenness in China's political and economic development and the resulting unevenness in the development of the revolution.

Comrades, so much for the positive side of the question. Now let me take up its negative side, namely, the question that certain elements of the national bourgeoisie are often past masters at deceiving the people. Why? Because apart from the genuine supporters of the people's revolutionary cause, many others of this class may for a time appear as revolutionaries or semi-revolutionaries, and in that capacity are able to deceive the people and make it hard for the people to see through their lack of thoroughness and their affected airs and graces. This increases the responsibility of the Communist Party to criticise its allies, to unmask the false revolutionaries and to win hegemony. To deny that during a great upheaval the national bourgeoisie may vacillate and join the revolution, is to abandon or at least belittle our Party's task of winning hegemony. For if, like the landlords and compradors, the national bourgeoisie appeared with the hideous features of traitors, then our Party might very well disregard its task of fighting for hegemony or at least take it lightly.

In making a general analysis of the attitude of the Chinese landlord class and bourgeoisie in a great upheaval, another aspect should be pointed out, namely, that even within the camp of the landlords and compradors there is no complete unity. This results from the circumstances of a semi-colony, *i.e.* circumstances in which many imperialist powers are contending for China. When our struggle is directed against Japanese imperialism, the pet dogs of the United States or even Britain may, in obedience to the varying tones of their masters' command, engage in a veiled strife or even an open conflict with the Japanese imperialists and their pet dogs. There have been many instances of such dog-fights in the past and we are not going to dwell upon them. We will only mention now that even Hu Han-min,[15] a Kuomintang politician once imprisoned by Chiang Kai-shek, put his signature not very long ago to the document of our Six-Point Programme for Resistance to Japan and Salvation of the Nation.[16] Warlords of the Kwantung and Kwangsi cliques[17] who form Hu Han-min's backing have also set themselves against Chiang Kaishek under the deceitful slogans "Recover the lost territory" and "Resistance to Japan side by side with annihilation of the bandits".[18] (Chiang Kai-shek's slogan being "Annihilation of the bandits before resistance to Japan".) You see, isn't this rather strange? It is not strange at all; it is merely a particularly interesting instance of a fight among big and small dogs, well-fed and under-fed dogs; it represents a crack which is neither big nor small, and a contradiction which at once tickles and hurts. But this fight, crack or contradiction is indeed useful to the revolutionary people. We must make a collection of all the fights, cracks and contradictions within the enemy camp to direct them against the principal enemy of the moment.

Summing up the problem of class relations, we may say that, along with the basic change in the situation caused by the Japanese invasion into China Proper, the relationship among the various classes in China has changed, with an increase in the strength of the camp of the national revolution and a decrease in the strength of the camp of the national counter-revolution.

Now we shall deal with the conditions in the camp of China's national revolution.

First, the condition of the Red Army. Comrades, as you have seen, for nearly a year and a half the three main contingents of China's Red Army have carried out a colossal shift of positions. After Comrade Jen Pi-shih[19] and others led the Sixth Army Group to shift its position in August last year towards where Comrade Ho Lung's army was stationed,[20] we started our shift immediately in October.[21] In March this year the Red Army in the Szechwan-Shensi border area[22] also began to shift its position. All three contingents of the Red Army abandoned their old positions and shifted to new regions. This colossal shift turned the old areas into guerrilla zones. In the course of these shifts the Red Army was considerably weakened. If we take into consideration this aspect of the total situation, we see that the enemy won a temporary and partial victory, while we met with a temporary and partial defeat. Is this statement correct? I think it is, for it is a statement of fact. But some people (Chang Kuo-t'ao[23] for instance) say that the Central Red Army[24] met with failure. Is this statement correct? No. For that is not the fact. When a Marxist approaches a problem, he should not only look at the parts, but see the whole. A frog squatting at the bottom of a well says, "The sky is only the size of the mouth of a well". That is wrong, for the sky is not limited to the size of the mouth of a well. But if it says, "A certain portion of the sky is only the size of the mouth of a well", it will be right, for that tallies with the fact. Thus, we say the Red Army has failed in one respect (in preserving its original bases), but has achieved victory in another respect (in fulfilling the plan of the Long March). The enemy, on the other hand, has won victory in one respect (in occupying our original bases), but has failed in another respect (in realising his plan of "encirclement and annihilation" and of "pursuit and annihilation"). Only this statement is correct, for we have in fact completed the Long March.

Speaking of the Long March, I should like to ask, "what is its significance?" We say that the Long March is the first of its kind ever recorded in history, that it is a manifesto, an agitation corps and a seeding-machine. Since P'an Ku divided heaven from earth and the Three Sovereigns and Five Emperors[25] reigned, has there ever been in history a long march like ours? For twelve months we were under daily reconnaissance and bombing from the air by scores of planes; we were encircled, pursued, obstructed and intercepted on the ground by a big force of several hundred thousand men; we encountered untold difficulties and great obstacles on the way, but by keeping our two feet going we swept across a distance of more than 20,000 *li* through the length and breadth of eleven provinces. Well, has there ever been in history a long march like ours? No, never. The Long March is also a manifesto. It proclaims to the world that the Red Army is an army of heroes and that the imperialists and their jackals, Chiang Kai-shek and his like, are perfect nonentities. It announces the bankruptcy of the encirclement, pursuit, obstruction and interception attempted by the imperialists and Chiang Kai-shek. The Long March is also an agitation corps. It declares to the approximately two hundred million people of eleven provinces that only the road of the Red Army leads to their liberation. Without the Long March, how could the broad masses have known so quickly that there are such great ideas in the world as are upheld by the Red Army? The Long March is also a seeding-machine. It has sown many seeds in eleven provinces, which will sprout, grow leaves, blossom into flowers, bear fruit and yield a harvest in the future. To sum up, the Long March ended with our victory and the enemy's defeat. Who led the Long March to victory? The Communist Party. Without the Communist Party, such a long march would have been inconceivable. The Chinese Communist Party—its leading bodies, its cadres and its members—is not afraid of difficulties or hardships. Whoever is sceptical of our ability to lead the revolutionary war will fall into the muddy pit of opportunism.

A new situation arose as soon as the Long March was concluded. In the battle at the town of Chihlo, the Central Red Army and the north-western Red Army, in brotherly solidarity, shattered the traitor Chiang Kai-shek's campaign of "encirclement and annihilation" against the Shensi-Kansu border area[26] and thus laid the cornerstone for the Party centre's task of establishing the national headquarters of the revolution in the North-west.

Such being the case with the Red Army's main forces, what about the guerrilla warfare in various southern provinces? The guerrilla warfare in the South received some setbacks, but it has not been stamped out. And in many places it is just reasserting itself, and is growing and expanding.[27]

In the Kuomintang-controlled areas, the workers' struggle is now developing from inside the factory to the outside, from an economic struggle into a political struggle. The heroic struggle against the Japanese and the traitors on the part of the working class is now in intense ferment and, judging by the situation, will burst forth before long.

The peasants' struggle has never ceased. Plagued by foreign aggression, internal warfare and natural calamities, the peasants have started extensive struggles in the form of guerrilla war, mass uprisings, famine riots, etc. An anti-Japanese guerrilla war is going on in the North-eastern provinces and eastern Hopeh[28] in reply to the attacks of Japanese imperialism.

The student movement has advanced in big strides and will advance farther. But only when it is co-ordinated with the struggle of the workers, peasants and soldiers can this movement be kept up, overriding the martial law of the traitors and the policy of disruption and massacre carried out by the police, spies, educational racketeers and fascists.

We have already dealt with the possibility for the national

bourgeoisie and the rich peasants and small landlords in the countryside to vacillate and even participate in the anti-Japanese struggle.

The national minorities, especially the Inner Mongolians, who are directly menaced by Japanese imperialism, are now rising up in struggle. In future their struggle will merge with the people's struggle in North China and the Red Army's activities in the North-west.

All this indicates that the revolutionary situation is changing from a localised into a nation-wide one and changing gradually from a state of unevenness into one of relative evenness. We are now on the eve of a great change. The task of the Party is to form a united national revolutionary front by integrating the activities of the Red Army with all the activities of the workers, peasants, students, the petty bourgeoisie and the national bourgeoisie of the whole country.

THE NATIONAL UNITED FRONT

Having surveyed the situation both on the side of the revolution and on that of the counter-revolution, we shall find it easy to elucidate the Party's tactical tasks.

What is the basic tactical task of the Party? It is none other than to form a broad national revolutionary united front.

When changes take place in the revolutionary situation, there should be corresponding changes in revolutionary tactics and in the method of revolutionary leadership. While the task of the Japanese imperialists and the collaborators and traitors is to reduce China to a colony, our task is to transform China into an independent and free country with territorial integrity.

To win China's independence and freedom is a great task. Towards this end we must fight foreign imperialism and the domestic counter-revolutionary forces. Japanese imperialism has made up its mind to bluster and bludgeon its way into China. And the domestic counter-revolutionary forces of the landed gentry and the comprador class are still, at the present moment, stronger than the people's revolutionary forces. The task of overthrowing Japanese imperialism and the Chinese counter-revolutionary forces cannot be accomplished in a day, so we must be prepared to devote a long time to it; nor can it be accomplished by small forces, so we must accumulate large forces. The counter-revolutionary forces in China and throughout the world are weaker than they used to be, whereas the revolutionary forces in China and throughout the world have become much stronger. This is a correct estimate, an estimate made from one angle. But at the same time we must also say that the counter-revolutionary forces in China and throughout the world are still stronger than the revolutionary forces. This, too, is a correct estimate, an estimate made from another angle. From the unevenness in China's political and economic development ensues the unevenness in the development of the revolution. The revolution generally starts, develops and triumphs in places where the counter-revolutionary forces are comparatively weak, while in places where they are strong, it either has not arisen or is developing only very slowly. Such was the situation which the Chinese revolution faced during a long period in the past. It may be anticipated that, at certain stages in the future, although the general revolutionary situation will have developed farther ahead, the unevenness will still remain. The transformation of such unevenness into general evenness still demands prolonged efforts, and a correct tactical line for the Party. If the revolutionary war led by the Communist Party of the Soviet Union[29] was concluded in three years, then, to the revolutionary war led by the Chinese Communist Party, we should be prepared to give, as is necessary, more time, besides the long years already devoted to it, in order to dispose finally and thoroughly of the domestic and foreign counter-revolutionary forces; such impetuosity as we once showed will never do. Sound revolutionary tactics must also be set forth and if we keep on milling around in narrow circles we shall never achieve great things. I am not saying that things in China can only be done at a slow tempo; they must be done boldly, for the danger of national subjugation will not allow us a moment's slackening. From now on the revolution will certainly develop at a much greater speed than before, for both China and the world are entering a new stage of war and revolution. For all that, the Chinese revolutionary war remains a protracted one, as determined by the strength of imperialism and the uneven development of the revolution.

We have said that the characteristic of the present situation is that a new upsurge of national revolution is coming, that China is on the eve of a great new nation-wide revolution; and this is the characteristic of the present revolutionary situation. This is a fact, or one aspect of the fact. But now we also say that imperialism is still a force to be seriously reckoned with, that the unevenness in the development of the revolutionary forces is still a serious defect, and that to defeat our enemies we must be prepared to fight a protracted war; such is another characteristic of the present revolutionary situation. This is also a fact, or another aspect of the fact. Both characteristics, both facts teach us and urge us to adapt ourselves to the situation, revise our tactics, and change our ways of disposing our forces and carrying on the war. The present situation demands that we boldly give up closed-door sectarianism, form a broad united front and curb adventurism. Before the time is ripe for a decisive battle, or before we have adequate strength for it, we must not rashly wage a decisive battle.

I shall not mention here the relation between closed-door sectarianism and adventurism, or the dangers that adventurism may bring about when momentous events unfold themselves in future; we can put this off for future discussion. I shall only point out here that the tactic of the united front and the tactic of closed-door sectarianism are tactics diametrically opposed to each other.

The one is to accumulate large forces so as to surround our enemies and annihilate them.

The other is to rely on a single horseman to wage a desperate fight with a formidable enemy.

The one holds that without an adequate appraisal of how the Japanese attempt to colonise China will change the battle array of the revolution and the counter-revolution in China, we shall be unable to appraise adequately the possibility of forming a broad national revolutionary united front. Without an adequate appraisal of the strength as well as the weakness of the Japanese counter-revolutionary forces, of the Chinese counter-revolutionary forces, and of the Chinese revolutionary forces, we shall be unable to appraise adequately the necessity of organising a broad national revolutionary united front, to take resolute measures to break down closed-door sectarianism, be unable to wield the united front as a weapon to organise and rally millions upon millions of people and all potential friendly forces of the revolution to advance and attack our centremost objective—Japanese imperialism and its jackals, the Chinese traitors—or to use our tactics as a weapon to attack the central objective confronting us, but on the contrary shall set up diverse objectives and consequently our bullets would hit the lesser enemies or even our allies rather than the principal enemy. This means that we shall be unable to pick out the right enemy and shall waste our ammunition. In this manner we shall be unable to drive the enemy into a narrow isolated position. In this manner we shall be unable to draw over from the enemy's camp and his front all those who have joined them under compulsion, those who were our enemies yesterday but may become our friends today. In this manner we shall be actually helping the enemy, retarding and isolating the revolution, causing it to dwindle and decline, and even to take the road to defeat.

The other would say: all such arguments are erroneous. The forces of the revolution must be pure and absolutely pure, and the road of revolution must be straight and absolutely straight. Only what is recorded in the "Bible" is correct. The national bourgeoisie is destined to be entirely and eternally counter-revolutionary. Not a single inch is to be yielded to the rich peasants. As regards the yellow trade unions, we should fight them tooth and nail. If we must shake hands with Ts'ai T'ing-k'ai, then while shaking his hand, we ought to call him a "counter-revolutionary". Has there even been a cat that does not love meat or a warlord who is not a counter-revolutionary? The intellectuals can remain revolutionary only for a day or two, and it is dangerous to recruit them. Hence the conclusion: closed-door sectarianism is the only magic wand, and the united front is the tactic of opportunism.

Comrades, which is right, the idea of a united front or the idea of closed-door sectarianism? Of which does Marxism-Leninism approve? I shall definitely answer: It approves of a united front and not of closed-door sectarianism. Three-year-old tots may have many correct ideas, but cannot be entrusted with serious affairs of the state and the world, because they do not yet understand them. Marxism-Leninism is opposed to the infantile disorder found among the revolutionary ranks. Those who insist upon the tactic of closed-door sectarianism are merely spreading a series of such infantile disorders. The path of revolution, like the road of every activity in the world, is always tortuous, never straight. The battle array of the revolution and the counter-revolution may change, just as everything else in the world may change. The Party's new tactic to form a broad united front starts from the two basic facts that Japanese imperialism is determined to reduce the whole of China to its colony and that there are still serious weaknesses in China's revolutionary forces at present. In order to attack the counter-revolutionary forces the revolutionary forces today need to organise millions upon millions of the people and manœuvre a huge revolutionary army. Only such a force can crush the Japanese imperialists and the collaborators and traitors: this is a truth obvious to everybody. Therefore, only the tactic of the united front is a Marxist-Leninist tactic. The tactic of closed-door sectarianism is, on the contrary, the tactic of a "lonely overlord". In the manner of "sending fish to the water and birds to the woods", closed-door sectarianism will drive the "millions upon millions" and the "huge army" to the enemy's side, to his great satisfaction. Closed-door sectarians are, in fact, the loyal slaves of the Japanese imperialists and of the collaborators and traitors. What the closed-door sectarians call "pure" and "straight" is the very thing which will receive a slap in the face from Marxism-Leninism, but praise from Japanese imperialism. We shall definitely reject closed-door sectarianism; what we want is the national revolutionary united front that will be fatal to the Japanese imperialists and the collaborators and traitors.

THE PEOPLE'S REPUBLIC[30]

If we say that our government has hitherto been one based on the alliance of the workers, peasants and the urban petty bourgeoisie, then from now on it must be so transformed as to represent, besides the workers, peasants and the urban petty bourgeoisie, members of all other classes who are willing to take part in the national revolution.

For the present, this government's basic task is to oppose the attempt of Japanese imperialism to annex China. This government will broaden its scope of representation: not only the representatives of those who are interested only in the national revolution but not in the agrarian revolution may join the government, but also the representatives of those who will not oppose European and American imperialism because of their affiliations, but will oppose Japanese imperialism and its lackeys, may join the government if they want to. Therefore this government's programme should as a matter of principle fit in with the main task of fighting Japanese imperialism and its jackals, and we should modify our past policies accordingly.

The special feature of the revolution at present is that there are a well-steeled Communist Party and a well-steeled Red Army. This is a matter of the utmost importance. Great difficulties would arise if there were no well-steeled Communist Party and Red Army. Why? Because the collaborators and the traitors are numerous and powerful in China and are sure to devise every means to break up this united front; they will employ such measures as intimidation and bribery, manipulation of alignments and alliances, to sow dissension and discord, and use armed strength to oppress and crush separately all those forces that are weaker than themselves and are willing to part company with the traitors and join us to fight Japan. In the absence of the two vital factors, the Communist Party and the Red Army, in the anti-Japanese government and the anti-Japanese army, the disruption of the united front could hardly be averted. The revolution in 1927 failed chiefly because the opportunist line then existing in the Communist Party made no effort to expand our own ranks (the workers' and peasants' movement and the armed forces led by the Communist Party), but relied solely on a temporary ally, the Kuomintang. As a result, imperialism ordered its jackals, the landed gentry and the comprador class, to stretch out thousands of tentacles to drag over first Chiang Kai-shek and then Wang Ching-wei, thereby landing the revolution in failure. In the revolutionary united front of that time there was no mainstay, no strong revolutionary armed troops; when defections took place on all sides, the Communist Party, forced to fight single-handed, was powerless to foil the tactic adopted by the imperialists and the Chinese counter-revolutionaries of crushing their opponents separately. Though there was then an army under Ho Lung and Yeh T'ing, it was not yet a politically consolidated body, and moreover, as the Party was not good at leading it, it too ended in defeat. This was a lesson learnt at the cost of blood, showing how the revolution failed because of the lack of a nuclear revolutionary force.

But changes have taken place today in this respect; there are already a strong Communist Party and a strong Red Army, as well as the base areas of the Red Army. The Communist Party and the Red Army are not only acting at present as the initiators of the Anti-Japanese National United Front but will inevitably become the powerful mainstay of the anti-Japanese government and anti-Japanese army, preventing the Japanese imperialists and Chiang Kai-shek from attaining their ultimate end in their policy of disrupting the national united front. We must be very vigilant, because the Japanese imperialists and Chiang Kai-shek will undoubtedly employ in every conceivable way such measures as intimidation, bribery and the manipulation of alignments and alliances.

Of course we cannot expect every section of the broad ranks of the Anti-Japanese National United Front to be as consolidated as the Communst Party and the Red Army. In the course of action some bad elements under the enemy's influence may withdraw from the united front. However, we are not afraid of the withdrawal of such people. Some bad people may drop out under the enemy's influence, but good people will join in under ours. So long as the Communist Party and the Red Army live and grow, the Anti-Japanese National United Front, too, will live and grow. Such is the hegemony of the Communist Party and the Red Army in the national united front. The Communists, now no longer little children, are able to take care of themselves and to get along with their allies. If the Japanese imperialists and Chiang Kai-shek can employ such measures as manipulation of alignments and alliances against the revolutionary forces, the Communist Party can do the same against the counter-revolutionary forces. If they can draw over to them the bad elements from our ranks, naturally we can also draw over to us the "bad elements" (good elements to us) from theirs. If we can draw over a greater number of people from their ranks, then the enemy forces will be reduced and ours increased. In short, at present two basic forces are struggling against each other; it is a matter of course that all the intermediate forces must attach themselves either to one side or to the other. The policies of subjugating and of betraying China, pursued by the Japanese imperialists and Chiang Kai-shek respectively, cannot but drive many forces to our side, either to join directly the ranks of the Communist Party and the Red Army or to form a united front with us. This prospect will be realised so long as our tactic is not one of closed-door sectarianism.

Why should we change the workers' and peasants' republic into a people's republic?

Our government represents not only the workers and peasants but the whole nation. This was originally implied in the slogan of a workers' and peasants' democratic republic, because the workers and peasants constitute from 80 to 90 per cent of the nation's population. The Ten-Point Programme[31] adopted by the Sixth National Congress of our Party stands not only for the interests of the workers and peasants but also for the interests of the nation. But the present situation makes us change the slogan and alter it into one of a people's republic. This is because Japanese invasion has altered the class relations in China and it is now possible not only for the petty bourgeoisie but also for the national bourgeoisie to join the anti-Japanese struggle.

Beyond doubt, the people's republic does not represent the interests of the enemy classes. On the contrary, the people's republic stands in direct opposition to the jackals of imperialism, the landed gentry and the comprador class, and does not include them in the "people". This is comparable to the fact that Chiang Kai-shek's "National Government of the Republic of China" represents only the richest men but not the common people, who are not counted as "citizens". As from 80 to 90 per cent of China's population is made up of the workers and peasants, the people's republic is first and foremost to represent their interests. But should the people's republic remove imperialist oppression and make China free and independent, should it remove the oppression of the landlords and make China free from semi-feudalism, it would benefit not only the workers and peasants but other sections of the people as well. The sum total of the interests of the workers, peasants and other sections of the people constitutes the interests of the Chinese nation. Though the comprador and the landlord classes also live on Chinese soil, they do not care about the interests of the nation; their interests clash with those of the majority of the people. As we part company only with this small number of landlords and compradors and clash only with them, we have the right to call ourselves the representatives of the whole nation.

There is also a clash of interest between the working class and the national bourgeoisie. We cannot successfully expand the national revolution if we do not give political and economic rights to its vanguard and enable the working class to exert its strength to cope with imperialism and its jackals, the traitors. But if the national bourgeoisie joins the united front against imperialism, then the working class and the national bourgeoisie will have interests in common. The people's republic will not, in the era of the bourgeois-democratic revolution, abolish non-imperialist and non-feudalist private property but will encourage the development of industrial and commercial enterprises of the national bourgeoisie rather than confiscate them. We shall protect any national bourgeois so long as he does not support the imperialists and traitors. In the stage of democratic revolution, a limit is set to the struggle between labour and capital. While the labour law of the people's republic protects the interests of the workers, it is not opposed to the profit-making of the national bourgeoisie or the development of their industrial and commercial enterprises, because such development is detrimental to imperialism and beneficial to the Chinese people. It is thus clear that the people's republic represents the interests of the people of the various strata who are opposed to imperialism and the feudal forces. The government of the people's republic is based principally on the workers and peasants, but will at the same time admit the representatives of all other classes that are opposed to imperialism and the feudal forces.

But isn't it dangerous to let the representatives of such classes join the government of the people's republic? No. The workers and peasants form the basic section of the masses of the republic. In giving the urban petty bourgeoisie, the intellectuals and other elements who support the anti-imperialist and anti-feudal programme the right to voice their opinion and to work in the government of the people's republic, the right to elect and to be elected, we are not jeopardising the interests of the basic section of the masses—the workers and peasants. The essential part of our programme must be the protection of the interests of the basic section of the masses—the workers and peasants. The majority formed in this government by the representatives of the basic section of the masses, the workers and peasants, and the leadership and activities of the Communist Party in it, combine to ensure that the participation of the representatives of those people involves no danger. It is perfectly obvious that the Chinese revolution at the present stage is still a bourgeois-democratic revolution, not a proletarian-socialist one. Only the counter-revolutionary Trotskyites[32] will talk such nonsense as that China has already completed her bourgeois-democratic revolution and that any further revolution can only be a socialist one. The revolution of 1924–7 was a bourgeois-democratic revolution which was not completed but failed. The agrarian revolution led by us from 1927 up to the present is also a bourgeois-democratic revolution, because its task is to oppose imperialism and feudalism, not capitalism. The revolution will remain such for quite a long time to come.

The motive forces of the revolution are still, in the main, the workers, the peasants and the urban petty bourgeoisie, but now there may be in addition the national bourgeoisie.

The transition of the revolution is a thing of the future. In the future the democratic revolution will inevitably be transformed into a socialist revolution. As to when the transition will take place, it depends on whether the conditions for it are ripe; it will certainly take quite a long time. Until all the necessary political and economic conditions are ripe, until the transition is not detrimental but beneficial to the greatest majority of the people throughout the country, we should not glibly talk about the transition. It is wrong to doubt this and to expect that a transition will take place within a very short time, as did some of our comrades in the past who maintained that the moment the democratic revolution began to triumph in key provinces a transition in the revolution would begin. They did that because they failed to see what kind of country China is politically and economically, because they did not know that it is much more difficult and requires a good deal more time and effort for China than for Russia to complete her democratic revolution politically and economically.

INTERNATIONAL SUPPORT

Finally, a word is necessary about the interrelationship of the Chinese revolution with the world revolution.

Ever since that monster imperialism came into being, things in the world have been organically connected with one another, and it is impossible to attempt to separate them. We Chinese people possess the heroic spirit to wage the bloody war against the enemies to the finish, the determination to recover our lost territory through our own efforts, and the ability to stand on our own feet in the family of nations of the world. But this does not mean that we can dispense with international support; no, international support is necessary for the revolutionary struggle today in any country or of any nation. As the ancients put it, "There were no just wars in the Era of Spring and Autumn".[33] This is even more true of imperialism today, and it is only the oppressed nations and the oppressed classes that can wage just wars. All those wars in the world in which the people rise to fight their oppressors are just wars. The February and October Revolutions in Russia were just wars. The revolutions of the people in various European countries after the First World War were just wars. In China, the Anti-Opium War,[34] the War of the T'aip'ing

Heavenly Kingdom,[35] the Boxer War,[36] the Revolutionary War of 1911,[37] the Northern Expedition of 1926–7, the Agrarian Revolutionary War from 1927 up to the present, and the present war against Japan and the traitors are all just wars.

In the present nation-wide anti-Japanese upsurge and world-wide anti-fascist upsurge, just wars will spread all over China and the globe. All just wars should support each other and all unjust wars should be turned into just ones—this is the Leninist line.[38] Our anti-Japanese war needs the support of the people of the world, above all the support of the people of the Soviet Union; and they will certainly support us, because we and they are concerned with each others' weal and woe. In the past the Chinese revolutionary forces were cut off for a time from the world revolutionary forces by Chiang Kai-shek and in this sense we were isolated. But now the situation has turned in our favour. From now on the situation will continue to turn even more to our advantage. We shall no longer be isolated. That is an essential condition for China to achieve victory in her Anti-Japanese War and in her revolution.

December 27, 1935.

STRATEGIC PROBLEMS OF CHINA'S REVOLUTIONARY WAR

This is a summary of the experience of the Second Revolutionary Civil War (1927–38). The result of a major Inner-Party debate over military problems during the Second Revolutionary Civil War, it gives the views of one military line as opposed to those of another. The controversy was settled at the Tsunyi meeting of the Party centre in January 1935, at which Comrade Mao Tse-tung's correct views were adopted and those of the erroneous line rejected.

The Party centre was moved to northern Shensi in October 1935, and in December Comrade Mao made his report "On the Tactics of Fighting Japanese Imperialism", in which he solved systematically the problem of the political line in the Second Revolutionary Civil War. A year later he wrote this booklet to give a systematic explanation of the strategic problems of China's revolutionary war.

The five chapters here published were originally delivered as lectures at the Red Army College in northern Shensi. The Sian Incident and its sequel kept Comrade Mao too busy to round off the work with chapters on the strategic offensive, political work and other problems.

CHAPTER I

HOW TO STUDY WAR

I. THE LAWS OF WAR ARE DEVELOPMENTAL

The laws of war—this is a problem which anyone directing a war must study and solve.

The laws of a revolutionary war—this is a problem which anyone directing a revolutionary war must study and solve.

The laws of China's revolutionary war—this is a problem which anyone directing China's revolutionary war must study and solve.

We are now engaged in a war; our war is a revolutionary war; and our revolutionary war is being waged in this semi-feudal and semi-colonial country of China. Thus we must not only study the laws of war in general but also study the laws of a particular revolutionary war and moreover study the laws of the even more particular revolutionary war in China.

Everyone knows that, in doing a thing, if one does not

understand its circumstances, its characteristics and its relations to other things, then one cannot know its laws, cannot know how to do it, and cannot do it well.

War is the highest form of struggle, existing ever since the emergence of private property and social classes, for settling contradictions between classes, between nations, between states, or between political groups at given stages of their development. Without understanding the circumstances of war, its characteristics, and its relations to other things, we cannot know the laws of war, cannot know how to direct it, and cannot win victory.

Revolutionary war—a revolutionary class war or a revolutionary national war has its special circumstances and characteristics in addition to circumstances and characteristics of war in general. Thus besides the general laws of war, it has some special laws of its own. Without understanding these special circumstances and characteristics and without understanding its special laws, we cannot direct a revolutionary war and win victory in it.

China's revolutionary war—whether a civil war or a national war, it is waged in the special environment of China; and compared with war in general or the revolutionary war in general, it again has its special circumstances and special characteristics. Thus, besides the laws of war in general and of revolutionary war in general, it has also some special laws of its own. If we do not understand them, we cannot win victory in China's revolutionary war.

Therefore, we must study the laws of war in general, we must also study the laws of revolutionary war, and, finally, we must study the laws of China's revolutionary war.

One group of people hold an incorrect view, and we refuted it long ago. They declare that it is enough to study merely the laws of war in general or, specifically, that it is enough to follow the military rules published by the reactionary Chinese government or the reactionary military academies in China. They do not see that these rules represent only the laws of war in general and moreover are entirely copied from abroad; if we copy them and apply them mechanically without the slightest change in form or content, it will be like whittling down the feet to fit the shoes, and we shall be defeated. Their argument is: such things were learned at the cost of blood by people in the past, why are they of no use? They do not see that although we must cherish the experiences acquired by people in the past at the cost of their blood, we must also cherish experiences acquired at the cost of our own blood.

Another group of people hold a second incorrect view, and we also refuted it long ago. They declare that it is enough to study Russia's experiences of revolutionary war or, specifically, that it is enough to follow the guiding laws of the civil war in the Soviet Union and the military directives published by the military leadership there. They do not see that these laws of war and military directives in the Soviet Union embody the special characteristics of the civil war and the Red Army of the Soviet Union; if we copy them and apply them mechanically and allow no change whatsoever, it will also be like whittling down the feet to fit the shoes, and we shall be defeated. Their argument is: our war, like the war in the Soviet Union, is a revolutionary war; since the Soviet Union has won victory, how can there be any alternative but to follow its example? They do not see that although we must especially cherish the Soviet experiences of war because they are the most recent experiences of revolutionary war and have been acquired under the guidance of Lenin and Stalin, we must also cherish the experiences of China's revolutionary war, because there are a great number of conditions special to the Chinese revolution and the Chinese Red Army.

Another group of people hold a third incorrect view, and we also refuted it long ago. They declare that the experiences of the Northern Expedition of 1926–7 are the most valuable and that we must learn from them; or specifically, that we must learn from them to drive straight forward to seize the big cities. They do not see that while the precedents in the Northern Expedition must be studied, they should not be copied mechanically, because the circumstances of our present war are different. We should adopt only those measures in the Northern Expedition that are still suitable in the present circumstances, and we should work out our own measures according to our present circumstances.

12

Thus the difference in the circumstances of wars determines the difference in the guiding laws of wars: the differences of time, place and character.

Considering the condition of time, war and the guiding laws of war are both developmental; as each historical stage has its characteristics, the laws of war in each historical stage have their characteristics and cannot be mechanically applied in a different stage.

Considering the character of war, as revolutionary war and counter-revolutionary war each has its own characteristics, the laws of each also have their own characteristics, and the laws governing one cannot be mechanically applied to the other.

Considering the condition of place, as each state or nation, especially a big state or a big nation, has its peculiarities, the laws of war in each state or nation have their peculiarities and cannot be copied mechanically either.

In studying the guiding laws of war of different historical stages, of different characters, of different places and of different nations, we must keep our eyes on their respective characteristics and their development, and must oppose a mechanical approach to the problem of war.

That is not all. It marks a progress and development on the part of a commander capable at first of commanding only a small unit to become capable of commanding a big one. There is also a difference between operating in one and the same place and operating in many different places. It marks also a progress and development on the part of a commander capable at first of operating only in a place he knows well, to become capable of operating in many other places. Owing to the technological, tactical and strategic developments on the enemy side and on our own, the conditions at each stage of a war are also different. It marks even further progress and development on the part of a commander capable of directing a war in its elementary stage, to become capable of directing it in its advanced stage. To be competent only in commanding a certain military unit at a certain place or at a certain stage in the development of a war means making no progress or showing no development. There are some people who, contented with a single talent or a peep-hole view, never make any progress; they may play some part in the revolution at a given place and time, but not a significant part. We need commanders in war who can play a significant part. All guiding laws of war develop as history develops and as war develops; nothing remains changeless.

2. THE AIM OF WAR LIES IN ELIMINATING WAR

War, this monster of mutual slaughter among mankind, will be finally eliminated through the progress of human society, and in no distant future too. But there is only one way of eliminating it, namely, to oppose war by means of war, to oppose counter-revolutionary war by means of revolutionary war, to oppose national counter-revolutionary war by means of national revolutionary war, and to oppose counter-revolutionary class war by means of revolutionary class war. There are only two kinds of wars in history, just and unjust. We support just wars and oppose unjust wars. All counter-revolutionary wars are unjust, all revolutionary wars are just. We will put an end to man's warring era with our hands, and the war we are waging is undoubtedly part of the final war. But the war we are confronted with is also undoubtedly part of the greatest and most ruthless of all wars. The greatest and most ruthless of all unjust counter-revolutionary wars is pressing on us; and if we did not raise the banner of a just war, the majority of mankind would suffer destruction. The banner of a just war of mankind is the banner for the salvation of mankind; the banner of China's just war is the banner for the salvation of China. A war which will be waged by the overwhelming majority of mankind and of the Chinese people will undoubtedly be a just war—it will be incomparably the most honourable undertaking for saving mankind and China, and will form a bridge leading world history into a new era. When human society advances to the point where classes and states are eliminated, there will no longer be any wars, whether revolutionary or counter-revolutionary, just or unjust, and that will be an era of lasting peace for mankind. Our study of the laws of revolutionary war starts from our will to eliminate all wars—this is the dividing line between us Communists and all exploiting classes.

3. STRATEGY STUDIES THE LAWS OF A WHOLE MILITARY SITUATION

Wherever there are military operations, there is a whole military situation. A whole military situation may cover the entire world, it may cover an entire country, or it may cover an independent guerrilla area or a major independent operational front. Whenever there are various phases and stages to be taken into consideration there is a whole military situation.

The task of strategy is to study the laws for directing operations that may affect a whole military situation. The task of operational or tactical direction is to study the laws for directing military operations which are of a partial character.

Why should a campaign or battle commander have some understanding of the laws of strategy? Because a comprehension of the whole makes it easier for one to handle the part and because the part belongs to the whole. The view that strategic victory is achieved by tactical successes alone is erroneous, because it overlooks the fact that the first and the foremost problem in deciding the outcome of a war is whether or not the whole situation and its various stages are properly taken into consideration. If there are serious shortcomings or mistakes in the appraisal of the whole situation and the various stages of a war, the war will certainly be lost. "Make a single careless move and the entire game is lost" refers to a move which is linked with the whole, *i.e.* a move decisive for the whole situation, not to a move of a partial nature, *i.e.* a move which is not decisive for the whole situation. This is as true of war as a game of chess.

But the whole situation cannot detach itself from its parts and become independent of them; the whole situation is made up of all its parts. Sometimes certain parts suffer destruction or defeat, yet the whole situation is not vitally affected, because those parts are not decisive for the whole situation. In a war, some defeats or failures in battles or campaigns do not lead to a change for the worse in the whole military situation, because they are not defeats of decisive significance. But if most of the campaigns making up a whole military situation are lost or one or two decisive campaigns are lost, the whole situation will change immediately. In that case, "most of the campaigns" and "the one or two campaigns" are decisive. In the history of war, there are instances where, after a succession of battles won, defeat in a single battle nullifies all the previous achievements and there are also instances where, after many defeats, victory in a single battle opens up a new situation. In such instances "a succession of battles won" and "many defeats" are of a partial nature and are not decisive for the whole situation, while the "defeat in a single battle" and "victory in a single battle" are both decisive. All these instances explain the importance of taking the whole situation into consideration. For the person in command of the whole situation, the most important thing is to devote his attention to appraising the whole military situation. The main thing is that, on the basis of existing circumstances, he should consider the problem of the grouping of his military units and formations, of the relations between campaigns, of the relations between various operational stages, and of the relations between the sum total of the enemy's activities and that of his own—all these require the maximum effort; if he overlooks them and is preoccupied with secondary considerations, he can hardly avoid setbacks.

As to the relationship between the whole and the parts, it holds not only between war strategy and operational direction but also between operational direction and tactics. The relation between the action of a division and that of a regiment or battalion, and the relation between the action of a company and that of a platoon or squad, are concrete illustrations. The commanding officer at any level should centre his attention on the most important and most decisively significant problem or action in the whole situation he is handling, and not on other problems or actions.

The importance or decisive significance of a thing is not determined according to circumstances in general or in the abstract, but according to the concrete circumstances. In a military operation the selection of the direction and the point of a surprise attack should be determined according to the situation of the enemy, the character of the terrain and the strength of our own forces at the moment. Where supplies are

abundant, care should be taken that the soldiers do not over-
eat, but where there is a shortage of supplies, care should be
taken that they do not suffer from hunger. In a White area the
mere leakage of a piece of information may cause defeat in a
subsequent engagement, but in a Red area the leakage of information does not as a rule form a very serious problem. The
officer in higher command has to take a personal part in
certain campaigns, but not in others. For a military academy,
the most important problem is selecting a director and instructors and laying down an educational programme. For a mass
rally, care should be taken chiefly in mobilising the masses to
attend it and in proposing suitable slogans. And so on and so
forth. In a word, the only principle is to centre our attention on
the important links which have a bearing on the whole situation.

To learn the guiding laws of a whole military situation we
must do some hard thinking. We cannot take in the whole
situation with our eyes and we comprehend it only by using
the mind; there is no other way. But as the whole situation is
made up of its parts, people experienced in a partial situation or
in operational or tactical direction can comprehend those
things on a higher plane if they will use their minds. Such
strategic problems as the relation between the enemy and ourselves, of the relation between various campaigns or between
various operational phases, certain parts that are significant
(decisive) for the whole situation, the characteristics of the
whole situation, the relation between the front and the rear,
and the distinction as well as the connection between losses
and replacements, between fighting and resting, between concentration and dispersion, between attack and defence, between
advance and retreat, between sheltered and exposed positions,
between the main attack and supplementary attacks, between
surprise attack and containment, between centralised command
and decentralised command, between protracted war and war
of quick decision, between positional warfare and mobile warfare, between our forces and friendly forces, between one service
and another, between higher and lower ranks, between cadres
and soldiers, between veterans and new recruits, between senior
and junior cadres, between old and new cadres, between Red

and White areas, between old and new Red areas, between the central and border districts, between warm and cold weather, between victory and defeat, between large and small operational formations, between regular army and guerrilla forces, between annihilating the enemy and winning over the masses, between expanding and consolidating the Red Army, between military and political work, between past and present tasks, between present and future tasks, between tasks dictated by different circumstances, between fixed and unfixed fronts, between civil and national wars, between one historical stage and another, etc., etc.—none of these can we see with our eyes, yet, if we think hard, we can comprehend, grasp and master them all. This means that we can raise all important problems of a war or of operations to a higher level of principle and solve them. The task in studying strategic problems is to achieve this aim.

4. THE IMPORTANT PROBLEM IS TO BE GOOD AT LEARNING

Why have we organised the Red Army? Because we want to use it to defeat the enemy. Why do we study the laws of war? Because we want to apply them to war.

Learning is no easy matter, but to apply what one has learnt is even more difficult. In classrooms or in books people may all deal with military science in a knowing manner, but in actual fighting some people win and others are defeated. Both military history and our own war experience prove this.

Where then does the crux lie?

In actual life we cannot ask for an invincible general, there have been very few such generals since ancient times. We ask for a general who is both brave and wise, who usually wins battles in the course of a war—a general who combines wisdom with courage. To attain the combination of wisdom and courage, we must learn one method—a method to be employed in learning as well as in applying what we have learnt.

What is the method? It is to familiarise ourselves with all aspects of the enemy's situation as well as our own, to discover the laws of the actions of both sides, and to take these laws into account in our own actions.

The collections of military rules and orders promulgated in

many countries point out the necessity of "applying principles elastically according to the situation", as well as the measures to be taken in a defeat. The former requires a commander not to commit mistakes subjectively through too flexible an application of principles, while the latter tells him how to cope with a situation when he has already committed mistakes or when unexpected and irresistible changes occur in the circumstances.

Why are mistakes committed? Because the disposition of forces in the war or battle or the directing of them does not fit in with the conditions of a certain time and a certain place, because the directing does not correspond with or dovetail into realities, in other words, because the contradiction between the subjective and the objective is not solved. People can hardly avoid coming up against such a situation in performing any task, only some are more and others are less competent in performing it. We demand greater competence in performing tasks, and in war we demand more victories or, conversely, fewer defeats. The crux here lies precisely in making the subjective and the objective correspond well with each other.

Let us take an example in tactics. If the point selected for attack falls on a particular flank of the enemy which happens to be exactly his weak spot, and consequently the assault is a success, then the subjective corresponds with the objective, or the commander's reconnaissance, judgment and decision correspond with the enemy's actual situation and dispositions. If the point selected for attack falls on another flank or the centre and the attack is up against a snag and makes no headway, then such correspondence is lacking. If the attack is properly timed, if reserves are thrown into action neither too late nor too early, and if other battle dispositions and operational actions are all favourable to us and unfavourable to the enemy, then the subjective direction corresponds perfectly with the objective situation in the entire engagement. Such perfect correspondence is rarely found in a war or battle, because both contestants in a war or battle are groups of armed human beings who keep their secrets from each other, and this is quite unlike dealing with inanimate objects or routine matters. But if a general correspondence between the direction and the situation is attained, namely, between those decisive parts of the direction and the situation, there is a basis for victory.

The commander's correct dispositions ensue from correct decisions, his correct decisions ensue from correct judgments, and his correct judgments ensue from a comprehensive and indispensable reconnaissance as well as a systematic deliberation on the various data gathered through such reconnaissance. Employing all possible and necessary methods of reconnaissance, a commander subjects various data thus gathered about the enemy's situation to such deliberation as discards the crude and selects the refined, eliminates the false and retains the true, proceeds from one point to another, and goes through the outside into the inside; then, in addition, he takes into account the conditions on his own side, and studies the differences and similarities between the two sides, thereby forming his judgment, making up his mind and mapping out his plans—this is the complete process of knowing a situation which a military man goes through before he formulates the plan of strategy, of a campaign, or of a battle. But a careless military man, instead of doing this, bases his military plan upon his own wishful thinking, hence his plan is fantastic and does not correspond with actualities. A reckless military man relying solely upon enthusiasm cannot but be tricked by the enemy, or enticed by the superficial or partial situation of the enemy, or swayed by the irresponsible suggestions of his subordinates that are based neither on real knowledge nor on deep insight, and consequently he cannot but run his head against a brick wall because he either does not know or is unwilling to know that any military plan must be based on an indispensable reconnaissance and a careful deliberation over his own situation and the enemy's as well as over the interrelations of the two.

The process of knowing the situation goes on not only before but also after the formulation of a military plan. The carrying out of a plan, from its very beginning to the conclusion of an operation, is another process of knowing the situation, *i.e.* the process of putting it into practice. In this process, there is need to examine anew whether the plan mapped out in the earlier process corresponds with the actualities. If the plan does not correspond or does not fully correspond with them, then we must, according to fresh knowledge, form new judgments and make new decisions to modify the original plan in order to meet the new situation. There are partial modifications in almost every operation, and sometimes even a complete change. A hothead who does not know how to change his plan, or is unwilling to change it but acts blindly, will inevitably run his head against a brick wall.

The above applies to a strategical action, a campaign, or a battle. If an experienced military man is modest and willing to learn, and has familiarised himself with the conditions of his own forces (officers and men, arms, supplies, etc., and their totality) as well as those of the enemy (similarly, officers and men, arms, supplies, etc., and their totality), and with all other conditions relating to war, such as politics, economy, geography and weather conditions, he will be more confident in directing a war or an operation and will be more likely to win it. This is because over a long period of time he has learnt the situation on both the enemy side and his own, discovered the laws of action, and solved the contradiction between the subjective and the objective. This process of knowing is very important; without such a long period of experience it is difficult to understand and grasp the laws of an entire war. No truly able commander of a high rank can be made out of one who is a mere beginner in warfare or one who knows warfare only on paper; and to become such a commander one must learn through warfare.

All military laws and theories partaking of the character of principle represent past military experiences summed up by people in both ancient and modern times. We should carefully study the lessons which were learnt in past wars at the cost of blood and which have been bequeathed to us. This is one point. But there is another point, namely, we must also put conclusions thus reached to the test of our own experience and absorb what is useful, reject what is useless, and add what is specifically our own. The latter is a very important point, for otherwise we cannot direct a war.

Reading books is learning, but application is also learning and the more important form of learning. To learn warfare through warfare—this is our chief method. A person who has had no opportunity to go to school can also learn warfare, which means learning it through warfare. As a revolutionary war is the concern of the masses of the people, it is often undertaken without previous learning but is learnt through undertaking it —undertaking is itself learning. There is a distance between a civilian and a soldier, but that distance is not as long as the Great Wall and can be quickly eliminated; to take part in revolution and war is the method of eliminating it. To say that learning and application are difficult means that it is difficult to learn thoroughly and apply skilfully. To say that civilians can very quickly become soldiers means that it is not difficult to get them initiated. In summarising these two aspects we may apply an old Chinese adage: "Nothing is difficult in the world for anyone who sets his mind on it." Initiation is not difficult and mastery is also possible so long as one sets one's mind on them and is good at learning.

Military laws, like the laws governing all other things, are a reflection in our mind of objective realities; everything is objective reality except our mind. Consequently what we want to learn and know includes things both on the enemy side and our own, and both sides should be regarded as the object of our study and only our mind (thinking capacity) is the subject that makes the study. Some people are intelligent in knowing themselves but stupid in knowing their opponents, and others are the other way round; neither kind can solve the problem of learning and applying the laws of war. We must not belittle the saying in the book of Sun Wu Tzu,[1] the great military expert of ancient China, "Know your enemy and know yourself, and you can fight a hundred battles without disaster", a saying which refers both to the stage of learning and to the stage of application, both to knowing laws of the development of objective realities and to deciding on our own action according to them in order to overcome the enemy facing us.

War is the highest form of struggle between nations, states, classes, or political groups, and all laws of war are applied by a nation, a state, a class, or a political group waging a war to win victory for itself. It is beyond question that success or failure in a war is mainly determined by the military, political, economic and natural conditions on both sides. But not entirely so; it is also determined by the subjective ability on each side in directing the war. A military expert cannot expect victory in war by going beyond the limits imposed by material conditions, but within these limits he can and must fight to win. The stage of action of a military expert is built upon objective material conditions, but with the stage set, he can direct the performance of many lively dramas, full of sound and colour, of power and grandeur. We Red Army commanders must, therefore, on a given material basis—military, political, economic and natural conditions—display our power and lead the whole army to crush the national and class enemies, and to change this evil world. This is where our ability in directing war can and must be exercised. We do not allow any of our Red Army commanders to become rash and reckless hotheads and must encourage every one of them to become a hero who, at once brave and wise, possesses not only the courage to override all obstacles but the ability to control the changes and developments in an entire war. Swimming in an immense ocean of war, a commander must not only keep himself from sinking but also make sure to reach the opposite shore with measured strokes. The laws of directing wars constitute the art of swimming in the ocean of war.

So much for our methods.

CHAPTER II

THE CHINESE COMMUNIST PARTY AND CHINA'S REVOLUTIONARY WAR

China's revolutionary war, which began in 1924, has passed through two stages, *i.e.* the stage of 1924-7 and the stage of 1927-36; from now on it will enter the stage of the national anti-Japanese revolutionary war.

The revolutionary war in all three stages has been and will be led by the Chinese proletariat and its party, the Chinese Communist Party. The chief enemies in China's revolutionary war are imperialism and the feudal forces. Although the Chinese bourgeoisie may take part in the revolutionary war on certain historical occasions, yet owing to its selfish character and its lack of political and economic independence, it is neither willing nor able to lead China's revolutionary war to complete victory. The masses of the Chinese peasantry and of the urban petty bourgeoisie are willing to take part actively in the revolutionary war and to bring about its complete victory. They are the main forces in the revolutionary war, yet small-scale production, which is their characteristic and limits their political outlook (a section among the unemployed being imbued with anarchist ideology), renders them unable to give correct leadership in the war. Thus, in an era when the proletariat has already appeared on the political stage, the responsibility of leadership in China's revolutionary war inevitably falls on the shoulders of the Chinese Communist Party. At such a time any revolutionary war will certainly end in defeat if the leadership of the proletariat and the Communist Party is lacking or is forsaken. For of all the social strata and political groups in semi-colonial China, only the proletariat and the Communist Party are the most open-minded and unselfish, possess the most far-sighted political outlook and the highest organisational quality, and are also the readiest to learn with an open mind from the experiences of the advanced world proletariat and its parties as well as to apply what they have learnt in their own undertakings. Hence only the proletariat and the Communist Party can lead the peasantry, the urban petty bourgeoisie and the bourgeoisie, overcome the narrow-mindedness of the peasantry and the petty bourgeoisie, the destructiveness of the unemployed masses, and the vacillation and lack of thoroughness of the bourgeoisie (provided no mistake is made in the Communist Party's policy), and thereby lead the revolution and the war to the path of victory.

The revolutionary war of 1924–7 was waged, basically speaking, under the political influence which the world proletariat and the Chinese proletariat and their parties exerted on the Chinese national bourgeoisie and its party, as well as through the political co-operation between the former and the latter. But this revolutionary war failed at a critical moment primarily because of the betrayal of the big bourgeoisie and also because of the voluntary surrender of leadership in the revolution by the opportunists within the revolutionary ranks.

The Agrarian Revolutionary War from 1927 to the present

time has been waged under new circumstances. The enemy in this war is not only imperialism but also the big bourgeoisie and the big landlords in alliance with each other. Moreover the national bourgeoisie has become the tail of the big bourgeoisie. As the Communist Party alone has been leading the revolutionary war, it has taken absolute leadership in the war. This absolute leadership of the Communist Party is the most important condition for resolutely carrying on the revolutionary war to the end. Without it, one cannot conceive that the revolutionary war could have been carried on with such pertinacity.

The Chinese Communist Party has led China's revolutionary war with courage and determination and for fifteen long years the Party has shown to the Chinese people that it is their friend and that it always stands in the forefront of the revolutionary war, fighting for their interests and for their freedom and liberation.

The Chinese Communist Party, with its experience in arduous struggles, through the bloodshed and martyrdom of hundreds of thousands of its brave members and tens of thousands of its brave cadres, has played a great educational role among hundreds of millions of the whole nation. The great historic achievements of the Communist Party in the revolutionary struggle have created the condition for the salvation and survival of China at this critical juncture of the invasion of a national enemy, in other words, such achievements have given rise to a political leadership enjoying the confidence of the great majority of the people, a leadership which is chosen after long years of being tested. The pronouncements of the Communist Party are now more readily accepted by the people than those of any other party. Without the arduous struggles of the Communist Party in the last fifteen years, it would have been impossible to save the nation from the new menace of extinction.

Besides the mistakes of the Right opportunism of Ch'en Tu-hsiu[2] and the "Left" opportunism of Li Li-san,[3] the Chinese Communist Party has committed the following two errors in the revolutionary war. The first was the "Left" opportunism of 1931–4,[4] which brought extremely serious losses to the Agrarian Revolutionary War, resulting in our failure to defeat the enemy during our fifth campaign against "encirclement and annihilation", the loss of the base areas and the weakening of the Red Army. This error was corrected at the enlarged meeting of the Central Political Bureau at Tsunyi in January 1935. The second was the Right opportunism of Chang Kuo-t'ao in 1935-6,[5] which developed to such an extent as to undermine the discipline of the Party and the Red Army and to bring serious loss to a part of the Red Army's main forces; but by virtue of the correct leadership of the Central Committee and the political consciousness of the Party members and commanders and men in the Red Army, this error was also rectified in the end. All these errors were of course harmful to our Party, to our revolution and to the war, but in the end they were all rectified; in overcoming these errors our Party and our Red Army steeled themselves and became even stronger.

The Communist Party has led and continues to lead the stupendous, sublime, glorious and victorious revolutionary war. This war is not only the banner of China's liberation, but is pregnant with significance for world revolution. The eyes of the revolutionary masses throughout the world are upon us. In the new stage of our national anti-Japanese revolutionary war we will lead the Chinese revolution to its completion and also exert a far-reaching influence on the revolution in the East as well as in the whole world. Our past revolutionary wars prove that we need not only a correct Marxist political line but also a correct Marxist military line. Fifteen years of revolution and war have forged such a political line and such a military line. In the new stage of the war from now on these lines will, we believe, be further developed, substantiated and enriched under new circumstances, so that our aim of defeating the national enemy will be attained. History tells us that correct political and military lines do not emerge and develop spontaneously and smoothly, but only in the course of struggles. On the one hand, they have to struggle against "Left" opportunism and on the other against Right opportunism. Without struggling against and thoroughly overcoming such harmful tendencies that endanger the revolution and the revolutionary wars, the establishment of a correct line and victory in the revolutionary war are impossible. It is for this purpose that in the present booklet I often touch upon the erroneous views.

CHAPTER III

CHARACTERISTICS OF CHINA'S REVOLUTIONARY WAR

I. THE IMPORTANCE OF THE SUBJECT

People who will not admit, who do not know, or who do not care to know that China's revolutionary war has its own characteristics have treated the war waged by the Red Army against the Kuomintang forces as similar in nature to wars in general or the civil war in the Soviet Union. The experience of the civil war in the Soviet Union directed by Lenin and Stalin has indeed a world-wide significance. All Communist Parties, including the Chinese Communist Party, regard this experience and its theoretical summing-up by Lenin and Stalin as their guiding compass. Yet this does not mean that we are to make use of this experience mechanically under our own conditions. China's revolutionary war is distinguished by many characteristics from the civil war in the Soviet Union. Failure to reckon with these characteristics or denial of them is of course erroneous. This point has been fully proved in the ten years of our war.

Our enemy also made similar mistakes. He refused to admit that fighting the Red Army requires strategy and tactics different from those for fighting other forces. Relying on his superiority in various respects, he under-estimated us and stuck to his old methods of warfare. This was the case both before and during his fourth campaign of "encirclement and annihilation" in 1933; as a result, he courted a series of defeats. The reactionary Kuomintang general Liu Wei-yuan first—and after him Tai Yo—suggested a new approach to the Kuomintang army. Their recommendations were eventually accepted by Chiang Kai-shek. This was how Chiang Kai-shek established his Officers Training Corps at Kuling[6] and acquired the new reactionary military principles[7] he applied in his fifth campaign of "encirclement and annihilation".

But when the enemy modified his military principles to suit the conditions of warfare against the Red Army, there appeared in our own ranks a group of people who returned to the "old way". Advocating a return to conditions of a general nature and refusing to reckon with any special circumstances, they rejected the experience in the history of the Red Army's bloody fights, under-estimated the strength of imperialism and the Kuomintang as well as that of the Kuomintang army, and deliberately ignored the new reactionary principles the enemy had adopted. As a result, all the revolutionary bases were lost except the Shensi-Kansu border area, the Red Army was reduced from 300,000 to a few tens of thousands, the membership of the Chinese Communist Party was reduced from 300,000 to a few tens of thousands, and the Party organisations in Kuomintang areas were almost entirely wiped out. In short, we received an extremely great historical punishment. This group of people called themselves Marxist-Leninists, but had actually not learnt even an iota of Marxism-Leninism. Lenin said that "the most essential thing in Marxism, the living soul of Marxism", is "the concrete analysis of concrete conditions".[8] These comrades had forgotten exactly this point.

It can thus be seen that failure to understand the characteristics of China's revolutionary war means inability to direct it or lead it to victory.

2. WHAT ARE THE CHARACTERISTICS OF CHINA'S REVOLUTIONARY WAR?

What then are the characteristics of China's revolutionary war?

I think there are four.

The first is that China is a vast semi-colonial country which is unevenly developed both politically and economically, and which has gone through the revolution of 1924–7.

This characteristic indicates that it is possible for China's revolutionary war to develop and attain victory. We pointed this out (at the First Party Conference of the Hunan-Kiangsi Border Area[9]) when, in late 1927 and early 1928 soon after guerrilla warfare was started in China, some comrades in the

Hunan-Kiangsi border area—the Chingkang mountains—
raised the question: "How long can the red flag be kept flying?"
For this was a most fundamental question; without answering
the question whether China's revolutionary base areas and the
Chinese Red Army could exist and develop, we would not
advance a single step. The Sixth National Congress of the
Chinese Communist Party in 1928 again answered the question.
Henceforth the Chinese revolutionary movement has been
provided with a correct theoretical basis.

Let us now analyse this characteristic.

The unevenness of political and economic development in
China—the coexistence of a frail capitalist economy and a
preponderant semi-feudal economy; the coexistence of a few
modern industrial and commercial cities and the boundless
expanses of stagnant rural districts; the coexistence of several
millions of industrial workers on the one hand and, on the other,
hundreds of millions of peasants and handicraftsmen under the
old régime; the coexistence of big warlords controlling the
Central government and small warlords controlling the provinces; the coexistence of two kinds of reactionary armies, *i.e.*
the so-called Central army under Chiang Kai-shek and the
troops of miscellaneous brands under the warlords in the
provinces; and the coexistence of a few railway and steamship
lines and motor roads on the one hand and, on the other, the
vast number of wheel-barrow paths and trails for pedestrians
only, many of which are even difficult for them to negotiate.

China is a semi-colonial country—the disunity among the
imperialist countries has caused the disunity among the various
ruling blocs in China. A semi-colonial state controlled by
several countries is different from a colony controlled by a
single country.

China is a vast country—"When the east is still dark, the
west is lit up; when night falls in the south, the day breaks in
the north"; hence one need not worry about whether there is
room enough to move round.

China has gone through a great revolution which has provided us with the seeds of the Red Army, the Chinese Communist Party which leads the Red Army, and the masses who
have participated in a revolution.

We have said, therefore, that the first characteristic of China's revolutionary war is that China is a vast semi-colonial country which has gone through a revolution and is unevenly developed politically and economically. This characteristic basically determines not only our political strategy and tactics, but also our military strategy and tactics.

The second characteristic is the great strength of the enemy.

What is the situation of the Kuomintang, the enemy of the Red Army? It is a party that has seized political power and has relatively stabilised it. It has gained the support of the principal counter-revolutionary countries in the world. It has remodelled its army, which has thus become different from any other army in Chinese history and on the whole similar to the armies of the modern states in the world; its army is supplied much more abundantly with arms and other equipment than the Red Army, and is greater in numerical strength than any army in Chinese history, even than the standing army of any country in the world. There is a world of difference between the Kuomintang army and the Red Army. The Kuomintang controls the key positions or lifelines in the politics, economy, communications and culture of China; its political power is nation-wide in character.

The Chinese Red Army is confronted with such a powerful enemy. This is the second characteristic of China's revolutionary war. This characteristic inevitably makes the war waged by the Red Army different in many ways from wars in general, from the civil war in the Soviet Union and from the Northern Expedition.

The third characteristic is that the Red Army is weak and small.

The Chinese Red Army was born after the failure of the first great revolution, starting as guerrilla units. It finds itself existing not only in a period of reaction in China but in a period of relative political and economic stability in the reactionary capitalist countries in the world.

Our political power is dispersed and isolated in mountainous or remote regions, and is deprived of any outside help. In economic and cultural conditions the revolutionary base areas are more backward than the Kuomintang areas. The revolutionary bases embrace only rural districts and small towns. They were extremely small in the beginning and have not grown much larger since. Moreover, they are often shifted and the Red Army possesses no really consolidated bases.

The Red Army is small in numbers, its arms are poor, and its access to food, bedding, clothing and other supplies is extremely difficult.

This characteristic presents a sharp contrast to the preceding one. The strategy and tactics of the Red Army are based on this sharp contrast.

The fourth characteristic is the Communist Party's leadership and the agrarian revolution.

This characteristic is the inevitable result of the first one. It gives rise to the following two features. On the one hand, China's revolutionary war, though taking place in a period of reaction in China and throughout the capitalist world, can yet be victorious because it is led by the Communist Party and supported by the peasantry. Because we have secured the support of the peasantry, our base areas, though small, possess great political power and stand firmly opposed to the political power of the Kuomintang which encompasses a vast area; in a military sense this creates colossal difficulties for the attacking Kuomintang troops. The Red Army, though small, has great fighting capacity, because its men under the leadership of the Communist Party have sprung from the agrarian revolution and are fighting for their own interests, and because officers and men are politically united.

On the other hand, our situation contrasts sharply with that of the Kuomintang. Opposed to the agrarian revolution, the Kuomintang is deprived of the support of the peasantry. Despite the great size of its army it cannot arouse the bulk of the soldiers or many of the lower-rank officers, who used to be small producers, to risk their lives voluntarily for its sake. Officers and men are politically disunited and this reduces its fighting capacity.

3. OUR STRATEGY AND TACTICS ENSUING FROM THESE CHARACTERISTICS

A vast semi-colonial country that is unevenly developed politically and economically and that has gone through a great revolution; a powerful enemy; a weak and small Red Army; and the agrarian revolution—these are the four principal characteristics of China's revolutionary war. They determine the guiding line for China's revolutionary war and its strategic and tactical principles. The first and fourth characteristics determine the possibility of the Chinese Red Army growing and defeating its enemy. The second and third characteristics determine the impossibility of the Chinese Red Army growing speedily or defeating its enemy quickly, or in other words, they determine the protracted nature of the war and, if things go wrong, the possibility of the war ending in failure.

These are the two aspects of China's revolutionary war. They exist simultaneously, that is, there are favourable as well as difficult conditions. This is the fundamental law of China's revolutionary war, from which many other laws are derived. The history of ten years of our war has proved the validity of this law. He who has eyes but does not see these laws of a fundamental nature cannot direct China's revolutionary war, cannot lead the Red Army to win victories.

It is quite clear that, in order to determine correctly our strategic direction, it is necessary to solve correctly all problems of principle, as for instance: *against* adventurism during offensive operations, *against* conservatism while on the defensive, and *against* flight-ism when shifting our forces; *against* guerrilla-ism in the Red Army, yet *for* its guerrilla character; *against* protracted campaigns and a strategy of quick decision, and *for* a strategy of protracted war and campaigns of quick decision; *against* fixed operational fronts and positional warfare, and *for* fluid operational fronts and mobile warfare; *against* the mere routing of the enemy, and *for* a war of annihilation; *against* the principle of striking with both fists, and *for* the principle of striking with one fist;[10] *against* a large rear area and *for* a small rear area; *against* absolute centralised command and *for* a relatively centralised command; *against* the purely military viewpoint and the idea of roving insurgents,[11] but *for* the view that the Red Army is a propagandist and organiser of the Chinese revolution; *against* banditry[12] and *for* strict political discipline; *against* warlordism and *for* a democratic way of life within limits and authoritative military discipline; *against* an incorrect sectarian cadres policy and *for* a correct cadres policy; *against* isolationism and *for* the winning over of all possible allies; and finally, *against* keeping the Red Army at its old stage and *for* striving to bring it to a new stage.

In our discussion of the problems of strategy, we are going to explain these matters clearly on the basis of the lessons of the history of the ten years' bloody war of the Chinese revolution.

CHAPTER IV

CAMPAIGNS OF "ENCIRCLEMENT AND ANNIHILATION" AND COUNTER - CAMPAIGNS — MAIN FORMS OF CHINA'S CIVIL WAR

For ten years, *i.e.* since the day guerrilla warfare began, around every dependent unit of the Red guerrillas or the Red Army, or around every revolutionary base area, we have been regularly confronted by the enemy's campaigns of "encirclement and annihilation". The enemy looks upon the Red Army as a monster and wants to capture it as soon as it appears. He is always hot on the heels of the Red Army and always tries to encircle it. For ten years this form of warfare has not changed; if there is no national war to replace the civil war, the pattern will remain the same until the day when the enemy becomes the weaker contestant and the Red Army the stronger.

The Red Army's operations take the form of campaigns against "encirclement and annihilation". Victory for us means chiefly success in our campaigns against the enemy's "encirclement and annihilation", that is, strategic and operational victory. Each fight against "encirclement and annihilation" constitutes a campaign which is usually made up of several or even scores of big and small battles. Even though many battles have been won, there is yet no strategic victory or victory of the whole campaign until the enemy's campaign of "encirclement and annihilation" is basically smashed. The history of the Red Army's ten years of war is a history of campaigns against "encirclement and annihilation".

In the enemy's campaign of "encirclement and annihilation" and the Red Army's counter-campaign, just as in all wars, ancient or modern, in China or elsewhere, two forms of fighting are employed, the offensive and the defensive. However, what characterises China's civil war is the prolonged alternation of the two. In each campaign of "encirclement and annihilation" the enemy employs the offensive against the Red Army's defensive, and the Red Army employs the defensive against the enemy's offensive—this is the first stage of a counter-campaign. Then the enemy employs the defensive against the Red Army's offensive, and the Red Army employs the offensive against the enemy's defensive—this is the second stage of the counter-campaign. Every such campaign consists of these two stages, alternating over an extended period.

By "alternation" we mean the alternation of the two forms of fighting both in the operation as a whole and in each battle. This is a fact obvious to everybody. The campaign of "encirclement and annihilation" and its counter-campaign are the alternating forms of war. The first stage in which the enemy meets our defensive with his offensive and we meet his offensive with our defensive, and the second stage in which the enemy meets our offensive with his defensive and we meet his defensive with our offensive, are alternating forms of battle in each campaign.

As to the content of a battle or war, there is each time not only alternation but also variation. This, too, is a fact obvious to everybody. In this connection, it has become the rule that the scale of a campaign or counter-campaign each time becomes larger, the situation more complicated, and the fighting more intense.

This does not mean, however, that there are no fluctuations. After the fifth campaign of "encirclement and annihilation", as the Red Army was greatly weakened, as all the base areas in the South were lost, and as the Red Army, having shifted to the North-west, no longer held an important position threatening the internal enemy as it did in the South, the scale of the campaigns became somewhat smaller, the situation simpler and the fighting less intense.

What constitutes failure for the Red Army? Strategically speaking, only when a campaign against "encirclement and annihilation" is altogether unsuccessful can it be called a failure, and only a partial and temporary one at that. For the Red Army's ultimate failure in the civil war would mean its complete annihilation, but this has never happened. The loss of extensive bases and the shifting of the Red Army represent a temporary and partial failure, not a final and complete one, even though the word "partial" here implies the loss of 90 per cent of the bases, of the Party membership and of the armed forces. We call this the continuation of the defensive, and the enemy's pursuit the continuation of the offensive. That is to say, in the enemy's campaign of "encirclement and annihilation" and our counter-campaign we failed to turn from the defensive to the offensive but, on the contrary, our defensive was broken by the enemy's offensive; thus our defensive became a retreat and the enemy's offensive became a pursuit. But when the Red Army reached a new area, for example, when we shifted from Kiangsi and other places to Shensi, the alternation of the campaign of "encirclement and annihilation" and the counter-campaign began afresh. Therefore we say that the Red Army's strategic retreat (the Long March)[13] was a continuation of its strategic defensive, and the enemy's strategic pursuit was a continuation of his strategic offensive.

There are only two basic forms of fighting, attack and defence, in the Chinese civil war as well as in any war, ancient or modern, in China or elsewhere. The distinctive feature of China's civil war lies in the prolonged alternation of the campaigns of "encirclement and annihilation" and the counter-campaigns, the continuous alternation of the two forms of fighting, attack and defence, including such a feature as the great strategic shift of forces (the Long March) over more than twelve thousand kilometres.

Failure on the part of the enemy means the same thing. Strategic failure for him means that his campaign of "encirclement and annihilation" is smashed by us and that consequently our defensive becomes an offensive, while he turns to the defensive and has to reorganise his forces before he can launch another campaign. He has had no occasion to resort to such a strategic shift of forces over more than twelve thousand kilometres as we had, because he is ruler of the whole country and is much stronger than we are. But partial shifts of forces on his side have occurred. In some of our base areas, enemy forces in White strongholds surrounded by the Red Army sometimes broke through our encirclement and withdrew to the White areas to organise a new offensive. If the civil war continues and if the Red Army's victories become larger in scale, such shifts will happen more often. But the enemy cannot end up in the same way as the Red Army, because he does not enjoy the support of the people and his officers and men are not united. If he were to imitate the Red Army's long-distance shift of forces, he would certainly be annihilated.

In the period of Li Li-san's line in 1930, Comrade Li Li-san, unaware of the protracted nature of the Chinese civil war, was unable to discern the law of the Chinese civil war, namely, that there is a prolonged alternation of the campaigns of "encirclement and annihilation" and their smashing (at that time there had already been three campaigns of "encirclement and annihilation" in the Hunan-Kiangsi border areas and two in Fukien), and consequently, in an attempt to achieve a quick nation-wide victory for the revolution, ordered an attack on Wuhan by the Red Army, then still in its infancy, and a nation-wide armed uprising. Thus he committed the error of "Left" opportunism.

Nor did the "Left" opportunists during 1931–4 believe in the law of the continuous alternations of the campaigns of "encirclement and annihilation" and counter-campaigns. The theory of "auxiliary forces" appeared in the base area in the Hupeh-Honan-Anhwei border area where some responsible comrades considered that the Kuomintang's forces, after their failure in the third campaign of "encirclement and annihilation", could only fight as "auxiliary forces", and that for further attacks on the Red Army, the imperialists themselves would have to come to the fore as the main forces. On the basis of this estimation, the strategic directive was for the Red Army to attack Wuhan. This agreed in principle with the views of those comrades in Kiangsi who urged that the Red Army should attack Nanchang, who opposed making the various base areas into a contiguous territory and luring the enemy deep into our territory, but held that the capture of the capital and other metropolitan cities was the basis for the "victory in a province", who believed that "the fight against the fifth campaign of 'encirclement and annihilation' was the decisive engagement between the revolutionary way and the colonial way", etc. This "Left" opportunism sowed the seeds of the erroneous line adopted in the battles against the fourth campaign of "encirclemwnt and annihilation" in the Hupeh-Honan-Anhwei border area as well as in the battles against the fifth campaign of "encirclement and annihilation" in the Central area in Kiangsi, thereby reducing the Red Army to a helpless position before the enemy's fierce campaigns of "encirclement and annihilation" and entailing enormous losses to the Chinese revolution.

Linked directly with "Left" opportunism which denies the alternation of the enemy's campaigns of "encirclement and annihilation" and our counter-campaigns, is another entirely erroneous view that the Red Army should under no circumstances adopt defensive measures.

A revolution or a revolutionary war is an offensive—this statement is of course correct in a sense. Throughout the process of its emergence and development—from being a small force to being a big force, from the non-possession of political power to the seizure of it, from the absence of a Red Army to its creation, and from the absence of revolutionary base areas to their establishment—a revolution or a revolutionary war has always to be an offensive and cannot be conservative, and tendencies to conservatism must be opposed.

The only statement that is entirely correct is: that a revolution or a revolutionary war is an offensive yet has also its defensive phase and retreat. To defend in order to attack, to retreat in order to advance, to take a flanking action in order to take a frontal action, and to be devious in order to go direct— these are inevitable occurrences in the process of development of many things, and military movements cannot be otherwise.

Of the two statements above, the first may be correct politically but incorrect when applied in the military sphere.

Moreover, it would be correct politically only under certain circumstances (when the revolution is advancing), but incorrect under other circumstances (when the revolution is retreating: a wholesale retreat like that in Russia in 1906[14] and that in China in 1927, or a partial retreat like that in Russia at the time of the Brest Litovsk Treaty of 1918[15]). Only the second statement is entirely correct and true. The "Left" opportunism of 1931–4, which mechanically opposed the employment of defensive military measures, merely represented an extremely infantile way of thinking.

When will the pattern of the alternation of the campaigns of "encirclement and annihilation" come to an end? In my opinion, if the civil war drags on, the alternation will come to an end when a fundamental change takes place in the relative strength between the enemy and ourselves. Once the Red Army becomes stronger than its enemy, such an alternation will come to an end. Then it will be for us to encircle and annihilate the enemy, and for the enemy to resort to the counter-campaigns; but political and military conditions will not permit the enemy to gain the same position as that of the Red Army in its counter-campaigns. We can say with confidence that by then the pattern of the alternation of the campaigns of "encirclement and annihilation" and the counter-campaigns, even though not altogether ended, will generally come to an end.

CHAPTER V

STRATEGIC DEFENSIVE

Under this heading I am going to discuss the following problems: (1) active defence and passive defence; (2) preparation for a campaign against "encirclement and annihilation"; (3) strategic retreat; (4) strategic counter-offensive; (5) problems of starting the counter-offensive; (6) problems of troop concentration; (7) mobile warfare; (8) war of quick decision; and (9) war of annihilation.

1. ACTIVE DEFENCE AND PASSIVE DEFENCE

Why should we begin by discussing defence?

After the failure of China's first national united front of

1924–7, the revolution became an extremely intense and ruthless class war. The enemy is the ruler of the whole country, while we have only small armed forces; consequently from the very beginning we have been fighting against the enemy's campaigns of "encirclement and annihilation". Our offensives are closely linked with our attempt to break up these campaigns and the prospect of our development depends entirely upon whether we can succeed. The process of breaking them up is usually circuitous rather than straightforward. Our first and most serious problem is how to conserve our strength and wait for an opportunity to defeat the enemy. Thus the strategic defensive is the most complicated and most important problem in the Red Army's operation.

In the ten years of our war two deviations often occurred with regard to the strategic defensive: one was to under-estimate the enemy and the other was to cower before the enemy.

As a result of under-estimating the enemy, many guerrilla units were defeated and the Red Army failed to break up several of the enemy's campaigns of "encirclement and annihilation".

When the revolutionary guerrilla units first arose, their leaders often failed to estimate correctly the enemy's situation and our own. They usually under-estimated the enemy because when they succeeded in a sudden armed uprising at a certain place or in a mutiny in the White troops, they noticed only the favourable circumstances at the moment or rather failed to realise the critical situation. Moreover, they did not understand their own weaknesses (their lack of experience and the smallness of their forces). The objective fact was that the enemy was strong and we were weak, yet, unwilling to ponder over it and ignoring defence and retreat these people talked only of taking the offensive and thus disarmed themselves spiritually in the matter of defence and misdirected their actions. Many guerrilla units were defeated on account of this.

Examples of the Red Army's failure to break up the campaign of "encirclement and annihilation" due to the same cause were its defeat in 1928 in the Haifeng and Lefung area, Kwangtung,[16] and its loss of freedom of action in the Hupeh-Honan-Anhwei border area in the fourth counter-campaign in

1932, when it was misled by the theory about the Kuomintang being an "auxiliary force".

There are many instances of setbacks due to our cowering before the enemy.

Contrary to those who under-estimated the enemy, some people over-estimated him and under-estimated themselves; consequently they adopted an unwarranted policy of retreat, also disarming themselves spiritually in the matter of defence. The result was the defeat of the guerrilla units, the defeat of the Red Army in certain campaigns, or the loss of a base.

The most conspicuous example of the loss of a base is the loss of the Central base in Kiangsi in the fifth campaign against "encirclement and annihilation". The mistake here resulted from a Right viewpoint. The leaders, who feared the enemy as if he were a tiger, set up defences everywhere and resisted on successive lines, and dared not launch an attack on the enemy's rear, which would have been to our advantage, nor play a bold hand by luring the enemy troops to penetrate deep into our territory so as to herd them together and annihilate them; as a result, the whole base was lost and the Red Army took to the Long March of more than 12,000 kilometres. But such a mistake is usually preceded by the "Left" mistake of under-estimating the enemy. The military adventurism of attacking metropolitan cities in 1932 was precisely the root cause of the line of passive defence adopted subsequently in coping with the enemy's fifth campaign of "encirclement and annihilation".

The most striking example of cowering before the enemy was Chang Kuo-t'ao's line, a policy of retreat. The defeat of the Western Column of the Red Army's Fourth Front Army west of the Yellow river[17] spelt its final bankruptcy.

Active defence is also called offensive defence or defence by decisive engagements. Passive defence is also called exclusive or pure defence. In practice real defence is not passive but active, defence for the sake of counter-attack and advance. As far as I know, there is no military text-book of any value, no military expert with any sense, in ancient or modern times, in China or elsewhere, who is not opposed to passive defence, strategical or tactical. Only the greatest idiot or megalomaniac would cherish passive defence as a trump card. However, such people do exist in the world and such things do take place. This is a mistake in war, a symptom of military conservatism which we must oppose resolutely.

Military experts of new and rapidly developing imperialist countries like Germany and Japan positively boast of the advantages of strategic offensive and condemn strategic defensive. Such an idea is fundamentally unsuitable for China's revolutionary war. Such military experts point out that the great shortcoming of defence lies in the fact that, instead of gingering up the people, it demoralises them. But that applies only to countries where class contradictions are sharp and the war benefits only the reactionary ruling strata or the reactionary groups in power. Our case is different. Under the slogan of safeguarding the revolutionary base areas and safeguarding China, we can rally the greatest majority of the people to fight single-mindedly, because we are the victims of oppression and aggression. The Red Army of the Soviet Union defeated its enemies also by defensive warfare during the civil war. It not only carried on the war under the slogan of defending the Soviets when the imperialist powers organised the Whites for an onslaught, but also carried out military mobilisation under the slogan of defending the capital when the October Uprising was being prepared. Defensive battles in a just war can not only exercise a lulling influence on the politically alien elements but mobilise the backward sections of the masses to join in the war.

When Marx said that once an armed uprising is started there must not be a moment's pause in the attack, [18] he meant that the masses, having taken the enemy by surprise in an uprising, must not allow the reactionary ruling classes any chance to retain or recover their political power, but must seize this moment to spring a surprise attack on the nation's reactionary ruling forces, and that they must never feel satisfied with the victories they have won, underrate the enemy, relent in their attacks on the enemy, or hesitate to go forward so as to miss the chance of annihilating the enemy and court failure for the revolution. This is correct. This does not mean, however, that we revolutionaries should not adopt defensive measures even when we are already locked in a battle with an enemy stronger than ourselves and are hard pressed by him. Anyone who thinks so would be a prize idiot.

Our past war was on the whole an offensive against the Kuomintang, though militarily it assumed the form of smashing the enemy's campaigns of "encirclement and annihilation".

In military terms, our warfare consists in the alternate adoption of the defensive and the offensive. It makes no difference to us whether our offensive is regarded as following the defensive or preceding it, because the turning-point comes when we smash the campaigns of "encirclement and annihilation". It remains a defensive until a campaign of "encirclement and annihilation" is smashed, and then it immediately begins as an offensive; they are but two phases of the same thing, as one campaign of "encirclement and annihilation" of the enemy is closely followed by another. Of the two phases, the defensive phase is more complicated and more important than the offensive phase. It involves numerous problems of how to smash the campaign of "encirclement and annihilation". The basic principle is for active defence and against passive defence.

In the civil war, when the Red Army surpasses the enemy in strength, there will no longer be any use for strategic defensive in general. Then our only directive will be strategic offensive. Such a change depends on an overall change in the relative strength of the enemy and ourselves. The only defensive measures that remain will be of a partial character.

2. PREPARATION FOR A CAMPAIGN AGAINST "ENCIRCLEMENT AND ANNIHILATION"

If we are not adequately and sufficiently prepared against the enemy's planned campaign of "encirclement and annihilation" we shall be inevitably forced into a passive position. To accept battles on the spur of the moment and in a flurry cannot ensure victory. Therefore it is indeed absolutely necessary that, simultaneously with the enemy's preparation for a campaign of "encirclement and annihilation", we proceed with the preparation for a counter-campaign. The view which opposes such preparation, once held in our own ranks, is ridiculous and childish.

Here is a difficult problem which easily arouses controversy. The problem is: when should we conclude our offensive and turn to the phase of preparing for the next counter-campaign?

When we are victoriously advancing, the enemy is in a defensive position and his preparation for the next campaign of "encirclement and annihilation" is carried on in secret so that it is difficult for us to know when his offensive will begin. If we start to prepare for the counter-campaign too early, the gains that will result from our attack may be diminished and sometimes even undesirable effects may be produced on the Red Army and the people. For the chief measures in the preparatory phase are the military arrangements and political mobilisation for retreat. Sometimes when we start the preparation too early, we shall have to wait for the enemy; we may wait for a long time without the enemy appearing and then we have no alternative but to launch a new offensive. Sometimes just as our new offensive is beginning, the enemy starts his offensive, and we are put in a difficult position. Therefore choosing the right moment to begin our preparation becomes an important problem. The right moment should be determined according to both the enemy's situation and ours and the relation between the two. In order to understand the enemy's situation, we should collect data on his political, military and financial conditions, and on the state of public opinion in his territory. In analysing such data we must take the total strength of the enemy fully into account, and, while we must not exaggerate the extent of his past defeats, we must also consider the contradictions within his own camp, his financial difficulties and the effect of his past defeats, etc. As to ourselves, while we must not exaggerate the extent of our past victories, we must also take their effect fully into account.

As to the moment for starting the preparation, the general advice is "better too early than too late". This is because preparation started too early entails smaller loss than preparation started too late, and the advantage of early preparation lies in that preparedness eliminates mishaps and places us in a fundamentally invincible position.

The important problems in the phase of preparation are arrangements for the retreat of the Red Army, political mobilisation, recruiting of new soldiers, preparations in finance and food supply, and treatment of politically alien elements.

For the Red Army, to prepare for retreat means to make sure that it does not head in a direction disadvantageous to retreat, that it does not advance too far, and that it does not become too fatigued. The main forces of the Red Army must bear this in mind on the eve of the enemy's all-out offensive. At such a time, the Red Army must attend mainly to the opening up of battle-fields, the acquisition of provisions, and the expansion and training of its forces.

Political mobilisation is the most important problem in a campaign against "encirclement and annihilation". That is to say, we must clearly, resolutely and fully inform the rank and file of the Red Army and the people in the base area of the inevitable and impending enemy offensive, of the grave peril such an offensive means to them, and at the same time, of the weakness of the enemy, the favourable conditions of the Red Army, our indomitable will to victory, the general plan of our work, etc. The Red Army and the entire population must be called upon to fight against the campaign of "encirclement and annihilation" and for the defence of the base area. Except for military secrets, political mobilisation must be carried out openly and extensively so as to reach all possible supporters of the revolutionary cause. The vital point here is to convince the cadres.

In recruiting new soldiers, we should proceed along two lines; on the one hand, we should note the level of political consciousness of the people and the density of the population; on the other, we should consider the existing conditions of the Red Army and the possible extent of its losses in the course of the entire counter-campaign.

Finance and food supply are, needless to say, of great importance for a counter-campaign. That the enemy may prolong his campaign should be taken into consideration. There must be an estimation of the minimum material requirements, chiefly of the Red Army and also of the people in the revolutionary base area, for the entire duration of the counter-campaign.

We must be vigilant towards politically alien elements, but

14

not so unduly apprehensive of their treachery as to adopt excessive preventive measures. Distinctions should be made between the landlords, the merchants and the rich peasants, and the main thing is to explain our policy to them, to win their neutrality, and to organise the masses of the people to keep an eye on them. It is only to the most dangerous few that stern measures like detention should be meted out.

The extent of success in a counter-campaign is closely related to the degree of fulfilling the preparatory task of this stage. Negligence in preparation due to an under-estimation of the enemy and panic due to fear of the enemy's attack are both harmful tendencies to be resolutely opposed. An enthusiastic but calm state of mind, and intense but orderly work, are what we need.

3. STRATEGIC RETREAT

A strategic retreat is a planned strategic step which an inferior force, unable to smash quickly the offensive of a superior force, adopts in order to conserve its strength and wait for an opportune moment for beating the enemy. But military adventurists will hear nothing of such a step and advocate "halting the enemy beyond the gate".

We all know that when two strong men fight, the wise one usually yields a step, while his stupid opponent, charging furiously puts forth all his might and skill at the first onset, with the result that he is often floored by the man who yields.

In *Water Margin*,[19] the pugilist Hung, challenging Lin Ch'ung to a fight at Ch'ai Chin's house, snarled repeatedly, "Come on!" "Come on!" "Come on!"; in the end it was the retreating Lin Ch'ung who sought out Hung's weak point, and floored him with one kick.

During the Era of Spring and Autumn, Lu and Ch'i were at war.[20] At first the Duke of Lu would order an attack before the Ch'i troops tired themselves out, but he was stopped by Ts'ao Kuei and adopted instead the policy "the enemy tires, we attack"; the army of Ch'i was defeated and the battle became a classic example in China's military history of how a weak force can defeat a strong enemy. Please read the account given by the historian Tso Ch'iu-ming:[21]

"In the spring the Ch'i troops invaded us. The Duke was about to fight. Ts'ao Kuei asked for an audience. The inhabitants of Ts'ao's district said, 'War is the business of meat-eating officials, why should you meddle?' Ts'ao replied, 'Meat-eaters are narrow-minded; they cannot plan ahead'. So he went to see the Duke. He asked, 'With what are you going to fight?' The Duke replied, 'I never dare to keep food and clothing to enjoy them all by myself but always share them with others'. Ts'ao said, 'Such paltry charity is not universally bestowed, the people will not follow you'. The Duke replied, 'I never offer to the gods less sacrifice, jade or silk than I have promised them, so my faith is absolute'. Ts'ao said, 'This petty faith is not recognised universally, the gods will not bless you'. The Duke said, 'Though it is beyond me to attend personally to the details of all trials, small and big, I always demand the facts', Ts'ao said, 'That bespeaks your devotion to your duty and now you are able to fight a battle. When you fight, I beg to be with you.' The Duke rode with him. The battle was fought at Changshuo. When the Duke was about to drum for the warriors to advance, Ts'ao said, 'Not yet'. After the troops of Ch'i had drummed thrice, Ts'ao said, 'Now we can drum'. The army of Ch'i was routed. The Duke was ready for pursuit. Ts'ao again said, 'Not yet'. He dismounted from his chariot and examined the enemy's wheel-tracks and then climbed on to the chariot's hand-rest and surveyed the situation. And he said, 'Yes'. The Duke's army then began to pursue the Ch'i troops. After the victory the Duke inquired. Ts'ao explained: 'A battle depends upon courage. The first drum arouses the spirit, at the second it flags, and with the third it is exhausted. When the enemy's spirit runs out, ours is full, hence we win. But it is difficult to fathom the moves of a big state, and I was afraid that there might be an ambush. But when I found the enemy's tracks criss-crossed and his banners drooping in disorder, I recommended pursuit."

This was the case of a weak state resisting a strong state. The story indicates the political preparation made before a battle—

to inspire faith among the people; and it gives an account of the favourable terrain for switching over to the counter-offensive—Changshuo, the favourable time to start the counter-offensive—when the enemy's spirit was exhausted and one's own was full, and the occasion to start the pursuit—when the enemy's tracks criss-crossed and their banners drooped in disorder. Though it was not a big campaign, it also illustrates the principles of strategic defensive. In China's military history, there are numerous instances of victories won according to these principles. In such famous battles as that between Ch'u and Han at Chengkao,[22] between Hsin and Han at Kunyang,[23] between Yuan and Ts'ao at Kwantu,[24] between Wu and Wei at Chihpi,[25] between Wu and Shu at Yiling,[26] and between Ch'in and Chin at Feishui,[27] the contestants were unequal in strength, and the weaker one, yielding a step at first, pinned down the stronger one through delayed action and defeated him.

Our war began in the autumn of 1927 when we had no experience at all. Both the Nanchang Uprising[28] and the Canton Uprising[29] failed, and in the Autumn Harvest Uprising[30] the Red Army on the Hunan-Hupeh Kiangsi border area also suffered several defeats and shifted to the Chingkang mountains on the Hunan-Kiangsi border. In the following April the units which survived the unsuccessful Nanchang Uprising also arrived by way of southern Hunan. Since May 1928, however, a basic principle, simple in character, with regard to guerrilla warfare was already set forth in keeping with the conditions of the time, namely, the formula in sixteen key words: "enemy advances, we retreat; enemy halts, we harass; enemy tires, we attack; enemy retreats, we pursue". This military principle in a sixteen-word formula had been accepted by the Party centre prior to the domination of Li Li-san's line. Later on our operational principle developed a step farther. When the first campaign against "encirclement and annihilation" was conducted in the Kiangsi base area, the principle of "luring the enemy to penetrate deep" was put forward and successfully carried out. After the enemy was defeated in his third campaign of "encirclement and annihilation", a complete set of operational principles for the Red Army was formulated. This was the period of a new development of our military principles which were greatly enriched in content and considerably modified in form, mainly in the sense that although they remained basically the same sixteen-word formula, they transcended their original character of simplicity. The formula included the basic principles of the campaign against "encirclement and annihilation", covering both of its phases, strategic defensive and strategic offensive, as well as both phases in the defensive, strategic retreat and strategic counter-offensive. Later developments were but an elaboration of the formula.

But beginning from January 1932, after the publication of the Party's resolution on "Winning Victory First in One or Several Provinces After Smashing the Third Campaign of 'Encirclement and Annihilation'", a resolution which contained serious mistakes in principle, the "Left" opportunists started to attack and finally disavowed these correct principles, and established another complete set of so-called "new principles" or "regular principles", which were the very opposite. Thenceforth the old principles could no longer be considered regular and were rejected as "guerrilla-ism". An atmosphere of opposition to guerrilla-ism prevailed for three whole years. In the first stage of this period military adventurism appeared, only to turn in the second stage into military conservatism and emerge finally in the third stage as flight-ism. It was not until January 1935 when the Party centre called an enlarged meeting of its Political Bureau in Tsunyi, Kweichow, that this erroneous line was declared bankrupt and the correctness of the old line reaffirmed. But at what great price was this bought!

Those comrades who actively opposed guerrilla-ism argued as follows: It is wrong to lure the enemy to penetrate deep because we have to abandon so much territory. Though battles were won in this way, is not the present situation different from the past? Moreover, is it not better to defeat the enemy without abandoning any territory? And is it not still better to defeat the enemy in his own areas, or on the border between his and our areas? The old ways and means were devoid of any regularity and were only suitable for guerrillas. Now our own state has been established and our Red Army has become a regular force. Our fight against Chiang Kai-shek has become a war between one state and another, between one great army and another. History must not repeat itself and guerrilla-ism must be totally discarded. The new principles are "thoroughly Marxist", while the old ways and means were created by the guerrillas in the mountains where no Marxism existed. The new principles are opposed to the old: "Pit one against ten and ten against a hundred, fight bravely and determinedly, and make the most of a victory by hotly pursuing the enemy", "Go forth and attack on all fronts", "Seize the metropolitan cities", and "Strike with both fists". Measures to deal with the enemy's attack are: "Halt the enemy beyond the gate", "Take the first move to checkmate the enemy", "Don't break up the pots and pans", "Don't abandon an inch of territory", "Divide up the forces along six routes"; the new principles consist in "the decisive engagement between the revolutionary way and the colonial way", swift thrusts, a war of blockhouses, a war of attrition, a "protracted war", a great rear area, absolute centralised command, and, finally, house-moving on a large scale. Furthermore, anyone rejecting these principles is to be punished and labelled an opportunist, etc., etc.

Undoubtedly, all these theories and practices are erroneous. They amount to subjectivism. They are manifestations of the revolutionary hysteria and ultra-revolutionism of the petty bourgeois in favourable circumstances; but when the situation worsens, subjectivism changes into desperado-ism and further into conservatism and flight-ism. They are the theories and practices of hotheads and ignoramuses; they have not the slightest flavour of Marxism and are anti-Marxist.

Here we shall discuss only strategic retreat, which was called in Kiangsi "luring the enemy to penetrate deep" and in Szechwan "contracting the front". In the past no military theorist or practical soldier ever denied that this is the necessary measure for a weak army to take in the initial stage of a war against a strong force. Foreign military experts put it like this: "In strategically defensive operations any unfavourable battle of decision is usually to be avoided in the beginning, and to be sought only when conditions are favourable." That is entirely correct, and we have nothing to add to it.

The object of strategic retreat is to conserve strength and to prepare for the counter-offensive. The reason why retreat is necessary is that to yield not a step when facing the onset of a strong enemy inevitably endangers the very existence of the army. In the past, however, many people were stubbornly opposed to retreat, considering it to be an "opportunist line of pure defence". Our experience has proved that they were altogether mistaken.

To prepare for a counter-offensive, we must choose and create certain conditions favourable to ourselves but unfavourable to the enemy, so as to bring about a change in the relative strength between the enemy and ourselves and then enter the phase of the counter-offensive.

According to our past experience the situation generally cannot be considered favourable to ourselves and unfavourable to the enemy and we cannot switch to the counter-offensive unless we have secured during the phase of retreat at least two of the conditions listed below. These conditions are:

1. The people give active support to the Red Army;
2. The terrain is favourable for operations;
3. The main forces of the Red Army are completely concentrated;
4. The weak spots of the enemy are discovered;
5. The enemy is worn out both physically and morally; and
6. The enemy is induced to commit mistakes.

The first constitutes the most important condition for the Red Army. It also exists in the base area. Moreover, with this condition, conditions 4, 5 and 6 can be easily created or discovered. Therefore, when the enemy launches an all-out offensive, the Red Army invariably retreats from the White area into the base area, because the people there are the most active in giving support to its fight against the White army. There is also a difference between those parts near the border of a base area and its central section: in plugging the leakage of information, in reconnaissance, in transportation, in participation in fighting, etc., the people in the central section are more active than those on the border. Thus in coping with the first, second and third campaigns of "encirclement and annihilation" in

Kiangsi, the "terminuses of retreat" were fixed in places where the condition of the people was better or even the best. This characteristic of the base area caused a considerable change in the Red Army's methods of fighting, as distinguished from the methods of fighting in general, and was also the main reason why later on the enemy had to adopt the policy of building blockhouses.

For a retreating army, the advantage of fighting on the interior line is that it can choose freely the favourable terrain and force the attacking army to comply with its wishes. To defeat a strong army, a weak army has to study carefully the conditions of the terrain. But this condition alone is not enough and needs to be complemented by other conditions. First of all comes the condition of the people. Next comes the vulnerability of the enemy, *e.g.* an enemy who is exhausted or has committed blunders, or an advance column of the enemy comparatively low in fighting capacity. When these conditions are not present, we have to ignore the terrain, however excellent, and continue to retreat in order to secure the conditions we want. There is no lack of favourable terrain in the White areas, but there the favourable condition of the people is absent. When other favourable conditions are not yet created or discovered, the Red Army has no alternative but to retreat to its base area. Such is also the general difference between the central and border sections of a base area.

Except for local troops and containing forces, the principle for all assault troops should be concentration. When attacking an enemy who is on the strategic defensive, the Red Army often disperses itself. Once the enemy launches an all-out offensive, the Red Army carries on the so-called "retreat towards the centre". The terminus of the retreat is usually in the middle of the base area, but at times also in its front or rear part—this varies with the circumstances. Such a retreat towards the centre enables all the main forces of the Red Army to assemble.

Another essential condition for a weak army fighting a strong army is to pick out the weak spots for attack. But at the beginning of the enemy's offensive we often do not know which of the advancing columns of the enemy is the strongest, which next strong, which the weakest, and which the next weak; a process of reconnaissance is required. It often takes us considerable time to come by such knowledge. That is another reason why strategic retreat is necessary.

If the attacking enemy is far superior to us both in numbers and fighting capacity, we can attain the objective of bringing about a change in the relative strength only when the enemy force has been deeply drawn into our base area and has tasted to the full the bitterness of staying in the base area—as the chief-of-staff of a certain brigade of Chiang Kai-shek's army remarked during the third campaign of "encirclement and annihilation": "The stout have worn themselves thin and the thin have worn themselves to death", or as Ch'en Ming-shu, commander-in-chief of the Western Route Army of the Kuomintang army of "encirclement and annihilation" commented, "Everywhere the National Army gropes in the dark, while the Red Army walks in broad daylight". By this time the enemy, despite his strength, will have been greatly enfeebled; his soldiers are exhausted and demoralised and numerous vulnerable points are exposed. The Red Army, despite its weakness, will have conserved its strength and stored up energy, waiting at ease for the much-fatigued enemy. By then either the relative strength of the two sides will usually reach a certain degree of parity or the enemy's absolute superiority and our absolute inferiority will become relative; on some occasions the enemy even becomes inferior to us and we superior to him. In fighting against the third campaign of "encirclement and annihilation" in Kiangsi, the Red Army carried out a retreat to the extreme limit (assembling in the back part of the base area), without which it could not have defeated the enemy, because the numerical strength of the army of "encirclement and annihilation" was more than ten times that of the Red Army. When Sun Tzu said, "Avoid the enemy when he is full of dash, and strike him when he withdraws exhausted", he was referring to a way of exhausting and demoralising the enemy so as to reduce his superiority.

The last objective of retreat is to induce the enemy to commit mistakes and to detect them. We must realise that it is impossible for an enemy commander, however wise, not to commit a mistake of some sort over a comparatively long period

of time; consequently there is always the possibility of our
taking advantage of flaws on the part of the enemy. The enemy
makes mistakes just as we ourselves sometimes do, and he can
just as well take advantage of our mistakes as we do of his.
Moreover, we can skilfully induce the enemy to commit mistakes, by staging a "feint", as Sun Tzu called it (*i.e.* "make a
noise in the east but strike in the west", or in other words, stage
a false manœuvre in the east while attacking in the west). In so
doing, the terminus of retreat cannot be confined to a definite
area. Sometimes when a predesignated area is reached and as
yet no flaws can be taken advantage of, we must retreat farther
until the enemy betrays the flaws we can exploit.

The favourable conditions to be sought in the course of a
retreat are in general as described above. But this does not
mean that all the conditions must be present before a counter-
offensive can be undertaken. To obtain all the conditions at the
same time is neither possible nor necessary. But to secure
certain necessary conditions according to the existing situation
of the enemy is something which claims the attention of a weak
force operating on interior lines against a strong enemy; all
views to the contrary on this point are erroneous.

The choice of the terminus of retreat must be made in the
light of the whole situation. It is incorrect to fix the terminus
at a place where it is favourable for us to switch to the counter-
offensive only so far as the partial but not the whole situation
is concerned. For at the start of our counter-offensive we must
take subsequent developments into consideration, and our
counter-offensive invariably begins on a partial scale. Sometimes the terminus of retreat should be fixed in the front part
of the base area, as during our second and fourth campaigns
against "encirclement and annihilation" in Kiangsi and our
third counter-campaign in the Shensi-Kansu border area.
Sometimes it should be in the middle of the base area, as in the
first counter-campaign in Kiangsi. And sometimes in the rear
of the base area, as in the third counter-campaign in Kiangsi.
All these were determined by correlating the partial situation
with the whole situation. When our army never gave any
thought to retreat during our fifth counter-campaign in Kiangsi,
it was really behaving in a rash, blundering way, because it

paid no attention to either the partial or the whole situation. A situation is formed of conditions; in considering the relation between the part and the whole, one should examine both the enemy's conditions and our own as they are manifest in the partial as well as the whole situation and judge how favourable the conditions are for launching a counter-offensive.

The terminuses of retreat in a base area can be generally divided into three kinds: those in the front part, those in the middle part, and those in the rear part.

Does it mean that we refuse altogether to fight in the White areas? No. We refuse to do so only in coping with the enemy's big campaign of "encirclement and annihilation". Only when there is a wide disparity in strength between the enemy and ourselves, do we propose, on the principle of conserving our strength for crushing the enemy at an opportune moment, that we retreat to our base area and that the enemy should be lured to penetrate deep, because only by so doing can we create or discover favourable conditions for our counter-offensive. If the situation is not so serious, or if it is so serious that the Red Army cannot begin its counter-attack even in its base area, or if it does not favour a counter-offensive and a further withdrawal is necessary to bring about a change in the situation, then it would become permissible, theoretically at least, to fix the terminus of retreat in a White area, though in the past we have had very little experience of this kind.

In general, the terminuses of retreat in a White area can also be divided into three kinds: (1) those in front of a base area; (2) those on the flank of the base area; and (3) those behind the base area.

An example of a terminus of the first kind: during the first campaign against "encirclement and annihilation" in Kiangsi, if there had been no disunity inside the Red Army and no split in the local Party organisations, i.e. if the two difficult problems of Li-san's line and the A.-B. Group[31] had not existed, it was conceivable that we could have concentrated our forces at a point within the triangle formed by Kian, Nanfeng and Changshu, and launched a counter-offensive. For the enemy force advancing at the time between the Kan and Fu rivers was not overwhelmingly superior to the Red Army in strength

(100,000 against 40,000). Though the condition of the people there was inferior to that in the base area, the condition of favourable terrain was present; moreover, it would have been possible to smash the enemy columns separately as they advanced by separate routes.

An example of a terminus of the second kind: during the third campaign against "encirclement and annihilation" in Kiangsi, if the enemy's offensive had not been on such a large scale and if one of the enemy's columns had been advancing from Kienning, Lichwan and Taining on the Fukien-Kiangsi border, and if the strength of that column had rendered it a suitable object for our attack, it is conceivable that the Red Army could have massed its forces in the White area in western Fukien and crushed that column first without having to make a big detour of a thousand *li* through Juikin to Hsingkuo.

An example of a terminus of the third kind: again during the third campaign against "encirclement and annihilation" in Kiangsi, if the enemy's main force had not headed for the west but for the south instead, we might have been compelled to retreat to the Hweichang-Sunwa-Anyuan district (which was in the White area) so that we could lure the enemy to go farther south; then the Red Army could have turned around and driven back northward into the base area and by this time the enemy force in the northern part of the base area would not have been a very big one.

All these cases are hypothetical; we had no actual experience of them, and can only regard them as something exceptional and not turn them into general principles. For us, when the enemy launches a big campaign of "encirclement and annihilation", the general principle is to lure him to penetrate deep into our territory and to retreat into the base area and then fight him, because this is the surest way for us to smash his offensive.

Those who advocate "halting the enemy beyond the gate" oppose strategic retreat on the ground that retreat means losing territory, endangering the people ("breaking up the pots and pans", so to speak), and creating an unfavourable impression on the outside world. During the fifth campaign against "encirclement and annihilation" they argued that every time we yielded a step, the enemy's line of blockhouses would advance a step, and thus the base area would shrink daily and we would have no way of recovering our loss. If luring the enemy to penetrate deep into our territory had been very useful in the past, it was now useless in the fifth campaign of "encirclement and annihilation", with the enemy resorting to the strategy of building blockhouses. To cope with the fifth campaign of "encirclement and annihilation" only such measures as dividing up our forces for resistance and making swift thrusts were to be adopted.

It is easy to refute such ideas, and our history has already refuted them. As to the loss of territory, it often happens that loss can be saved only through loss: This is the principle of "In order to take, we must first give". If what we lose is territory and what we gain is victory over the enemy, plus recovery and even expansion of territory, then it is a profitable business. In business transactions, if a buyer does not give his money, he cannot obtain the goods; if a seller does not give his goods, he cannot obtain the money. The loss which a revolutionary movement incurs is destruction, and what it gains is progressive reconstruction. Time is lost during sleep and rest, yet energy is gained for tomorrow's work. Should any foolish person who does not understand this refuse to sleep, he will have no energy left the next day, and that will be a losing business. We did a losing business in the enemy's fifth campaign of "encirclement and annihilation" precisely on this account. Unwillingness to lose a part of the territory resulted in the loss of all the territory. Abyssinia lost all her territory because she put up an inflexible fight, though that was not the sole cause of her disaster.

The same holds true with the problem of endangering the people. If we will not let the pots and pans of a section of inhabitants be broken for once, then the pots and pans of the whole population will go on being broken for a long time. The fear of a temporarily unfavourable political impression will entail a long-lasting unfavourable impression. After the October Revolution, if the Russian Bolsheviks had followed the suggestions of the "Left Communists" and refused to sign a

peace treaty with the Germans, the new-born Soviets would
have incurred the danger of imminent extinction.[32]

Such seemingly revolutionary "Left" views originate from
the ultra-revolutionism of the petty-bourgeois intellectuals as
well as the narrowness and conservatism of the small peasant
producers. Looking at a problem only one-sidedly, without
being able to take a comprehensive view of the whole, they are
unwilling to link today's interests with those of tomorrow, or
partial interests with those of the whole, clinging for dear life
to things partial and temporary. It is true that we should cling
tenaciously to those parts that are, in view of all the circumstances, favourable to the whole situation at that time, and to
the entire period, especially to that sector of time and space
which is of decisive significance, otherwise we shall be advocates
of letting things take their course. That is why there must be a
terminus for retreat. But we must not rely on the short-
sightedness of the small producer. We must learn the wisdom
of the Bolsheviks. When our naked eyes are not enough, we
must avail ourselves of the aid of a telescope or microscope.
The method of Marxism serves as a telescope or microscope in
matters political and military.

Of course, there are difficulties in a strategic retreat. To
time its beginning, to choose a terminus for it, and to convince
the cadres and the people politically are all difficult problems
that must be solved.

The problem of timing the beginning of a retreat is of
momentous significance. Had our retreat in the first campaign
against "encirclement and annihilation" in Kiangsi not been
made at the right time, that is, had it been delayed, the extent
of our victory, to say the least, would have been affected. Both
premature and belated retreats will of course incur losses.
But generally speaking, a belated retreat causes more damage
than a premature retreat. Timely retreat places us entirely
on our own initiative, and helps greatly our switching to the
counter-offensive when we have reached the terminus, re-
grouped our forces, and waited at ease for the much-fatigued
enemy. In smashing the enemy's first, second and fourth
campaigns of "encirclement and annihilation" in Kiangsi,
we were able to handle the enemy with poise and ease. In the

third campaign, however, as the enemy had suffered such a terrible defeat in the second campaign, we did not expect him to open his new offensive so quickly (we ended our second counter-campaign on May 29, 1931, and Chiang Kai-shek began his third campaign on July 1); the Red Army, assembled after making hasty detours, was greatly fatigued. How to time the retreat depends wholly on collecting the necessary intelligence and making decisions in the light of the general situation existing between the enemy and ourselves, in the same way as timing the beginning of the preparatory phase of a counter-offensive mentioned above.

To convince the cadres and the people of the necessity of strategic retreat is an extremely difficult task when they have yet had no experience of it and when the army leadership, necessarily entrusting the decision on strategic retreat to a few people or even to one person, is not yet so authoritative that it enjoys the confidence of the cadres. Owing to the cadres' lack of experience and of faith in strategic retreat, great difficulties were encountered on this score at the beginning of the first and fourth counter-campaigns and during the entire fifth counter-campaign. In the first counter-campaign the cadres, under the influence of Li Li-san's line, had been in favour of attack until they were convinced of the necessity of retreat. In the fourth counter-campaign the cadres, under the influence of military adventurism, objected to making preparations for retreat. In the fifth counter-campaign, the cadres at first persisted in the military adventurist view opposed to luring the enemy to penetrate deep into our territory, which subsequently developed into military conservatism. A concrete example is that Chang Kuo-t'ao's line did not admit the impossibility of establishing our bases in the Tibetan and the Mohammedan regions [33]—not until it ran up against a brick wall. Experience is necessary for the cadres, and failure is indeed the mother of success. But open-minded acceptance of other people's experience is also necessary, and it is sheer "narrow-minded empiricism" to insist on having experience in everything oneself and stubbornly adhering to one's opinions while rejecting other people's experience. Our war has suffered from this in no small measure.

The people's disbelief in the necessity of strategic retreat due to their lack of experience was most striking in the first counter-campaign in Kiangsi. At that time all the local Party organisations and the masses of the people in the counties of Kian, Hsingkuo and Yungfeng were opposed to the Red Army's retreat. But once they had experience in this counter-campaign, such a problem did not arise at all in the subsequent counter-campaigns. All were convinced that the loss of the base area and the suffering of the people were temporary and all had faith in the Red Army's ability to smash the campaigns of "encirclement and annihilation". However, the faith of the people is closely linked with that of the cadres, hence the main and primary task is to convince the cadres.

The sole purpose of strategic retreat is to switch to the counter-offensive, and strategic retreat constitutes merely the first phase of strategic defensive. The decisive link in the entire strategy is whether victory can be won in the phase of counter-offensive which follows.

4. STRATEGIC COUNTER-OFFENSIVE

To defeat the attack of an enemy who enjoys absolute superiority we rely on the new situation created out of the phase of strategic retreat, which is favourable to ourselves but unfavourable to the enemy, which has changed since the beginning of the enemy's offensive, and which is made up of various conditions. We have pointed this out above.

However, the presence of conditions and a situation favourable to ourselves and unfavourable to the enemy does not yet mean the defeat of the enemy. Such conditions and such a situation contain only the possibilities of our victory or the enemy's defeat, but they do not yet constitute victory or defeat and for neither of the contestants has victory or defeat become an actuality. In order to transform the possibility of victory or defeat into an actuality, it is necessary for the contestants to have a decisive engagement. And only a decisive engagement can settle the question as to who wins and who is defeated. That is the sole task in the phase of strategic counter-offensive. The counter-offensive is a long process, the most dramatic, the liveliest, and also the final phase of a defensive campaign. What is called active defence means chiefly a strategic counter-offensive that is in the nature of a decisive engagement.

Conditions and situation are created not only in the phase of strategic retreat but continue to be created in the phase of counter-offensive. In the latter phase the situation and conditions are not exactly the same in form or character as in the former phase.

What may remain the same in form and character is, among other things, the fact that the enemy troops are even more fatigued and further reduced in number—this is nothing but a continuation of the fatigue and reduction in the previous phase.

But wholly new conditions and a new situation will certainly arise. For instance, when the enemy has suffered one or several defeats, the conditions favourable to ourselves but unfavourable to the enemy will be not merely the enemy's fatigue, etc., but in addition the new condition that he has met with defeats. New changes will arise in the situation. As the enemy troops begin to move in disorder and to act at haphazard, the relative strength of the opponents naturally becomes different from what it was before.

But if it is not the enemy but we ourselves who have suffered one or several defeats, then the advantages or disadvantages of conditions and situation will be reversed. This means that the enemy's disadvantages will diminish and ours will begin to appear and even multiply. That again will be something entirely new and different.

The defeated side, no matter which it is, will immediately have to make a new effort, an effort to save its disastrous situation, to extricate itself from the newly arisen conditions and situation unfavourable to itself but favourable to its opponent, and to recreate the conditions and situation favourable to itself and unfavourable to its opponent so that it can bring pressure on the latter.

The effort of the winning side will be just the opposite: it will strive to expand its victory and inflict greater losses on the enemy, to multiply the conditions and further improve the situation favourable to itself, and to prevent its opponent from achieving his aim of extricating himself from the unfavourable situation and averting disaster.

Thus, for either of the two sides, the struggle at the stage of the decisive engagement is the most intense, the most complicated, the most kaleidoscopic, the most difficult and the most trying, and, for a commander, the hardest juncture in the whole war or campaign.

There are many problems connected with the counter-offensive, chiefly the timing of the beginning of the counter-offensive, the concentration of troops, mobile warfare, war of quick decision, and war of annihilation.

Whether in a counter-offensive or in an offensive, the principles for dealing with these problems are basically the same. In this sense we may say that a counter-offensive is but an offensive.

But a counter-offensive is not exactly an offensive. The principles of the counter-offensive are applied when the enemy is on the offensive. The principles of the offensive are applied when the enemy is on the defensive. In this sense, therefore, there are certain differences between the two.

For this reason, although many operational problems have been included in the discussion of the counter-offensive under the category of strategic defensive and, to avoid repetition, other problems are only discussed under the category of strategic offensive, yet in applying them we should not overlook either their similarities or their differences.

5. PROBLEMS OF STARTING THE COUNTER-OFFENSIVE

Problems of starting a counter-offensive are problems of the so-called "first battle" or "prelude".

Many bourgeois military experts advise caution in the first battle, whether in strategic defensive or strategic offensive, but more especially in the defensive. In the past we also seriously raised this problem. The campaigns against the enemy's "encirclement and annihilation" in Kiangsi, from the first to the fifth, have given us abundant experience and a study of them is not without profit.

In the first campaign the enemy, about 100,000 men deployed

in eight columns, advanced southward on the base area of the Red Army along the line between Kian and Kienning. The Red Army was then about forty thousand strong, concentrated in the district of Hwangpei and Siaopu in Ningtu, Kiangsi.

The situation at that time was as follows:

1. The enemy forces of "annihilation" numbered no more than 100,000 and none of them were Chiang Kai-shek's personal troops; the general situation was not very grave.

2. The enemy division under Lo Lin was defending Kian, stationed alone on the west bank of the Kan river.

3. The three enemy divisions under Kung Ping-fan, Chang Hui-tsan and T'an Tao-yuan occupied the Futien-Tungku-Lungkang-Yuantow district, to the south-east of Kian and to the north-west of Ningtu. The main forces of Chang's division were quartered at Lungkang and those of T'an's division at Yuantow. It was not advisable to open up a battlefield in Futien and Tungku where the inhabitants, misled by the A.-B. Group, had as yet no faith in the Red Army and were even opposed to it.

4. The enemy division under Liu Ho-ting was far away in Kienning in the White area of Fukien, and it might not break into Kiangsi.

5. The two enemy divisions under Mao Ping-wen and Hsu K'e-hsiang had reached the Towpei-Lokow-Tungshao sector between Kwangchang and Ningtu. Towpei was in a White area, Lokow in a guerrilla area, and Tungshao, with the presence of the A.-B. Group there, was a loophole from which information might easily leak out. Furthermore, if we were to drive westward after beating Mao Ping-wen and Hsu K'e-hsiang, the enemy divisions under Chang Hui-tsan, T'an Tao-yuan and Kung Ping-fan might join forces, thus making it difficult for us to win a decisive victory and impossible for us to conclude the campaign.

6. The two enemy divisions under Chang Hui-tsan and T'an Tao-yuan, which made up the main forces of the army of "encirclement and annihilation", were the personal troops of Lu Ti-p'ing, commander-in-chief of the campaign and Chairman of the Provincial Government of Kiangsi, and Chang Hui-tsan was concurrently the field commander. If these two

divisions were annihilated, the campaign of "encirclement and annihilation" would be practically smashed. The two divisions had about fourteen thousand men each, with Chang Hui-tsan's division disposed at two points; so we would have an absolute superiority by attacking one division at a time.

7. The Lungkang-Yuantow sector, garrisoned by the main forces of Chang's and T'an's divisions, was close to the point where our troops were concentrated; moreover, the condition of the people was good and they could shield our approach.

8. The terrain in Lungkang was good. Yuantow was not easy to attack. But should the enemy there advance to Siapow to attack us, the terrain would be good too.

9. We could mass the largest possible number of troops at Lungkang. In Hsingkuo, some tens of *li* to the south-west of Lungkang, we had an independent division of over one thousand men, which could manœuvre to the enemy's rear.

10. If our troops effected a breakthrough and created a breach in the enemy's front, his columns to the east and west would be cut into two distantly separated groups.

For the above reasons, we decided to launch our first battle against—and in fact hit—the main force under Chang Hui-tsan, his two brigades and his division headquarters, and we captured the entire force of nine thousand men including the divisional commander himself; not a man or a horse escaped. This victory in a single engagement so scared T'an's and Hsu's divisions that they fled towards Tungshao and Towpei respectively. Our army then pursued T'an's division and annihilated half of it. We fought two battles in five days (from December 27, 1930, to January 1, 1931), and the enemy forces in Futien, Tungku and Towpei, afraid of being beaten, pulled out helter-skelter; thus ended the first campaign.

The situation in the second campaign of "encirclement and annihilation" was as follows:

1. The enemy forces employed in the campaign numbered 200,000, with Ho Ying-ch'in as the commander-in-chief, who stayed at Nanchang.

2. As in the first campaign, none of the forces were the personal troops of Chiang Kai-shek. The Nineteenth Route Army under Ts'ai T'ing-k'ai, the Twenty-sixth Route Army

under Sun Lien-chung and the Eighth Route Army under Chu Shao-liang were very strong or comparatively strong, while all the rest were weak.

3. The A.-B. Group had been cleaned up, and the entire population of the base area supported the Red Army.

4. The Fifth Route Army under Wang Chin-yu, newly arrived from the North, was apprehensive, and generally speaking, so were the two divisions constituting its left wing under Kuo Hua-tsung and Ho Meng-lin respectively.

5. If our troops attacked Futien first and then swept to the east, we could expand the base area in the Kienning-Lichwan-Taining sector on the Fukien-Kiangsi border and amass provisions for smashing the next campaign of "encirclement and annihilation". If we struck westward instead, then we would come up against the Kan river, where we would have no room for expansion after the conclusion of the battle. To turn eastward again after finishing the battle would fatigue the army and waste our time.

6. Though the numerical strength of our army was slightly reduced from that in the first campaign to little more than thirty thousand, our men had had four months to rehabilitate themselves and store up energy.

For these reasons, we decided to seek our first battle in the Futien sector with the forces of Wang Chin-yu and of Kung Ping-fan (totalling eleven regiments). After winning the battle, we attacked successively the troops of Kuo Hua-tsung, Sun Lien-chung, Chu Shao-liang, and Liu Ho-ting. In fifteen days (from May 16 to May 30, 1931) we covered on foot a distance of seven hundred *li*, fought five battles, captured more than twenty thousand rifles, and smashed the campaign of "encirclement and annihilation" with great verve and gusto. When fighting Wang Chin-yu, we were situated between Ts'ai T'ing-k'ai and Kuo Hua-tsung, some ten *li* from Kuo and forty *li* from Ts'ai; so ridicule was poured on us for trying to "get through an oxhorn", but all the same we got through. This was mainly due to the condition of the base area, plus the disunity among the enemy's units. After Kuo's division was defeated, Ho's division fled post-haste to Yungfeng at night and thus saved itself.

The situation in the third campaign of "encirclement and annihilation" was as follows:

1. Chiang Kai-shek himself assumed supreme command with three commanders each in charge of a route—left, right and central. The central route was commanded by Ho Ying-ch'in who had his headquarters in Nanchang like Chiang, the right by Ch'en Ming-shu with his headquarters at Kian, and the left by Chu Shao-liang with his headquarters at Nanfeng.

2. The enemy forces employed in the campaign numbered 300,000. The main forces were Chiang's personal troops, which consisted of five divisions with nine regiments each, totalled about 100,000 men and were commanded respectively by Ch'en Ch'eng, Lo Cho-ying, Chao Kuan-t'ao, Wei Li-huang and Chiang Ting-wen. Next to these were the three divisions totalling forty thousand men under Chiang Kuang-nai, Ts'ai T'ing-k'ai and Han Te-ch'in. Then there was Sun Lien-chung's army of twenty thousand. The rest, comparatively weak, were not Chiang's personal troops either.

3. The enemy's strategy of the campaign was to "drive straight forward" into our territory—a strategy greatly different from that of "consolidating at every step" in the second campaign—with a view to pressing the Red Army back against the Kan river and annihilating it there.

4. There was only an interval of one month between the end of the second and the commencement of the third campaign. The Red Army (now about thirty thousand strong) had received neither rest nor replacements after much hard fighting; in addition, it had made a detour of one thousand *li* to reassemble in Hsingkuo in the western part of the base area in southern Kiangsi, when the enemy advanced right up against it in several columns.

In such a situation the first course we adopted was to break through at Futien by way of Hsing-kuo and Wanan, then sweep from west to east against the enemy's communication lines in the rear, thus making it quite futile for the main enemy forces to penetrate deep into our base area in southern Kiangsi—that was to be the first phase of our operation. As the enemy drew back northward, he would be greatly fatigued and we would take every opportunity to strike at his vulnerable points—that would be the second phase.

The main thing about this course was to avoid the enemy's main forces and to strike at his weak spots. But when our forces were advancing on Futien, we were detected by the enemy and the divisions under Ch'en Ch'eng and Lo Cho-ying rushed to the scene. We had to change our plan and fell back to the Kaohsing fair-ground (in the western part of Hsingkuo) which, together with its environs of several tens of square *li*, was then the only place left for us to reassemble in. Having reassembled there for a day, we decided to speed eastward in the direction of Lientang (in the eastern part of Hsingkuo), Liangtsun in the southern part of Yungfen, and Hwangpei (in the northern part of Ningtu). On the first day we passed under cover of darkness through the forty-*li* breach between Chiang Ting-wen's division and the forces of Chiang Kuang-nai, Ts'ai T'ing-k'ai and Han Te-ch'in, and veered to Lientang. On the second day our patrols skirmished with the forces under Shangkuan Yun-hsiang (who was in command of his own division and that of Ho Meng-ling). The first battle was fought on the third day with Shangkuan's division and the second on the fourth with Ho's; after making a three-day march we reached Hwangpei and fought the third battle with Mao Ping-wen's division. We won all three battles and captured over ten thousand rifles.

Then all the enemy's main forces that had been advancing westward and southward veered to the east; focusing their eyes on Hwangpei, they converged at furious speed to seek battle, and descended upon us in a big, compact encirclement. Then we sneaked through over a big mountain in the east in the twenty-*li* breach between the forces of Chiang Kuang-nai, Ts'ai T'ing-k'ai and Han Te-ch'in on the one side and those of Ch'en Ch'eng and Lo Cho-ying on the other, and reassembled within the borders of Hsingkuo to the west. By the time the enemy discovered this and began to advance westward, our forces had already had a half-month's rest, whereas the enemy forces, hungry, fatigued and low in morale, were now weakened and decided to retreat. Taking advantage of their retreat, we attacked the forces of Chiang Kuang-nai, Ts'ai T'ing-k'ai,

Chiang Ting-wen and Han Te-ch'in, and annihilated one brigade under Chiang Ting-wen and the entire division under Han Te-ch'in. Our engagement with the divisions under Chiang Kuang-nai and Ts'ai T'ing-k'ai resulted in stalemate and finally we let them get away.

The situation in the fourth campaign of "encirclement and annihilation" was as follows: The enemy forces were advancing in three columns on Kwangchang; the main force was in the east, while two divisions forming the western prong were exposed to us and very close to our concentration point. Thus we had the opportunity to attack first the western prong in the southern part of Yihwang and at one stroke we annihilated the two divisions under Li Ming and Ch'en Shih-chi. As the enemy dispatched two divisions from his eastern prong to co-ordinate with the central prong and make a further advance, we again had the opportunity to annihilate another of his divisions in the southern part of Yihwang. In the two battles more than ten thousand rifles were captured, and the campaign of "encirclement and annihilation" was basically broken.

In the fifth campaign of "encirclement and annihilation" the enemy advanced by means of the new strategy of building blockhouses, and first occupied Lichwan. However, in the hope of recovering it and halting the enemy beyond the border of the base area, we attacked Siaoshih, which was a strong enemy position in the White area north of Lichwan. When repulsed in that battle, we shifted our attack to Tzekichiao, also a strong enemy position in the White area south-east of Siaoshih, but again we gained no ground. Then we moved back and forth seeking battle between the enemy's main forces and his blockhouses and were reduced to a completely passive position. All through the fifth counter-campaign, which lasted a year, we did not show the slightest initiative or dynamic force. Finally we had no alternative but to withdraw from our base area in Kiangsi.

The experiences gained by our forces in the above-mentioned campaigns against "encirclement and annihilation", from the first to the fifth, prove that for the Red Army, which is in a defensive position, to smash the big, strong "annihilation" forces of the enemy, the first battle in the counter-offensive is of momentous importance. Its success or failure has a tremendous effect upon the whole situation, and affects even the final engagement. Hence we arrive at the following conclusions:

Firstly, win victory in the first battle by all means. We should strike only when we are positively sure that the enemy's situation, the terrain, the people and other conditions are all favourable to us and unfavourable to the enemy. Otherwise we should rather fall back and cautiously bide our time. There will always be opportunities, and we should not rashly accept battle.

In the first campaign against "encirclement and annihilation" our first thought was to strike at T'an Tao-yuan's forces; but solely because his forces never left the high commanding position of Yuantow, our troops advanced twice and twice gave up and withdrew, and a few days later we sought out Chiang Hui-tsan's forces which were vulnerable.

In the second counter-campaign our forces advanced to Tungku where, for the sole purpose of waiting for the troops under Wang Chin-yu to leave their strong position at Futien, and, willingly running the risk of the leakage of information and rejecting all impatient suggestions for a quick attack, we quartered ourselves close to the enemy for twenty-five days, and at last attained our aim.

In the third counter-campaign, although the situation was stormy, although our troops had returned by a forced march of one thousand *li*, and although our plan of outflanking the enemy was detected, yet we again gave up and withdrew, changed our plan to a breakthrough in the centre, and finally fought a successful first battle at Lientang.

In the fourth counter-campaign, after failing to capture Nanfeng in an attack, we resolutely adopted the course of retreat and, veering eventually to the enemy's right wing, we concentrated our forces in the Tungshao area and began our great victorious battle in the southern part of Yihwang.

It was only in the fifth counter-campaign that we completely failed to recognise the importance of the first battle: we were much alarmed at the loss of a single county town—that of Lichwan, and, in an attempt to recover it, we proceeded north

to meet the enemy; after our victory in an unexpected encounter
with the enemy at Sunkow (in which we annihilated one
enemy division), we failed to treat it as the first battle or to
foresee all the changes it would necessarily bring about, but
heedlessly launched an assault on Siaoshih with no assurance of
victory. We lost the initiative in our first move—certainly the
stupidest and worst way of fighting.

Secondly, the plan of the first battle must be the prelude in
the plan for the whole campaign and forms an organic part of
it. Without a good plan for the whole campaign it is absolutely
impossible to fight a really successful first battle. That is to say,
even though victory is won in the first battle, if the battle
prejudices the entire campaign rather than benefits it, then the
victory in such a battle can only be considered a defeat (*e.g.*
the battle of Sunkow in the fifth campaign of "encirclement
and annihilation"). Hence before fighting the first battle it
is necessary to have a general idea of how the second, third,
fourth, and even the final battles are to be fought, and to
consider what changes would ensue in the enemy's situation as
a whole if we should win the succeeding battles or if we should
lose them. Though the result may not turn out—and certainly
will never turn out—exactly as we anticipate, we must think
carefully and realistically in the light of the whole situation
confronting both the enemy and ourselves. Without grasping
the whole situation, it is impossible to make a really wise
move.

Thirdly, consideration must be given to the plan for the next
strategic phase of the war. We shall not have thoroughly
discharged our responsibility as directors of strategy if we are
occupied only with the counter-offensive and neglect the
measures to be taken subsequently in case we win the counter-
offensive or perhaps even lose it. When a director of strategy
finds himself in one strategic phase, he should take into
consideration many succeeding phases, or, at the very least,
the one that immediately follows. Even though future changes
are difficult to foresee and the farther away the perspective
the more blurred it seems, a general calculation is possible
and an appraisal of distant prospects is necessary. The method
of directing by which the director watches only the step he is

going to take is harmful not only in politics but in war as well. Every time one takes a particular step, one should watch what concrete changes result therefrom and modify or develop one's strategic and operational plans accordingly, otherwise one is liable to commit the mistake of reckless adventure and foolhardy action. Nevertheless, a generally thought-out long-term plan covering an entire strategic phase and even a number of strategic phases is certainly indispensable. Failure to prepare such a plan will result in the mistake of hesitating in a self-imposed predicament, thereby actually serving the enemy's strategic ends by landing ourselves in a passive position. It should be borne in mind that the enemy's supreme command has some strategic insight. It is only when we have trained ourselves to attain a level higher than the enemy's that strategic success will be possible. During the enemy's fifth campaign of "encirclement and annihilation", the mistake of the strategic direction of the "Left" opportunist line and Chang Kuo-t'ao's line lay mainly in the failure to do these things. In short, the phase of the counter-offensive must be taken into consideration when we are in the phase of the retreat, the phase of the offensive must be taken into consideration when we are in the phase of the counter-offensive, and the phase of the retreat must again be taken into consideration when we are in the phase of the offensive. To neglect all this and to be bound rigidly by the advantages and disadvantages of the moment is the way to disaster.

We must win the first battle, we must take into consideration the plan of an entire campaign, and we must take into consideration the strategic phase that immediately follows—these are the three principles which we must bear in mind when we begin a counter-offensive, *i.e.* when we fight the first battle.

6. PROBLEMS OF TROOP CONCENTRATION

Troop concentration seems to be easy, but is very difficult in practice. Everybody knows that the best method is to defeat the few with the many, but many people are incapable of doing that, and on the contrary often divide up their forces; this is because the directors of war, lacking a strategic mind and perplexed and enslaved by complicated circumstances, lose their initiative and take a line of muddling through.

No matter how complicated, critical and forlorn is the situation in which he finds himself, a military director is required, first of all, to organise and employ his own forces independently and with initiative. Though it often happens that he is forced by the enemy into a passive position, the important thing for him is to recover the initiative quickly. The outcome will be a defeat if he fails.

Initiative is not something illusory but concrete and material. Here the most important thing is conserving and massing the largest active force.

In fact, a defensive war is easily forced into a passive position and, compared with an offensive war, it is far less conducive to the fullest development of initiative. However, a defensive war, while passive in form, may comprise initiative in content and may change from a phase of passivity in form to a phase of initiative both in form and content. A thoroughly planned strategic retreat is in form made under compulsion, but its content is to conserve the forces and wait for an opportunity to crush the enemy, to lure the enemy to penetrate deep into our territory and to prepare for the counter-offensive. On the other hand, refusal to retreat and flurried acceptance of battle (as in the battle of Siaoshih) is a struggle for the initiative only in appearance but in reality a passive move. In a strategic counter-offensive not only is there initiative in content but even the passive form of a retreat is cast off. To the enemy, our counter-offensive means an effort to deprive him of his initiative as well as to put him into a passive position.

For achieving this aim thoroughly, concentration of troops, mobile warfare, war of quick decision and war of annihilation are all necessary conditions. And concentration of troops is the first and most essential condition.

Concentration of troops is necessary for reversing the situation between the enemy and ourselves.

Firstly, it serves to reverse the situation of advance and retreat. Formerly it was the enemy who advanced and we retreated, and now we seek to advance and make the enemy retreat. When we throw our concentrated troops into a battle and defeat the enemy, then in this same battle we shall have achieved this aim and produced an effect on the whole campaign as well.

Secondly, it serves to reverse the situation of offensive and defensive. To retreat until the terminus is reached belongs basically to the passive phase of defensive warfare, the phase of "defence". The counter-offensive belongs to the active phase, or the phase of "attack". Though such counter-offensive does not lose its defensive character in the whole strategically defensive war, yet compared with the retreat it is changed not only in form but also in content. The counter-offensive is a transitory phase between strategic defensive and strategic offensive and is in the nature of a prelude to strategic offensive—forces are concentrated precisely for this purpose.

Thirdly, it serves to reverse the situation of interior and exterior lines. A force operating on strategically interior lines labours under many disadvantages, especially in the case of the Red Army confronted with "encirclement and annihilation". But we can and absolutely must reverse the situation through campaigns or battles. We can turn the enemy's big campaign of "encirclement and annihilation" against us into a number of small, separate campaigns of encirclement and annihilation which our own troops carry out against the enemy. We can turn the enemy's strategic superiority over us into our superiority over him in an operational and tactical sense. We can reduce the enemy's strategically strong position to a position which is weak in an operational and tactical sense. At the same time we can reduce our strategic weakness by attaining an operationally and tactically strong position. This is what we call exterior-line operations on interior lines, encirclement and annihilation within "encirclement and annihilation", blockade within blockade, offensive in defensive, superiority in inferiority, strength in weakness, advantages in disadvantages, and initiative in passivity. To win victory in a strategic defensive thus depends basically on making a single move— concentrating the forces.

In the military history of the Chinese Red Army, this issue has often aroused important controversies. In the battle of Kian on October 4, 1930, we proceeded to advance and attack before

our forces were completely concentrated; fortunately the
enemy force (the division under Teng Ying) had fled of their
own accord, and our attack in itself was ineffective.

Beginning from 1932, there was the slogan "Launch attacks
on all fronts", which demanded that we should strike from the
base area in all directions—north, south, east and west. This is
wrong not only in strategic defensive but also in strategic
offensive. As long as there is no fundamental change in the
relative strength of the enemy and ourselves as a whole,
defensive and offensive, or containing action and assault,
always go hand in hand strategically or tactically, and it
rarely happens in practice that we can "Launch attacks on all
fronts". Such a slogan smacks of the military equalitarianism
which accompanies military adventurism.

In 1933, these advocates of military equalitarianism formulated the theory of "striking with both fists", demanding that
the main forces of the Red Army be divided into two groups to
win victories simultaneously in two strategic directions. As a
result, one fist remained idle while the other was over-fatigued
with fighting, and moreover we failed to score the biggest
possible victory at the time. In my opinion, when we are
confronted with a powerful enemy force, we should employ
our army, whatever its size, in only one main direction at a
given time, not two. I am not objecting to having two or more
operational directions, but at any given time there ought to be
only one main direction. The Chinese Red Army, appearing
in the arena of the civil war as a small and weak force, has
relied largely on the employment of concentrated strength in
repeatedly defeating its strong enemy and winning victories
that surprised the world. Any of its great victories can prove
this. When we say, "To pit one against ten and ten against a
hundred", we are talking about strategy, or the over-all ratio
between the enemy and ourselves in the entire war, and in this
sense we have actually been doing so. We are not, however,
talking about operational direction or tactics, and in that
sphere we must never apply it. In a counter-offensive or an
offensive, we have always massed a big force to strike against a
segment of the enemy. We suffered from an inadequate
concentration of our forces in such battles as were fought

against T'an Tao-yuan in the vicinity of Tungshao, Ningtu county, Kiangsi, in January 1931; against the Nineteenth Route Army in the vicinity of Kaohsing fair-ground, Hsingkuo county, Kiangsi, in August 1931; against Ch'en Chi-t'ang in the vicinity of the Shuikow fair-ground, Namyung county, Kwangtung, in July 1932; and against Ch'en Ch'eng in the vicinity of Tuantsun, Lichwan county, Kiangsi, in March 1934. Battles like those of the Shuikow fair-ground and Tuantsun were generally considered successes or even big successes (in the former we routed twenty regiments under Ch'en Chi-t'ang and in the latter twelve regiments under Ch'en Ch'eng), but we never like such victories and even regard them as defeats in a certain sense. For, in our opinion, a battle is of little significance when there are no spoils of war or when the spoils do not exceed our losses. Our strategy is "to pit one against ten", while our tactic is "to pit ten against one."—this is one of the fundamental principles on which we beat the enemy.

Military equalitarianism reached its extreme during the fifth campaign against "encirclement and annihilation" in 1934. It was thought that by "dividing up the forces along six routes" and "resisting on the whole front" we could get the upper hand of the enemy, but what happened was that the enemy got the upper hand of us, owing to our fear of losing territory. If we had concentrated our main forces in one direction and left only containing forces in other directions, of course we could not but incur losses in territory. But these would be only temporary and partial and their compensation would be the victory in the direction of our attack. When such a victory was won, the losses in the direction of our containing operations would naturally be recovered. The enemy's first, second, third and fourth campaigns of "encirclement and annihilation" all inflicted losses upon us, and in the third campaign especially, the Red Army's base in Kiangsi was almost completely lost; but in the end our territory was not only recovered but also expanded.

Failure to appreciate the strength of the people in the base area often gives rise to an unwarranted apprehension that the Red Army may move too far away from it. This was the case

when the Red Army in Kiangsi made a long drive to attack
Changchow, Fukien, in 1932, and also when it turned to attack
Fukien after the victory in the fourth campaign against
"encirclement and annihilation" in 1933. As it was feared, in
the first instance, that the entire base area might be occupied by
the enemy, and in the second, that part of it might be occupied,
concentration of forces was rejected in favour of dividing them
up for defence, but in both cases the final outcome proved this
to be wrong. In the enemy's eyes there was, on the one hand,
our base area which made him hesitate to advance and, on the
other, the Red Army invading the White areas, which constituted his main threat. His attention was invariably directed
to the whereabouts of the Red Army's main forces, and he rarely
left our main forces out of account to devote his whole attention
to our base area. Even when carrying out a defensive war, the
Red Army remained the centre of the enemy's attention. To
reduce our base area was part of his total plan, but when the
Red Army massed its main forces to annihilate one of his
columns, his supreme command was forced to devote greater
attention to, and employ larger forces against, the Red Army.
Hence it was possible to wreck his plan of reducing our base
area.

"During the period of the enemy's fifth campaign of 'encirclement and annihilation' based on the policy of building
blockhouses, we found it impossible to concentrate our forces
in our operations and could only divide them up for defence
and launch swift thrusts"—this view is incorrect. The
enemy's tactic of advancing and pushing forward—three,
five, eight, or ten *li* at a time—and building blockhouses
at each halt was actuated entirely by the Red Army's setting
up successive defence lines. The situation would certainly have
been different if in the interior line we had stopped doing so and,
when necessary and possible, advanced and charged into the
enemy's interior line. The principle of concentrating the forces
provides precisely the means to defeat the enemy's policy of
building blockhouses.

The concentration of forces we advocate does not imply the
abandonment of the operations of the people's guerrillas. The
abolition of small-scale guerrilla operations advocated by Li

Li-san's line—"Every single gun must go to the Red Army"— has long been proved incorrect. Considering the revolutionary war as a whole, the operations of the people's guerrillas and those of the main force, the Red Army, are complementary to each other like the right arm and left arm of a man, and it would be like a warrior with only one arm if there were only the latter without the former. In concrete terms and especially in respect to war, by "the condition of the people in the base area" we mean precisely that the people are armed. Mainly because of this, the enemy fears to approach our base area.

It is also essential to employ Red Army detachments in the direction of minor operations, and not to concentrate all the forces in the main direction. The concentration of forces we advocate is based on the principle of guaranteeing an absolute or relative superiority for operations on the battlefield. To cope with a strong enemy or to conduct operations on a front of vital importance, we must have an absolutely superior force— for example, in the first battle of December 30, 1930 in the first campaign against "encirclement and annihilation", a force of forty thousand was massed to beat Chang Hui-tsan's nine thousand. In dealing with a weak foe or operating on a front of no great importance, a relatively superior force is sufficient—for example, in the last battle of the second counter-campaign on May 19, 1931, only something over ten thousand Red Army men were employed to beat Liu Ho-ting's division of seven thousand men in Kienning.

This is not to say that we demand superiority in strength on every occasion. Under certain circumstances, we may appear on the battlefield with a relatively or absolutely inferior force.

An illustration of the employment of a relatively inferior force: when we have only a small detachment of the Red Army in a certain sector (this does not mean when we do have more troops but have not concentrated them), and when conditions such as the people, terrain and weather are very favourable, then, in order to repulse the attack of an enemy force of superior strength, it is of course necessary and possible to win victory by containing the centre and one of the flanks of that enemy force with guerrillas or small detachments, while concentrating the entire forces of the Red Army for a surprise attack on a segment of its other flank. When we do spring such a surprise attack we shall still be applying the principle of superiority over inferiority, of defeating the few with the many so far as the relative strength is concerned.

An illustration of the employment of an absolutely inferior force: when a guerrilla force springs a surprise attack on a powerful column of the White army, it is still applying the principle, since it attacks only a small segment of the enemy.

We should consider in the light of different conditions the theory that concentrating a great army in a single operational field is subject to the limitations of the terrain, roads, supplies and billeting facilities. There is a certain degree of difference in these limitations between the Red Army and the White army, because the former can stand greater hardships than the latter.

We defeat the many with the few—this we say to all the rulers of China. Yet we also defeat the few with the many— this we say to the separate units of the enemy forces that we meet on the battlefield. This is no longer a secret and the enemy in general is by now well acquainted with our habit. But he can neither deprive us of our victories nor avoid his losses, because he does not know when and where we shall strike. That we keep secret. The Red Army's operations are as a rule surprise attacks.

7. MOBILE WARFARE

Mobile warfare or positional warfare? Our answer is mobile warfare. When we do not have a large army, when we do not have replenishments of munitions, and when there is only a single detachment of the Red Army carrying on all the fighting in each base area, positional warfare is basically useless to us. To us, positional warfare is basically something which we cannot afford either in defence or in attack.

One of the outstanding characteristics of the Red Army's operations, which ensue from the fact that the enemy is strong and the Red Army is technologically weak, is the absence of a fixed operational front.

The Red Army's operational fronts vary with its operational direction. As its operational direction is subject to change, its operational fronts are fluid. Though the general direction does not change in a given period of time, the specific directions within it may change at any moment; when we are checked in one direction, we must turn to another. If we are checked in the general direction for a given period of time, then we must even change the general direction.

In a revolutionary civil war, the operational fronts cannot be fixed, and this happened even in the Soviet Union. The difference between the Soviet Army and ours is that our fronts are even more fluid. There cannot in any war be an absolutely fixed operational front, because possible changes like victory and defeat, advance and retreat, do not allow it. Generally speaking, however, there is usually a relatively fixed operational front in war. The only exception is the war waged by the Chinese Red Army at the present stage, when the disparity in strength between it and its enemy is so great.

Fluidity of operational fronts results in fluidity of the territory of our base area. As a rule it expands and contracts from time to time, and it often happens that while one base area emerges, another is submerged. Such fluidity of our territory originates entirely from the fluidity of the war.

Affected by the fluidity of the war and of our territory, the various kinds of construction work in our base area become fluid too. A construction plan drawn up for a number of months or years is unthinkable. The frequent change of plan is all in the day's work.

The affirmation of this characteristic will be of benefit to us. We proceed with our schedules on the basis of this characteristic and must not entertain the illusion of a war of steady advance without retreat, or take alarm at the temporary fluidity of our territory and of the rear of our army, or endeavour to form concrete, long-term plans. We must adapt our thought and our action to the circumstances, ready to sit down as well as to march on, never throwing away our ration bags. It is only by making efforts in today's fluid way of life that we can secure a less fluid one for tomorrow and a settled life in the end.

The strategic directive of "regular warfare", dominant in the fifth campaign against "encirclement and annihilation", denied this fluidity and opposed so-called guerrilla-ism. Comrades who were opposed to fluidity would have liked to manage affairs in the manner of the rulers of a big state, and the result was an extraordinary, colossal instance of fluidity—the Long March of 25,000 *li*.

Our workers' and peasants' democratic republic is a state, but today it is as yet an imperfect one. Today we are still in the phase of strategic defensive in the civil war, the form of our political power is still a long way from that of a perfect state, our army is still far inferior to the enemy both in numbers and in material equipment, our territory is still very small, and our enemy will never be happy for a moment until he has destroyed us. To define our policy on this basis, we must honestly admit the guerrilla character of the Red Army rather than repudiate guerrilla-ism wholesale. It is useless to feel ashamed on this score. On the contrary, this guerrilla character is precisely our distinguishing feature, our strong point, our means for defeating the enemy. We should prepare to discard this character, but we cannot yet discard it today. Some day this character will definitely become a thing to be ashamed of and therefore to be discarded, but today it is invaluable and must be firmly retained.

"Fight when we can win and run away when we cannot"—this is the popular interpretation of our mobile warfare today. No military expert anywhere in the world would approve of only fighting and disapprove of running away, though few people run away as much as we do. In our case, generally more time is spent in marching than in fighting and we would be doing well with an average of one big battle a month. All our "running away" is for the purpose of "fighting", and all our strategic and operational directives are formulated on the basis of "fighting". Nevertheless, there are a number of situations in which it is inadvisable for us to fight: in the first place it is inadvisable to fight when the enemy force confronting us is larger than ours; secondly, it is sometimes inadvisable when the force confronting us, though not large, is very close to other enemy forces in the vicinity; thirdly, generally speaking, it is inadvisable to fight when an enemy force is not isolated and is well entrenched; fourthly, it is inadvisable to continue an engagement in which victory is not in sight. Under any of these conditions we are prepared to "run away". Such "running away" is permissible as well as necessary. The recognition of the necessity of "running away" presupposes that of the necessity of fighting. Herein lies the fundamental characteristic of the Red Army's mobile warfare.

By saying that mobile warfare is basic we do not rule out any necessary and possible warfare. It should be granted that positional warfare is to be employed both in a strategic defensive when we stubbornly defend some key positions in a containing action, and in a strategic offensive when we are confronted with an isolated, unsupported enemy force. In the past we have had considerable experience of resorting to such positional warfare to defeat the enemy; many enemy cities, blockhouses and forts have been cracked open by us and the enemy's strongly fortified field positions have been broken through by us. We have to increase our efforts and remedy our shortcomings in this respect in the future. It is entirely proper for us to advocate an attack on positions or a defence of positions as circumstances require and permit. We are opposed only to adopting positional warfare in general or placing it on an equal footing with mobile warfare at this moment, for only that is impermissible.

Has there never been, during the ten years' civil war, the slightest change in the guerrilla character of the Red Army, in its lack of fixed operational front, in the fluidity of our domain, *i.e.* the base area, or in the fluidity of the work of construction in the base area?

Yes, there have been changes.

The period from the days in the Chingkang mountains up to the first campaign against "encirclement and annihilation" in Kiangsi was the first phase in which the guerrilla character and fluidity were very prominent, the Red Army being in its infancy and the base area being yet a guerrilla area. The period from the first campaign against "encirclement and annihilation" to the third one was the second phase in which the guerrilla character and fluidity diminished considerably, the front armies having been formed, and base areas with a population of several million having come into existence. The period from the end of the third to the fifth campaign against "encircle-ment and annihilation" was the third phase in which the guerrilla character and fluidity further diminished. A central government and a revolutionary military commission had been set up. The Long March constituted the fourth phase. From the erroneous rejection of minor guerrilla warfare and minor fluidity ensued major guerrilla warfare and major fluidity. Now we are in the fifth phase. As a result of our failure in smashing the fifth campaign of "encirclement and annihila-tion" and because of the major fluidity, the Red Army and the base area have been considerably reduced; yet we have also secured a foothold in the North-west and consolidated and developed our base area—the Shensi-Kansu-Ningsia border region. The three front armies which form the main forces of the Red Army have been brought under a unified command, which is something unprecedented.

According to the nature of the strategy adopted in the different periods, it may also be said that the period from the days in the Chingkang mountains to the fourth campaign against "encirclement and annihilation" was the first phase, the fifth campaign the second, and that from the Long March to the present the third. During the fifth campaign people erroneously discarded the correct directive of the past, and today we have in turn correctly discarded the erroneous direc-tive that was adopted during the fifth campaign and have reaffirmed the former correct directive. However, we are neither discarding everything in the fifth campaign, nor reaffirming everything before it. We have only reaffirmed the merits of the past, and discarded the errors committed in the fifth counter-campaign.

There are two aspects of guerrilla-ism. One is its irregu-larity, *i.e.* its decentralisation, non-uniformity, the lack of strict discipline, the simplicity of its methods of work, etc. All these things have emerged in the Red Army's infancy, and some of them answered precisely the needs of the time. But when the Red Army reaches a higher stage, we must gradually and con-sciously eliminate them so as to make the Red Army more centralised, more uniform, more disciplined and more methodi-cal and exact in its work—in short, more regular in character.

In operational command we should also gradually and consciously reduce the guerrilla element which is no longer required at the higher stage. Refusal to make progress in this respect and obstinate adherence to the old stage are impermissible and harmful and will not benefit large-scale operations.

The other aspect is the line of mobile warfare, the guerrilla character that is still needed at present in fighting both on a strategic and an operational scale, the inevitable fluidity of the base area, the flexibility and changeability of our construction plans in the base area, and the rejection of the untimely regularisation in building up the Red Army. To deny historical facts in this connection, to oppose the retention of what is useful, to leave rashly the present stage and to rush blindly towards a "new stage" which tantalises but has no real significance for the present, are equally impermissible and harmful and will not prove of any benefit to the operations at hand.

We are now on the eve of a new stage in the Red Army's technology and organisation. We must be prepared to reorientate ourselves to it. To refuse to be thus prepared is wrong and harmful to our future warfare. When in the future the Red Army's technological and organisational conditions are changed and when the building of the Red Army enters a new stage, its operational direction will become steadier and its front more fixed; positional warfare will increase; the fluidity of the war, the fluidity of our territory and of our construction work will be greatly diminished and finally eliminated; then things that handicap us at present, such as the superiority of the enemy and his entrenched positions, will no longer handicap us.

At present we are opposed on the one hand to the erroneous measures adopted in the period when "Left" opportunism was dominant, and on the other to the revival of the many irregular features of the Red Army in its infancy, features which are no longer needed. But we should resolutely reaffirm the many valuable principles of army building, of strategy and tactics, by means of which the Red Army has won victories all along. We must sum up all that was excellent in the past into a systematised, better-developed and further-enriched military policy, in order to strive to defeat our enemy today and prepare to shift to a new stage in the future.

There are numerous problems connected with the practice of mobile warfare, such as reconnaissance, judgment, decision, combat disposition, command, camouflage, concentration, advance, deployment, assault, pursuit, surprise attack, positional assault, positional defence, encounter action, retreat, night fighting, task operations, evading the strong and attacking the weak, besieging the enemy to strike at his reinforcements, feint, anti-aircraft devices, operating when hemmed in by enemy forces, by-passing operations, consecutive operations, operations without a rear, the need for conserving strength and storing up energy, etc. These problems have assumed many special features in the history of the Red Army, features which should be methodically treated and summed up in a study of operational direction, and I will not expatiate on them here.

8. WAR OF QUICK DECISION

A strategically protracted war and a campaign or battle of quick decision are two sides of the same thing, two principles to be emphasised simultaneously in the civil war, which are also applicable in the anti-imperialist war.

The revolutionary forces grow only gradually because of the great strength of the reactionary forces; this determines the protracted nature of our war. On this score impatience is harmful and advocacy of a "quick decision" incorrect. The ten years' revolutionary war we have fought may be surprising to other countries, but for us it is only like the presentation, amplification and preliminary exposition of the theme in an "eight-legged essay"[34] with many exciting paragraphs yet to follow. There is no doubt that future developments will be greatly accelerated under the domestic and international conditions. As changes have already taken place in the international as well as the domestic situation and greater changes will possibly ensue, it can be said that we have outgrown the past state of sluggish development and isolated fighting. But we should not expect overnight successes. The plucky determination to "wipe out the enemy before breakfast" is good, but any concrete plan to "wipe out the enemy before breakfast" is inadvisable. As China's reactionary forces are backed by many imperialist powers, our revolutionary war will remain a protracted war until China's revolutionary forces have built up enough strength to break through the main positions of domestic and foreign enemies, and until the international revolutionary forces have crushed or contained a greater part of the international reactionary forces. To start from this point and formulate a strategic plan for our long-term warfare is one of the important objectives in strategic direction.

The principle of operational and tactical direction is the opposite—not protraction but quick decision. All people, ancient or modern, Chinese or foreign, demand a quick decision in a campaign or battle. They all demand a quick decision in war and always regard a time-consuming, long drawn-out war as harmful. But China's war alone must be handled with the greatest patience and treated as a protracted one. During the period when Li Li-san's line prevailed, people ridiculed our way of doing things as "boxing tactics" (i.e tactics of fighting many see-saw battles before setting out to seize the big cities), and they sneered that we could not see the victory of the revolution until our hair turned white. Such a mood of ultra-revolutionism has long been proved incorrect.

But if the criticism of these people had been applied not to strategy but to operational and tactical direction, they would have been entirely correct. The reasons are: first, there is no source of replenishment of arms and especially of ammunition for the Red Army; secondly, as the White army consists of a number of detachments and the Red Army consists of only a single detachment, our army has to prepare itself speedily for another series of uninterrupted operations after smashing one campaign of "encirclement and annihilation"; and thirdly, though the various detachments of the White army advance separately, most of them keep rather close to each other, and if we do not quickly win a battle against one of the detachments, all the others will converge upon us. For these reasons we must wage battles of quick decision. It is usual for us to finish a battle in a few hours, or a day or two. It is only under the principle of "besieging the enemy to strike at his reinforcements", aimed at beating not the besieged enemy but his reinforcements, that we are prepared for a certain degree of protraction in our siege operations; with his reinforcements, however, we still seek a quick decision. Operational and tactical directives for protracted fighting are often given in a strategic defensive when we are stubbornly defending positions on the front of containment, or in a strategic offensive when we are attacking isolated, unsupported enemy forces or eliminating White strongholds within our base area. But such protracted warfare helps rather than hinders the main force of the Red Army in prosecuting battles of quick decision.

A quick decision cannot be successfully brought about simply because one wishes for it, but requires many specific conditions. The main requirements are: thorough preparation, correct timing, concentration of a preponderant force, the tactic of encirclement and outflanking, favourable positions, and attacks on an enemy force on the move or on a stationary enemy in an unconsolidated position. Without the fulfilment of these requirements, it is impossible to bring a campaign or battle to a quick decision.

In a major campaign to smash "encirclement and annihilation" we should still apply the principle of quick decision and not the principle of protraction. For the man-power, financial resources and armed strength of the base area do not permit of protraction.

But within the general principle of quick decision we must oppose undue impatience. It is entirely necessary that the supreme military and political leadership in a revolutionary base area, having considered the conditions of the base area as well as the situation of the enemy, should not be awed by his truculence, dispirited by such hardships as are yet bearable, or dejected by occasional setbacks, but should show forbearance and endurance. The first campaign of "encirclement and annihilation" in Kiangsi was smashed from the first to the last battle in a single week; the second was smashed in barely half a month; the third dragged on for three months; the fourth took three weeks; and the fifth taxed our endurance for a whole year. When we failed to smash the fifth campaign and were forced to effect a breakthrough, a kind of unjustified rashness was then manifested on our part. The circumstances made it possible to hold out for another two or three months to rest up and retrain the troops. If that had been done and if the leadership had become a bit wiser after the breakthrough, the situation would have been very different.

For all that, the principle of shortening by all means the duration of a campaign remains in force. Although the operational and tactical plans should call for a maximum effort for concentration of troops, mobile warfare, etc., and should thus ensure the annihilation of the enemy's man-power on the interior line (in the base area) and the quick termination of the encirclement, we must, when it is proved that the campaign of "encirclement and annihilation" cannot be terminated on our interior line, employ the main forces of the Red Army to break through the enemy's encirclement and then to smash it on our own exterior line, i.e. on the enemy's interior line. Today, as the enemy has developed the strategy of building blockhouses, this will be our regular method of operation. Two months after the commencement of the fifth campaign against "encirclement and annihilation", when the Fukien Incident[35] took place, the main force of the Red Army should undoubtedly have moved speedily to the Kiangsu-Chekiang-Anhwei-Kiangsi region, with Chekiang as the centre, to sweep over the length and breadth of the area of Hangchow, Soochow, Nanking, Wuhu, Nanchang and Foochow, transforming the strategic defensive into a strategic offensive by menacing the vital positions of the enemy and challenging him to battles in the vast zones that were devoid of blockhouses. By such means we would have been able to compel the enemy forces attacking southern Kiangsi and western Fukien to turn back to defend their vital positions, to smash their attack on the base area in Kiangsi, and to render aid to the people's government in Fukien—by such means we could certainly have rendered aid to it.

As this plan was not adopted, the fifth campaign of "encirclement and annihilation" could not be broken and the people's government in Fukien could not but collapse. Although after a whole year's fighting it became inopportune for us to advance on Chekiang, yet we could still have turned to the strategic offensive in another direction by moving our main forces towards Hunan, i.e. by driving into the middle section of Hunan without entering Kweichow, and so inducing the enemy to shift from Kiangsi to Hunan and annihilating him there. As this plan was also rejected, all hope of smashing the fifth campaign of "encirclement and annihilation" was finally dashed and there was no alternative but the Long March.

9. WAR OF ANNIHILATION

The advocacy of a "contest of attrition" is unsuited to the Chinese Red Army today. It is rather ridiculous that a "contest of treasures" should be held not between one dragon god and another but between a dragon god and a beggar.[36] For the Red Army which draws upon the enemy for almost all its supplies, the basic directive is war of annihilation. Only by annihilating the enemy's man-power can we smash the campaigns of "encirclement and annihilation" and expand the revolutionary base areas. The infliction of casualties on the enemy is adopted as a means for annihilating the enemy, otherwise it is meaningless. Since we incur losses ourselves in inflicting casualties on the enemy, and yet secure replenishments by annihilating him, not only are our losses compensated but our troops are strengthened. A battle is not basically decisive that ends only in routing an enemy of preponderant strength. A battle of annihilation, on the contrary, will produce a great and immediate effect on the enemy, whoever he may be. To wound all the ten fingers of a man is not so effective as to chop one of them off; to rout ten of the enemy's divisions is not so effective as to annihilate one of them.

Our directives dealing with the first, second, third and fourth campaigns of "encirclement and annihilation" were for battles of annihilation. Though the forces annihilated in each campaign constituted only a part of the enemy's total strength, all these campaigns of "encirclement and annihilation" were nevertheless smashed. During the fifth campaign against "encirclement and annihilation," however, we adopted an opposite directive which in fact helped the enemy to attain his goal.

A battle of annihilation on the one hand, and the concentration of a preponderant force and the tactic of outflanking and encirclement on the other, are of the same significance. Without the latter there cannot be the former. Conditions such as the people's support, favourable terrain, a vulnerable enemy force and surprise operations are all indispensable for the purpose of annihilation.

Routing an enemy force or even permitting it to escape has significance only when our main force is carrying on operations of annihilation against another definite enemy force in the battle or campaign as a whole, otherwise it is meaningless. And here again the losses become justified because of the gains.

We must not allow the establishment of our own war industry to foster in us a sense of exclusive reliance on it. Our basic directive is to rely on the war industries of the imperialist countries and of our enemy at home. We have a claim on the output of the arsenals of London as well as of Hanyang, and, what is more, it is to be delivered to us by the enemy's own transport corps. This is the sober truth, not a joke.

December 1936.

A STATEMENT ON CHIANG KAI-SHEK'S STATEMENT

In Sian, Chiang Kai-shek accepted the demand of Generals Chang Hsueh-liang and Yang Hu-ch'eng and the people of the North-west for resistance to Japan[1] and, as an initial step, ordered the troops engaged in the civil war to withdraw from the provinces of Shensi and Kansu; this marked the beginning of Chiang's reversal of his ten-year-old erroneous policy. A blow is thus dealt to the intrigues of the Japanese imperialists and the Chinese punitive group[2] who deployed the troops for civil war, fomented internal dissension, and tried to put Chiang into a death trap during the Sian Incident. The disappointment of the Japanese imperialists and the Chinese punitive group is already obvious. This indication of Chiang's awakening to reason may be regarded as a sign of the Kuomintang's willingness to end its ten-year-old erroneous policy.

On December 26 Chiang Kia-shek issued a statement in Loyang, the so-called "Admonition to Chang Hsueh-liang and Yang Hu-ch'eng", which, with its ambiguity and intricacy, is indeed an interesting piece of writing among China's political documents. If Chiang really wanted to derive a profound lesson from this incident, to exert himself for the rejuvenation of the Kuomintang, to end his old erroneous policy of seeking compromise in foreign affairs, waging wars at home, and oppressing the people, so that the Kuomintang will no longer be opposed to the wishes of the people, then, as a sign of his sincerity, he should have produced a better piece of writing, one in which he politically repented of the past and opened up a new prospect for himself. The statement of December 26 cannot satisfy the demands of the masses of the Chinese people.

In Chiang's statement there is one praiseworthy passage, in which he asserts that "all promises will be kept and actions resolutely taken". It means that, although he did not sign in Sian the terms set forth by Chang and Yang, yet he is willing to accept those terms which are beneficial to the state and the nation and will keep his promise in spite of the absence of his signature. We shall see whether, after he has withdrawn his troops, Chiang will act in good faith, whether he will carry out the terms he has accepted. These terms are:

(1) to reorganise the Kuomintang and the National Government by expelling the pro-Japanese clique and admitting the anti-Japanese elements;

(2) to release the patriotic leaders in Shanghai[3] and all other political prisoners and to guarantee the freedoms and rights of the people;

(3) to end the policy of "annihilating the Communists" and to enter into an alliance with the Red Army to resist Japan;

(4) to convoke a national salvation conference of all parties, all groups, all circles, and all armies to decide on the line for fighting Japan and saving the nation from extinction;

(5) to establish relations of co-operation with countries sympathetic to China's resistance to Japan; and

(6) to adopt other specific ways and means for national salvation.

The fulfilment of these terms requires first of all good faith and also some courage. We shall judge Chiang by his actions from now on.

But in Chiang's statement there is also the remark that the Sian Incident took place under the pressure of the "reactionaries". It is a pity that Chiang did not explain what kind of people he actually meant by the "reactionaries", nor do we know how the term "reactionaries" is defined in Chiang's dictionary. The Sian Incident certainly took place under the influence of the following forces:

(1) the rise of the indignation against Japan among Chang's and Yang's troops and among the revolutionary people of the North-west;

(2) the rise of the indignation against Japan among the people of the whole country;

(3) the growth of the left-wing forces in the Kuomintang;

(4) the demand of powerful groups in various provinces for resisting Japan and for saving the nation;

(5) the Communist Party's advocacy of an anti-Japanese national united front; and

(6) the development of the world peace front. All these are undeniable facts.

What Chiang calls the "reactionaries" are none other than these forces; other people call them "revolutionaries" while he dubs them "reactionaries"—that is all.

Since Chiang Kai-shek declared in Sian that he would fight Japan in earnest, presumably he will not again use his might and main to attack the revolutionary forces immediately after his departure from Sian; for not only his own political life and that of his clique hang upon his good faith, but athwart the path of practical politics there lies before him and his clique a force that has already expanded to their disadvantage, *i.e.* the so-called punitive group which tried to put Chiang into a death trap during the Sian Incident. We therefore advise Chiang to revise his political dictionary and change the word "reactionary" into "revolutionary", for it is better to change the name and make it correspond with the facts.

Chiang should remember that, apart from the efforts of Generals Chang and Yang, leaders in the Sian Incident, he owed his safe departure from Sian to the mediation of the Communist Party. Purely for the sake of the nation's survival, the Communist Party throughout the incident stood for a peaceful settlement and made considerable efforts to achieve it. Had the civil war become more widespread and had Chang and Yang kept Chiang Kai-shek in custody for long, the development of the incident could only have been favourable to the Japanese imperialists and the Chinese punitive group. It was in these circumstances that the Communist Party resolutely exposed the intrigues of the Japanese imperialists and of the Chinese punitive group, which included Wang Ching-wei, [4] Ho Ying-sh'in, [5] and others; and resolutely advocated a peaceful settlement of the incident, which coincided, though without any previous consultation, with the views of Generals Chang Hsueh-liang and Yang Hu-ch'eng and such Kuomintang members as T. V. Soong. [6] This is precisely the view of the people throughout the country, because they bitterly detest the present civil war.

Upon his acceptance of the Sian terms, Chiang was set free. From now on the question is whether he will carry out to the letter his own words that "all promises will be kept and actions resolutely taken", and conscientiously fulfil all the terms for national salvation. The people throughout the country will no longer allow Chiang any room for procrastination or modification of the terms. If Chiang hesitates to resist Japan and delays putting his words into practice, then the revolutionary tide of the people of the whole country will certainly sweep him away. The old saying has it: "If a man does not keep his word, what is he good for?" Chiang and his clique must pay close attention to this.

If Chiang can completely cleanse the dirt of the Kuomintang's ten-year-old reactionary policy, thoroughly rectify his basic mistake of making concessions in foreign affairs, of waging wars at home, and of oppressing the people, and immediately join the anti-Japanese front by uniting with all parties and groups, and can actually take both military and political steps for national salvation, the Communist Party will naturally extend its assistance to him. The Communist Party has, early in its letter to the Kuomintang on August 25,[7] promised such assistance to Chiang and the Kuomintang. That in the case of the Communist Party "all promises will be kept and actions resolutely taken" is a fact already acknowledged by the people throughout the country for fifteen years. The people throughout the country certainly have more confidence in the words and deeds of the Communist Party than in the words and deeds of any other party or group in the country.

December 28, 1936.

THE TASKS OF THE CHINESE COMMUNIST PARTY IN THE PERIOD OF RESISTANCE TO JAPAN

This is a report delivered at the national conference of the Communist Party of China, held in Yenan, May 1937.

THE PRESENT STAGE OF DEVELOPMENT OF CHINA'S EXTERNAL AND INTERNAL CONTRADICTIONS

1. The changes in China's international relations and internal class relations, arising from the fact that the contradiction between China and Japan has become the primary one and China's internal contradiction a secondary and subordinate one, have ushered in a new stage of development in the current situation.

2. China has long been riddled by two kinds of intense and basic contradictions—the contradiction between imperialism and China and that between feudalism and the great masses of the people. In 1927 the bourgeoisie, represented by the Kuomintang, betrayed the revolution and sold the national interests to imperialism, with the result that the workers' and peasants' régime stood in sharp antagonism to the Kuomintang régime and that the Chinese Communist Party could not but shoulder alone the task of the national and democratic revolution.

3. The situation since the Incident of September 18, 1931 and especially since the series of events in North China in 1935[1] has brought about the following changes in these contradictions:

A. The contradiction between China and imperialism in general gave way to a particularly sharp one between China and Japanese imperialism. Japanese imperialism is carrying out its policy of complete conquest of China. Consequently, the contradictions between China and certain other imperialist powers have been relegated to a secondary position and the rift is widened between these imperialist powers and Japan. The Chinese Communist Party and the Chinese people are therefore faced with the task of linking the Chinese Anti-Japanese

National United Front with the world peace front. That is to say, not only should China unite with the Soviet Union which has consistently been the good friend of the Chinese people, but she should, so far as possible, oppose Japanese imperialism in conjunction with those imperialist countries that are now willing to preserve peace and oppose new wars of aggression. Our united front should aim at resisting Japan, not at opposing all imperialist powers at once.

B. The contradiction between China and Japan has brought about a change in the class relations at home and has posed the question of survival to the bourgeoisie and even the warlords; thus a change in political attitude has gradually taken place among them as well as in their parties. This places before the Chinese Communist Party and the Chinese people the task of forming an Anti-Japanese National United Front. Our united front includes the bourgeoisie and all people who agree to defend the motherland; it embodies national solidarity against a foreign foe. This task not only must be, but can be, completed.

C. The contradiction between China and Japan has changed the situation of the great masses of the people throughout the country (the proletariat, the peasantry and the urban petty bourgeoisie) and of the Communist Party as well as the policy they sponsor. More and more people have risen to fight for national salvation. Since the Incident of September 18, the Communist Party's policy of concluding on three conditions (stop attacking the revolutionary base areas, guarantee the freedom and rights of the people, and arm the people) an agreement for resisting Japan with those groups in the Kuomintang that are willing to co-operate, has been developed into a policy for establishing an anti-Japanese united front of the whole nation. In line with this development successive steps have been taken by our Party, including the August declaration[2] and the December resolution,[3] both in 1935; the abandonment of the anti-Chiang Kai-shek slogan in May,[4] the August letter to the Kuomintang,[5] the September resolution on the democratic republic,[6] and the insistence on a peaceful settlement of the Sian Incident in December, all in 1936; and the February telegram to the Third Plenary Session of the Central Executive Committee of the Kuomintang in 1937.[7]

D. In face of the contradiction between China and Japan, a change has also been brought about in the Chinese warlords' independent régimes and the civil wars among them which arose from the imperialist policy of carving out spheres of influence as well as from the semi-colonial economic conditions in China. Japanese imperialism favours such independent régimes and civil wars which facilitate its exclusive possession of China. Certain other imperialist powers, in their own interests, temporarily favour China's unity and internal peace. The Chinese Communist Party and the Chinese people, on their part, are doing their utmost to oppose civil wars and splits and to fight for peace and unity.

E. The development of the contradiction between China and Japan has, in terms of political specific gravity, reduced the significance of the contradictions at home between the classes and between political blocs, making them something secondary and subordinate. But those contradictions still exist, and have by no means dwindled or been eliminated. The same is true of the contradictions between China and imperialist powers other than Japan. Hence the following task lies before the Chinese Communist Party and the Chinese people; to adjust properly those internal and external contradictions that can and must be adjusted at present so that they dovetail into the general task of uniting to resist Japan. Hence the Chinese Communist Party's policies for peace and unification, for democratic government, for the betterment of the people's living conditions, and for negotiations with foreign countries that are opposed to Japan.

4. The first stage of the new period in the Chinese revolution, which began on December 9, 1935, came to an end when the Kuomintang's Central Executive Committee held its third plenary session in February 1937. The major events in this stage were the movements for national salvation among the students, the cultural circles and the press, the Red Army's entry into the North-west, the Communist Party's agitation and organisational work on behalf of its policy and an Anti-Japanese National United Front, the anti-Japanese strikes in Shanghai and Tsingtao,[8] Britain's stiffening of her policy towards Japan in some degree,[9] the revolt in Kwangtung and

Kwangsi,[10] the war in Suiyuan and the support given to it,[11] Nanking's more or less stiffened attitude in the Sino-Japanese talks,[12] the Sian Incident, and finally, the Third Plenary Session of the Central Executive Committee of the Kuomintang in Nanking.[13] These events all centred round the basic contradiction—the antagonism between China and Japan, and immediately round the historical need of establishing an Anti-Japanese National United Front. The basic task of the revolution at this stage was to struggle for internal peace and stop internal armed conflicts so that there would be solidarity against Japan. The Communist Party during this stage issued the call to "stop the civil war and unite against Japan", a call which in the main evoked a good response, and this provides the first necessary condition for the actual formation of an Anti-Japanese National United Front.

5. Owing to the presence of the pro-Japanese clique within it, the Third Party Session of the Central Executive Committee of the Kuomintang neither made a definite and complete change in its policy, nor solved any problems concretely. However, the pressure from the people and the developments within itself forced the Kuomintang to begin to change its erroneous policy of the past ten years, *i.e.* to turn from civil war, dictatorship and non-resistance to Japan to the direction of peace, democracy and resistance to Japan, and to begin to accept the policy of an Anti-Japanese National United Front; such an initial change was clearly seen at the Third Plenary Session of the Central Executive Committee of the Kuomintang. From now on our demand is that the Kuomintang makes a complete change in its policy. Towards that end, we and the whole people must develop even more extensively the movement for resistance to Japan and for democracy; further criticise, push and urge the Kuomintang; unite with those of its members who stand for peace, democracy and resistance to Japan; push forward its wavering and hesitating members; and combat its pro-Japanese members.

6. The present stage is the second one in the new period. The previous stage and the present one are both transitional, leading to a nation-wide armed resistance to Japan. If the principal task in the previous stage was the fight for peace, then

the principal task in the present one is the fight for democracy. We must understand that a genuine and solid Anti-Japanese National United Front cannot be established either without internal peace or without democracy in the country. Hence the fight for democracy is the central link in the revolutionary task at the present stage. If we fail to see clearly the importance of democracy and slacken our efforts in the fight for it, we shall be unable to establish a genuine and solid Anti-Japanese National United Front.

THE STRUGGLE FOR DEMOCRACY AND FREEDOM

7. Japanese imperialism is intensifying its preparations for invading China Proper. In concert with the predatory wars for which Hitler and Mussolini are intensively preparing in the West, Japan in the East is exerting her utmost to bring about according to a definite plan the conditions for subjugating China at a single stroke—the internal military, political, economic and ideological conditions, the international diplomatic conditions, and the fostering of the pro-Japanese forces in China. Japan's propaganda about so-called "Sino-Japanese collaboration" and her mildness in certain diplomatic measures stem precisely from a tactical necessity on the eve of her war of aggression. China is now approaching the critical point of survival or extinction, and we must quicken the pace of our preparations for resisting Japan and saving the nation. We do not oppose preparation; what we oppose is the theory of long-term preparation, as well as the carefree idleness and self-indulgence of civil officials and military officers which imperil the nation; such things actually help the enemy and must be cleaned up speedily.

8. Political, military, economic and educational preparations for national defence are all necessary for armed resistance to save the nation and none of them should be delayed ior a moment. And the winning of political democratic rights is a central link in ensuring victory for armed resistance. Armed resistance requires nation-wide peace and solidarity, but without democratic rights, peace, though won, cannot be consolidated and internal solidarity cannot be strengthened.

Armed resistance requires the mobilisation of the people, but without democratic rights there is no way to proceed with mobilisation. Without consolidated peace and solidarity, without the mobilisation of the people, our armed resistance will face the same disastrous prospect as that in Abyssinia. Mainly because of her feudal régime, Abyssinia could not consolidate her internal solidarity or call forth the activity of her people, and consequently she failed. Without democracy China cannot establish a genuine and solid Anti-Japanese National United Front and accomplish its tasks.

9. China must at once start democratic reforms in the following two respects:

First with regard to the political system, the one-party and one-class reactionary government of the Kuomintang must be changed into a democratic form of government based on the co-operation of all parties and all classes. In this respect, we must first change the anti-democratic procedure of the elections to, and convocation of, the National Assembly, carry out democratic elections to the Assembly and ensure its freedom to conduct meetings, in order that a truly democratic constitution shall be drawn up, a truly democratic parliament be convoked, and a truly democratic government be elected to carry out truly democratic policies. Only by so doing can internal peace be really consolidated, internal armed rivalry discontinued, and internal solidarity strengthened so that the whole nation will be united to resist the foreign foe. The Japanese imperialists may begin their attacks before we complete our reforms. Thus in order to resist Japan's attacks at any moment and crush them thoroughly, we must quickly go ahead with the reforms and prepare to accomplish them fully during the armed resistance. The people of the whole country and the patriots in all parties should discard their old indifference towards the National Assembly and the constitution, and concentrate their strength on this specific movement for a national assembly and a constitution, a movement that has significance for national defence; they should severely criticise the Kuomintang, the party in power, pushing it and urging it to give up its one party and one class dictatorship, and to act according to the people's views. In the next few months of this year, a broad democratic movement must be started throughout the country, with the immediate objective of completing the democratisation of the national assembly and the constitution.

The second respect concerns the people's freedom of speech, assembly and association. Without these freedoms, the democratic reform of the political system cannot be carried out, nor can the people be mobilised to take part in the war for victoriously defending the motherland and recovering the lost territory. In the coming few months the democratic movement of the people throughout the country should strive for the minimum fulfilment of this task, including the release of political prisoners and the removal of the ban on political parties, etc. The democratic reform of the political system and the freedoms and rights of the people form an important part in the programme of the Anti-Japanese National United Front and are also necessary conditions for establishing a genuine and solid Anti-Japanese National United Front.

10. Our enemies—the Japanese imperialists, the Chinese collaborators, the pro-Japanese clique and the Trotskyites— have been trying with all their might to wreck every measure for peace and solidarity, democracy and freedom, and armed resistance to Japan. In the past when we were fighting strenuously for peace and solidarity, they did their utmost to foment civil wars and splits. At present and in the near future, as we fight strenuously for democracy and freedom, they will no doubt try again to wreck us. Their general objective is to foil us in our task of armed resistance in defence of the motherland, and to realise their aggressive plan for subjugating China. In the fight for democracy and freedom, from now on we must exert ourselves not only to conduct propaganda, agitation and criticism among the die-hards of the Kuomintang and the backward sections of the people, but to expose in every possible way and fight resolutely the intrigues of Japanese imperialism and its jackals, the pro-Japanese clique and the Trotskyites, for invading China.

11. For the sake of peace, democracy and armed resistance, and for the sake of establishing an Anti-Japanese National United Front, the Chinese Communist Party, in a telegram to the Third Plenary Session of the Central Executive Committee

of the Kuomintang, has pledged to them the following four things:

(1) the government in the Shensi-Kansu-Ningsia revolutionary base area that is under the leadership of the Communist Party shall be renamed as the Government of the Special Region of the Republic of China and the Red Army redesignated as part of the National Revolutionary Army, and they will accept the direction of the Central government in Nanking and its Military Council respectively;

(2) a thoroughly democratic system shall be introduced in areas under the Government of the Special Region;

(3) the policy of overthrowing the Kuomintang by armed force shall be discontinued; and

(4) the confiscation of the land of the landlords shall be discontinued. These pledges are necessary as well as permissible. Only thus can we, in line with the changes in terms of political specific gravity in China's internal and external contradictions, change the situation of antagonism between the two régimes at home and achieve solidarity against the enemy. These are principled and conditional concessions, made with the aim of obtaining in return what is necessary for the whole nation— peace, democracy and armed resistance. But there are limits to the concessions. To preserve the Communist Party's leadership in the Special Region and the Red Army, and to preserve the Communist Party's independence and freedom of criticism in its relations with the Kuomintang —such are the limits of the concessions beyond which it is impermissible to go. Concessions are to be made by both parties: the Kuomintang abandons the policy of civil war, dictatorship and non-resistance to the foreign foe, and the Communist Party abandons the policy of maintaining a rival régime. We exchange the latter for the former and resume our co-operation with the Kuomintang to fight for national salvation. To describe this as the capitulation of the Communist Party would only be Ah-Q-ism[14] or malicious slander.

12. Does the Communist Party agree with the Three People's Principles? Our answer is: Yes.[15]

The Three People's Principles have undergone historical changes. The revolutionary Three People's Principles of

Dr. Sun Yat-sen, resolutely put into practice by Dr. Sun in co-operation with the Communist Party, did win the confidence of the people and become the banner of the victorious revolution of 1924-7. In 1927, however, the Kuomintang persecuted the Communists (*i.e.* by the campaign to "purge the party"[16] and the anti-Communist war), and carried out an opposite policy, courting defeat for the revolution and landing the nation in a crisis; consequently, the people lost confidence in the Three People's Principles. At present, when the national crisis is extremely grave, the Kuomintang cannot continue to rule in the same old way without a change, and consequently the people of the whole country and the patriotic elements of the Kuomintang again urgently demand co-operation between the two parties. Therefore, what perfectly meets the historical need of the Chinese revolution and ought to be clearly grasped by every member of the Communist Party is that, reviving the spirit of the Three People's Principles, the two parties resume their co-operation in foreign policy under the Principle of Nationalism which aims at winning China's independence and liberation, and in domestic policy under the Principle of Democracy which aims at realising democracy and freedom, and the Principle of People's Welfare which aims at promoting the people's welfare, and furthermore jointly lead the people to put these resolutely into practice.

Communists will never abandon their ideal of socialism and communism, and will reach the stage of socialism and communism by going through that of bourgeois-democratic revolution. The Chinese Communist Party has its own political and economic programme. Its maximum programme is one of socialism and communism, which is different from the Three People's Principles. Even its programme in the period of democratic revolution is more thorough than that of any other party in the country. But the Communist Party's programme for a democratic revolution and the programme of the Three People's Principles as proclaimed by the Kuomintang's First National Congress are basically not in conflict with each other. Therefore, we not only accept the Three People's Principles, but are also willing to put them resolutely into practice; and furthermore we request the Kuomintang and call upon the whole people to put the Three People's Principles into practice jointly with ourselves. We hold that the Communist Party, the Kuomintang and the people of the whole country should struggle jointly for the three great objectives of securing national independence, democracy and freedom, and people's welfare.

13. Was our past slogan for a workers' and peasants' democratic republic wrong? No, it was not. Since the bourgeoisie, and particularly the big bourgeoisie, withdrew from the revolution, went over to the side of imperialism and the feudal forces, and turned into the enemy of the people, the only motive forces of revolution that remained were the proletariat, the peasantry and the urban petty bourgeoisie; the only revolutionary party that remained was the Communist Party; and the responsibility of organising the revolution could not but fall on the shoulders of the Communist Party, the only revolutionary party. The Communist Party alone continued to hold aloft the banner of revolution, preserved the revolutionary tradition, proposed the slogan of a workers' and peasants' democratic republic, and struggled arduously for this slogan for many years. The slogan of a workers' and peasants' democratic republic does not run counter to the bourgeois-democratic revolution but stands for the resolute carrying out of this revolution. None of the policies we adopt in our actual struggle has been unsuitable for this task. Our policy, including the confiscation of the land of the landlords and the enforcement of the eight-hour working day, never went beyond the private property system of capitalism and we did not at all put socialism into practice.

Who should compose the new democratic republic? They should be the proletariat, the peasantry, the urban petty bourgeoisie, the bourgeoisie, and all persons in the country who agree to undertake a national and democratic revolution, and the republic should be an alliance of these classes for the national and democratic revolution. The salient feature here is the inclusion of the bourgeoisie; this is due to the fact that under the present circumstances the bourgeoisie can participate once more in the resistance to Japan, and the party of the proletariat should not reject it but bring it into line and ally with it again for the common struggle, so as to facilitate the progress of the Chinese revolution. In order to end armed conflicts at home, the Communist Party is willing to discontinue the policy of confiscating the land of the landlords by force and is prepared to solve the agrarian problem by legislative and other appropriate means in the course of establishing the new democratic republic. Whether China's land should belong to the Japanese or to the Chinese—that is a problem which has to be solved first and foremost. Since the agrarian problem of the peasants is to be solved on the premise of national defence, it is entirely necessary for us to turn from the method of confiscation by force to new and appropriate methods.

It is correct both to have put forward the slogan of a workers' and peasants' democratic republic in the past and to drop it today.

14. In order to build up a national united front for a joint resistance to the enemy, certain internal contradictions must be adequately solved: the principle here is that this should strengthen and expand the Anti-Japanese National United Front and not weaken or reduce it. At the stage of the democratic revolution, contradictions and struggles between the classes, parties and political blocs in the country are unavoidable, but we can and must stop those struggles that are detrimental to solidarity and the resistance to Japan (such as civil war, partisan rivalry, local independent régimes, feudal political and economic oppression versus the policy of insurrections and excessive economic demands harmful to the resistance), and continue those struggles that benefit solidarity and the resistance to Japan (such as struggles for freedom of criticism, for independence of parties, and for the improvement of the political and economic conditions of the people).

15. In accord with the general task of fighting for an Anti-Japanese National United Front and a unified democratic republic, the tasks of the Red Army and the anti-Japanese base area are:

(1) To fit in with the conditions of the Anti-Japanese War, the Red Army should immediately be reorganised into the National Revolutionary Army, and, by improving its military,

political and cultural education, be made the model army group in the Anti-Japanese War.

(2) To change our base areas into a component part of the nation, to put into practice a democratic system adapted to new conditions, to reorganise the peace-preservation forces, and to clean up collaborators and saboteurs, so that these areas become the model region in resisting Japan and building up democracy.

(3) To carry out essential economic construction and improve the living conditions of the people in this region.

(4) To carry out essential cultural construction.

OUR RESPONSIBILITY OF LEADERSHIP

16. It is a law proved in China's history that, because of its economic and political flabbiness, the Chinese bourgeoisie which can take part in fighting imperialism and feudalism in certain circumstances will vacillate and turn traitor in others. History has therefore decided that China's anti-imperialist and anti-feudal bourgeois-democratic revolution can be completed not under the leadership of the bourgeoisie, but only under the leadership of the proletariat. Furthermore, it is only by fully calling forth the perseverance and thoroughness of the proletariat in the democratic revolution that the inherent vacillation and lack of thoroughness of the bourgeoisie can be overcome and that the revolution will not become abortive. Is the proletariat to follow the bourgeoisie, or is the bourgeoisie to follow the proletariat? This question of the responsibility of leadership in the Chinese revolution is the pivot upon which the success of the revolution depends. The experience of 1924–7 shows how the revolution forged ahead when the bourgeoisie followed the political leadership of the proletariat and how it suffered defeat as soon as the proletariat became politically the tail of the bourgeoisie (for which the Communist Party was responsible).[17] History should not be repeated.

In the present circumstances, the Anti-Japanese National United Front cannot be established, the objectives of peace, democracy and armed resistance cannot be attained, the motherland cannot be defended, and a unified democratic

republic cannot be realised without the political leadership of the proletariat and its party. This is proved by the
fact that the bourgeoisie, represented by the Kuomintang,
which for a long time dared not endorse the Anti-Japanese
National United Front initiated by the Communist Party, is
even today very passive and conservative. This situation
increases the responsibility of the political leadership of the
proletariat and its party. To function as the general staff in the
cause of resisting Japan and saving the nation is a responsibility
that the Communist Party cannot shift to others and an obliga-
tion it cannot refuse to fulfil.

17. How does the proletariat, through its party, exercise
political leadership over all the revolutionary classes in the
country?

Firstly, it puts forward a basic political slogan in accordance
with the development of history and, for the realisation of this
slogan, slogans of action for each stage of development as well
as for every major event. For instance, we have put forward
the basic slogan of "an Anti-Japanese National United Front
and a unified democratic republic", as well as the slogans, "end
the civil war", "fight for democracy", and "put up armed
resistance", as the specific aims of the concerted action of the
people throughout the country, for without such specific aims
there can be no political leadership to speak of.

Secondly, when the whole country has gone into action in
accordance with these specific aims, the proletariat, especially
its vanguard—the Communist Party, should fully demonstrate
its boundless activity and loyalty so as to set an example in
realising these specific aims. In fighting to fulfil all the tasks
of the Anti-Japanese National United Front and the democratic republic, Communists should see to it that they are the
most far-sighted, the most ready to make self-sacrifice, the most
resolute, and the most open-minded in sizing up a situation,
and that they rely on the majority of the masses and win the
support of the masses.

Thirdly, on the principle that in so far as its fixed political
objectives are not forfeited, it establishes proper relations
with its allies, and develops and consolidates this alliance.

Fourthly, by the expansion of the ranks of the Communist

Party, their unity in ideology, and the strictness of their discipline. The Communist Party's political leadership over the people of the whole country is brought about precisely through putting into practice the above-mentioned essentials. These essentials basically ensure our political leadership as well as the complete victory of the revolution against the possibility of any disruption through our allies' vacillation.

The Communist Party's political leadership over the people of the whole country is brought about precisely through putting into practice the above-mentioned essentials. These essentials basically ensure our political leadership as well as the complete victory of the revolution against the possibility of any disruption through our allies' vacillation.

18. When peace is realised and two-party co-operation established, the old methods of struggle, organisation and work which we have adopted to maintain a rival régime should be changed. Such a change will be mainly one from military to peaceful methods, and from illegal to legal methods. It is not easy to make such a change and we will have to learn from the very beginning. The retraining of cadres thus becomes a principal link.

19. Many comrades have raised questions concerning the nature and prospect of the democratic republic. Our answer is: as to its class nature, it is an alliance of all revolutionary classes, and as to its prospect, it may head towards socialism. Our democratic republic is to be established in the course of national armed resistance; it is to be established under the leadership of the proletariat; and it is to be established in the new international circumstances (the victory of socialism in the Soviet Union and the eve of a new period in the development of world revolution). Therefore, though according to the social and economic conditions it will still be a bourgeois-democratic state, yet according to the concrete political conditions it ought to be one based on the alliance of the working class, the peasantry, the petty bourgeoisie and the bourgeoisie, and therefore different from bourgeois republics in general. Thus, regarding perspectives, although it still may face towards capitalism, at the same time it may turn towards socialism, and the party of the Chinese proletariat should strive hard for the latter prospect.

20. To struggle against closed-door sectarianism and adventurism and at the same time against tail-ism is a necessary condition for carrying out the Party's tasks. In our Party's mass work there is a traditional tendency towards serious closed-door-ism, arrogant sectarianism, and adventurism—a bad tendency which hinders the Party from establishing an Anti-Japanese National United Front and winning over the majority of the masses. It is absolutely necessary to eliminate this tendency in every specific line of work. What we demand is to rely on the majority and to concern ourselves with the situation as a whole. We cannot allow a revival of Ch'en Tu-hsiu's tail-ism, which reflected bourgeois reformism in the ranks of the proletariat. It will inevitably lead the revolution to defeat if we weaken the Party's stand, blur its features, or sacrifice the interests of the workers and peasants in order to meet the demands of bourgeois reformists. What we demand is to carry out resolute revolutionary policies and win a complete victory in the bourgeois-democratic revolution. In order to overcome the bad tendencies mentioned above, it is entirely necessary to raise the Marxist-Leninist theoretical level of the whole Party, because Marxism-Leninism alone is the compass which can guide the Chinese revolution to victory.

May 3, 1937.

STRIVE TO WIN OVER MILLIONS UPON MILLIONS OF THE MASSES TO THE ANTI-JAPANESE NATIONAL UNITED FRONT

This is the concluding speech made at the national conference of the Communist Party of China in May 1937.

Comrades, after the discussion in the last few days, all comrades except a few who raised dissenting opinions have given their approval to my report, "The Tasks of the Chinese Communist Party in the Period of Resistance to Japan". In my concluding speech I shall discuss these dissenting opinions first because they are of some importance, and then take up some other problems.

THE QUESTION OF PEACE

Our Party has struggled for internal peace for nearly two years. After the Third Plenary Session of the Kuomintang's Central Executive Committee, we said that peace was already won, that the stage of "winning peace" was over, and that the new task was "consolidating peace"; and we also pointed out that this was linked with "winning democracy", *i.e.* consolidating peace through winning democracy. Some comrades, however, argue that this view cannot be maintained. Their conclusion is necessarily either an opposite one or one wavering midway. For they say, "Japan is retreating,[1] Nanking is vacillating all the more, and the contradiction between nations is dwindling while the contradiction within the country is intensifying". According to this appraisal, there naturally cannot be a new stage or new tasks, and the situation will return to the old stage, or even become worse. I consider this view incorrect.

When we said that peace was won, we did not mean that it was consolidated; on the contrary, we said that it was not. The realisation of peace and the consolidation of peace are two different things. Since there are Japanese imperialists, collaborators and pro-Japanese elements, history may reverse its course for a while and peace may meet with setbacks. But it is a fact that since the Sian Incident peace has been brought about by various factors (Japan's basic policy of invasion, the support of peace on the part of the Soviet Union as well as Britain, the United States and France, the pressure of the Chinese people, the Communist Party's peace policy during the Sian Incident and its abandonment of the policy of maintaining a rival régime, the differentiation within the bourgeoisie, the differentiation within the Kuomintang, etc.), and Chiang Kai-shek alone cannot make or unmake peace. To unmake it, he must fight against forces in many quarters and draw closer to the Japanese imperialists and the pro-Japanese elements. Beyond doubt, the Japanese imperialists and pro-Japanese elements are still endeavouring to prolong civil war in China. Therefore peace is not yet consolidated. In these circumstances our conclusion is not that we return to the old slogans, "stop the civil war" and "win peace", but that we should go a step farther and propose the new slogan, "win democracy"; only thus can we consolidate peace and bring about armed resistance. Why do we propose those three slogans which form an organic whole—"consolidate peace", "win democracy", and "bring about armed resistance"? Because we want to push the chariot-wheels of our revolution forward, and because circumstances already allow us to do so. If we denied the new stage and the new tasks, if we denied that the Kuomintang is "beginning to change", and, as a logical conclusion, denied of necessity the achievement made by the forces of all the groups in their struggle for peace during the past year and a half, then we would merely stay put at the same old position without taking a single step forward.

Why have these comrades made such an incorrect appraisal? The reason is that in examining the current situation they start not from the fundamentals but from any number of partial and transient phenomena (Sato's diplomacy, the Soochow trial,[2] the suppression of strikes, the eastward transfer of the Northeastern army,[3] and General Yang Hu-ch'eng's journey abroad,[4] etc.) and then draw a dismal picture. We say that the Kuomintang has begun to change, and we also add that it has not changed completely. It is inconceivable that the Kuomintang's ten-year-old reactionary policy should be completely changed without any new efforts, without more and greater efforts on our part and on the part of the people. Quite a number of people, reputedly "Lefts", used to denounce the Kuomintang bitterly and had during the Sian Incident advocated putting Chiang to death and "fighting our way out of the Tung pass";[5] but as soon as peace was realised and events like the Soochow trial occurred, they asked in a tone of astonishment, "Why does Chiang Kai-shek still do such things?" They should understand that the Communists and Chiang Kai-shek are not gods and are moreover not isolated persons but belong to a party or a class. The Communist Party has the ability to push the revolution forward step by step, but it has not the ability to clear away in a day all the bad things in the country. Chiang Kai-shek and the Kuomintang have all begun to change, but without greater efforts of the whole people, they certainly cannot wash off in a day the cumulative filth of the past ten years. We say that the movement is heading for peace, democracy and armed resistance, but we are not saying that such old pernicious things as civil war, dictatorship and non-resistance can be swept clean without any effort. It is only through struggle and hard work, and over a long period too, that the old pernicious things and the filth can be removed, and setbacks in the revolution, or its possible reversal, be averted.

"They are bent on destroying us." Yes, they always attempt to destroy us—I fully admit the correctness of this appraisal, and one must have fallen asleep not to have reckoned with this point. But the question is whether there has been a change in their method of destruction. I think there has been. A change from the policy of war and massacre to that of reform and deceit, from a stiff policy to a soft one, and from a military policy to a political one. Why has there been such a change? The bourgeoisie and the Kuomintang, confronted with Japanese imperialism, cannot but temporarily seek an ally in the proletariat, just as we have to seek an ally in the bourgeoisie. We should take this as the point of departure in considering the question. Internationally it is for the same reason that the French government has changed from being the Soviet Union's enemy into its ally.[6] Domestically our military tasks have also changed into political ones. We have no use for plotting and scheming; our aim is to unite with all those of the bourgeoisie and the Kuomintang who are sympathetic with the resistance to Japan in order jointly to defeat Japanese imperialism.

THE QUESTION OF DEMOCRACY

"It is wrong to emphasise democracy, and one should only emphasise resistance to Japan; without direct action against Japan, there can be no democratic movement; the majority of the people only want resistance to Japan but not democracy— it would be all right if only we could have another December 9 Movement."[7]

Let me first raise a few questions: Could one say in the past stage (from the December 9 Movement of 1935 to the Third Plenary Session of the Kuomintang's Central Executive Committee in February 1937) that most people only wanted resistance to Japan but not peace? Was it wrong to have emphasised peace in the past? Could there be a movement for peace without direct action against Japan (the Sian Incident and the Third Plenary Session of the Kuomintang's Central Executive Committee took place just after the resistance to Japan in Suiyuan had ended, and at this very moment we do not yet have anything like the resistance to Japan in Suiyuan or the December 9 Movement)? Who doesn't know that in order to resist Japan there must be peace, that without peace there can be no resistance to Japan, and that peace is the condition for resistance? All the direct and indirect actions against Japan in the previous stage (beginning with the December 9 Movement and ending with the Third Plenary Session of the Kuomintang's Central Executive Committee) centred round the struggle for peace; peace was the central link in the previous stage, the most essential thing in the anti-Japanese movement in the previous stage.

For the resistance to Japan, democracy is likewise the most essential thing in the new stage, and to work for democracy is to work for armed resistance to Japan. Resistance to Japan and democracy are conditions for each other, just as resistance to Japan and peace, peace and democracy, are conditions for each other. Democracy is the guarantee for resistance to Japan, and resistance to Japan can provide favourable conditions for the development of the democratic movement.

We hope there may be, and in fact there will be, many direct and indirect struggles against Japan in the new stage; these will expedite resistance to Japan and give great help to the democratic movement. But the core and essence of the revolutionary task which history entrusts to us is the winning of democracy. "Democracy", "democracy"—is it wrong to harp on it? I don't think so.

"Japan is retreating, Britain and Japan are approaching a state of equilibrium between themselves, and Nanking is vacillating all the more." This is an unwarranted worry that has arisen from an ignorance of the laws of historical development. If Japan finally drew back because of a revolution at home, that would be helpful to the Chinese revolution, that would be what we hope for and would mark the beginning of the collapse of the world front of aggression. Why should we worry? But that, after all, is not the case; Sato's diplomacy is a preparation for a major war and a major war is facing us. Britain's wavering policy can only be fruitless; this is determined by the divergence between the interests of Britain and Japan. If Nanking vacillates for long, it will become the enemy of the people of the whole country and its own interest will not allow this. A temporary phenomenon of retrogression cannot displace the general law of history. Hence one can deny neither the new stage nor the proposed task of democracy. Furthermore, the slogan of democracy can be adapted to any circumstances, and it is obvious to everybody that among the Chinese there is a deficiency, not a surplus, of democracy. Moreover, as shown by actual conditions, to point out the new stage and propose the task of democracy is to move a step closer to armed resistance. Events have moved forward; let us not attempt to drag them back.

"Why should the national assembly be emphasised?" Because it is something that may affect the whole of our life, because it is the bridge from reactionary dictatorship to democracy, because it forms part of national defence, and because it is legal. To recover eastern Hopeh and northern Chahar, to combat smuggling, to oppose "economic collaboration",[8] etc., as many comrades have proposed, are all quite correct, but these do not in the least contradict democracy or the convocation of the national assembly; the two are complementary to each other, but the central thing is the national assembly and civil rights.

It is entirely correct and indisputable that the day-to-day struggle against the Japanese and the people's struggle for livelihood must be co-ordinated with the democratic movement. But the central and essential thing at the present stage is democracy and freedom.

THE QUESTION OF THE PROSPECT OF THE REVOLUTION

A few comrades raised this question and my answer can only be brief.

Of an essay consisting of two parts, the second part can be written well only when the first part is. To give resolute leadership to the democratic revolution is the condition for winning victory for socialism. We are fighting for socialism, and in this we are different from any other followers of the revolutionary Three People's Principles. Our present effort is directed towards the great objective of the future, and if we lose sight of it, we shall no longer be Communists. But if we relax our efforts today, we shall not be Communists either.

We advocate the theory of the continuous development of revolution,[9] of the continuous development of a democratic revolution into a socialist revolution. The democratic revolution will undergo several stages of development, all under the slogan of a democratic republic. It is a long process of struggle from the hegemony of the bourgeoisie to the hegemony of the proletariat, a process of winning leadership, which depends on the condition that the Communist Party raises the level of consciousness and organisation of the proletariat, the level of consciousness and organisation of the peasantry and the urban petty bourgeoisie.

The staunch ally of the proletariat is the peasantry, and next to it, the urban petty bourgeoisie. It is the bourgeoisie that will dispute with us for hegemony.

It depends on the strength of the masses and on our correct policies to overcome the vacillation and the lack of thoroughness of the bourgeoisie; otherwise the bourgeoisie will turn round to overcome the proletariat.

A transition involving no shedding of blood is what we hope for and what we must fight strenuously for; the result will depend on the strength of the masses. We advocate the theory of the continuous development of revolution, but not the Trotskyite theory of a permanent revolution.[10] We stand for the attainment of socialism through all the necessary stages of the democratic republic. We are opposed to tail-ism, but we are also opposed to adventurism and ultra-revolutionism.

It is a Trotskyite approach, with which we cannot agree, to reject the participation of the bourgeoisie in the revolution because it can only be temporary and to describe the alliance with the anti-Japanese section of the bourgeoisie (in a semi-colonial country) as capitulationism. Such an alliance today is precisely a bridge that has to be crossed on our way to socialism.

THE QUESTION OF CADRES

To guide a great revolution there must be a great party and many excellent cadres. It would be impossible to carry out an unprecedented great revolution in a country like China with a population of 450,000,000 if the leadership were but a small group founded on a narrow basis; it would also be impossible if the leaders and cadres in the party were all narrow-minded and lacking in a sense of proportion, without insight or ability. The Chinese Communist Party has long been and still is a big political party in spite of its losses in the period of reaction; it has many good leaders and cadres, but there are not enough of them. The organisation of our Party must be expanded throughout the country; it must purposefully train tens of thousands of cadres and several hundreds of excellent mass leaders. These cadres and leaders must understand Marxism-Leninism, they must have political insight and ability to work, they must be full of the spirit of self-sacrifice, capable of solving problems independently; and they must remain firm in the midst of difficulties and work loyally and devotedly for the nation, the class and the Party. Only through these people can the Party be linked with its membership and the masses, and only through the firm leadership these people give to the masses can the Party succeed in defeating the enemy.

These people must not be tainted with selfishness, individual heroism or vaingloriousness, indolence or passivity, or arrogant sectarianism; they must be the selfless heroes of the nation and the class—such are the qualities and style in work which the members, cadres and leaders of the Party should have. Such is precisely the spiritual legacy handed down to us by tens of thousands of our members, thousands of our cadres, and scores of our best leaders who laid down their lives. Beyond doubt we ought to acquire these qualities in order to remould ourselves into better people and raise ourselves to a higher revolutionary level. But that is not enough; we have also to regard it as a task to discover many new cadres and leaders throughout the Party and throughout the country. Our revolution depends on the cadres, just as Stalin has said, "Cadres decide everything".[11]

THE QUESTION OF DEMOCRACY WITHIN THE PARTY

To attain our aims, democracy within the Party is necessary. To make the Party powerful, we must rely on practising the democratic centralism of the Party to arouse the activity of the whole Party. In the period of reaction and civil war centralism was more manifest. In the new period centralism should be closely linked with democracy. Through the practice of democracy the activity of the whole Party will be called forth. Through calling forth the activity of the whole Party great numbers of cadres will be steeled and brought to the fore, the remnants of sectarianism will be eliminated, and the whole Party will become solidly united as if forged from steel.

THE SOLIDARITY OF THE CONFERENCE AND THE SOLIDARITY OF THE WHOLE PARTY

The dissenting opinions on political problems expressed at this conference have, after clarification, given way to agreement, and the old difference between the Party centre's line and the line of retreat adopted under the leadership of certain comrades has also been settled[12]—an indication that our Party is already very solidly united. Such a solidarity is the most important basis for the present national and democratic revolution, for only through the solidarity of the Communist Party can the solidarity of the whole class and of the whole nation be achieved, and only through the solidarity of the whole class and of the whole nation can the enemy be defeated and the national and democratic revolution accomplished.

STRIVE TO WIN OVER MILLIONS UPON MILLIONS OF THE MASSES TO THE ANTI-JAPANESE NATIONAL UNITED FRONT

Our correct political line and solid unity aim at winning over millions upon millions of the masses to the Anti-Japanese National United Front. The broad masses of the proletariat, the peasantry and the urban petty bourgeoisie stand in need of our propaganda, agitation and organisation. And we must make further efforts to form an alliance with the anti-Japanese section of the bourgeoisie. To turn the Party's line into a mass line, we must make efforts, efforts long and persistent, constantly unrelenting, extraordinarily strenuous, and patient and tireless. Without such efforts, we can succeed in nothing. The formation and consolidation of the Anti-Japanese National United Front as well as the fulfilment of its tasks and the establishment of a democratic republic in China cannot in the least be separated from the efforts to win over the masses. If through these efforts millions upon millions of the masses are won over and come under our leadership, then our revolutionary task can be speedily fulfilled. Through our efforts we shall surely overthrow Japanese imperialism and realise complete national liberation as well as social liberation.

May 7, 1937.

ON PRACTICE

ON THE RELATION BETWEEN KNOWLEDGE AND PRACTICE—
BETWEEN KNOWING AND DOING

There used to be a group of doctrinaires in the Chinese Communist Party who, disregarding the experience of the Chinese revolution and denying the truth that "Marxism is not a dogma but a guide to action", for a long time bluffed people with words and phrases torn out of their context from Marxist works. There was also a group of empiricists who, for a long time clinging to their own fragmentary experience, could neither understand the importance of theory for revolutionary practice nor see the whole of the revolutionary situation, and thus worked blindly, though industriously. The Chinese revolution in 1931-4 was greatly damaged by the incorrect ideas of these two groups of comrades, particularly by those of the doctrinaires who, wearing the cloak of Marxism, misled large numbers of comrades. This article was written to expose from the viewpoint of Marxist theory of knowledge such subjectivist mistakes in the Party as doctrinairism and empiricism, especially doctrinairism. As its stress is laid on exposing doctrinaire subjectivism which belittles practice, this article is entitled "On Practice". These views were originally presented in a lecture at the Anti-Japanese Military and Political College in Yenan.

Pre-Marxist materialism could not understand the dependence of knowledge upon social practice, namely, the dependence of knowledge upon production and class struggle, because it examined the problem of knowledge apart from man's social nature, apart from his historical development.

To begin with, the Marxist regards man's productive activity as the most fundamental practical activity, as the determinant of all other activities. In his cognition man, depending mainly upon activity in material production, gradually understands nature's phenomena, nature's characteristics, nature's laws, and the relations between himself and nature; and through productive activity he also gradually acquires knowledge in varying degrees about certain human interrelations. None of such knowledge can be obtained apart from productive activity. In a classless society every person, as a member of society, joins in effort with the other members, enters into certain relations of production with them, and engages in productive activity to solve the problem of material life. In the various kinds of class society, on the other hand, members of society of all classes also enter, in different ways, into certain relations of production and engage in productive activity to solve the problem of material life. This is the primary source from which human knowledge develops.

Man's social practice is not confined to productive activity; there are many other forms of activity—class struggle, political life, scientific and artistic activity; in short, man in society participates in all spheres of practical social life. Thus in his cognition man, besides knowing things through material life, knows in varying degrees the various kinds of human interrelations through political life and cultural life (both of which are closely connected with material life). Among these the various forms of class struggle exert a particularly profound influence on the development of man's knowledge. In a class society everyone lives within the status of a particular class and every mode of thought is invariably stamped with the brand of a class.

The Marxist holds that productive activity in human society develops step by step from a lower to a higher level, and consequently man's knowledge, whether of nature or of society, also develops step by step from a lower to a higher level, that is, from the superficial to the deep and from the one-sided to the many-sided. For a very long period in history man was confined to a merely one-sided understanding of social history because, on the one hand, the biased views of the exploiting classes constantly distorted social history and, on the other, small-scale production limited man's outlook. It was only when the modern proletariat emerged along with the big forces of production (large-scale industry) that man could acquire a comprehensive, historical understanding of the development of social history and turn his knowledge of society into science, the science of Marxism.

' The Marxist holds that man's social practice alone is the criterion of the truth of his knowledge of the external world. In reality, man's knowledge becomes verified only when, in the process of social practice (in the process of material production, of class struggle, and of scientific experiment), he achieves the anticipated results. If man wants to achieve success in his

work, that is, to achieve the anticipated results, he must make
his thoughts correspond to the laws of the objective world
surrounding him; if they do not correspond, he will fail in
practice. If he fails he will derive lessons from his failure, alter
his ideas, so as to make them correspond to the laws of the
objective world, and thus turn failure into success; this is what
is meant by "failure is the mother of success", and "a fall into
the pit, a gain in your wit".

The theory of knowledge of dialectical materialism raises
practice to the first place, holds that human knowledge cannot
be separated the least bit from practice, and repudiates all
incorrect theories which deny the importance of practice or
separate knowledge from practice. Thus Lenin said, "Practice
is higher than (theoretical) knowledge because it has not only
the virtue of universality, but also the virtue of immediate
reality".[1]

Marxist philosophy, *i.e.* dialectical materialism, has two most
outstanding characteristics: one is its class nature, its open
declaration that dialectical materialism is in the service of the
proletariat; the other is its practicality, its emphasis on the
dependence of theory on practice, emphasis on practice as
the foundation of theory which in turn serves practice. In
judging the trueness of one's knowledge or theory, one cannot depend upon one's subjective feelings about it, but upon
its objective result in social practice. Only social practice can
be the criterion of truth. The viewpoint of practice is the first
and basic viewpoint in the theory of knowledge of dialectical
materialism.[2]

But how after all does human knowledge arise from practice
and in turn serve practice? This becomes clear after a glance at
the process of development of knowledge.

In fact man, in the process of practice, sees at the beginning
only the phenomena of various things, their separate aspects,
their external relations. For instance, a number of visitors
come to Yenan on a tour of observation: in the first day or two,
they see the topography, the streets and the houses of Yenan;
meet a number of people; attend banquets, evening parties
and mass meetings; hear various kinds of talk; and read various
documents—all these being the phenomena of things, the

separate aspects of things, the external relations between such things. This is called the perceptual stage of knowledge, namely, the stage of perceptions and impressions. That is, various things in Yenan affect the sense organs of the members of the observation group, give rise to their perceptions, and leave on their minds many impressions, together with an idea of the general external relations between these impressions: this is the first stage of knowledge. At this stage, man cannot as yet form profound concepts or draw conclusions that conform with logic.

As social practice continues, things that give rise to man's perceptions and impressions in the course of his practice are repeated many times; then a sudden change (a leap) takes place in the process of knowledge in man's mind, resulting in concepts. Concepts as such no longer represent the phenomena of things, their separate aspects, or their external relations, but embrace their essence, their totality and their internal relations. Conception and perception are not only quantitatively but also qualitatively different. Proceeding farther and employing the method of judgment and inference, we can then draw conclusions that conform with logic. What is described in the *Tale of the Three Kingdoms* as "knitting the brows one hits upon a stratagem", or in our workaday language as "let me think it over", refers precisely to the procedure of man's manipulation of concepts in his mind to form judgments and inferences. This is the second stage of knowledge.

When our visitors, the members of the observation group, have collected various kinds of data and, furthermore, "thought them over", they can come to the following judgment: "the Communist Party's policy of the Anti-Japanese National United Front is thorough, sincere and honest". Having made this judgment, they can, if they are honest about unity for national salvation, go a step farther and draw the following conclusion: "the Anti-Japanese National United Front can succeed". In the whole process of man's knowledge of a thing, conception, judgment and inference constitute the more important stage, the stage of rational knowledge. The real task of knowledge is to arrive at thought through perception, at a gradual understanding of the internal contradictions of objective things, their laws and the internal relations of various processes, that is, at logical knowledge. To repeat, the reason why logical knowledge is different from perceptual knowledge is that perceptual knowledge concerns the separate aspects, the phenomena, the external relations of things; whereas logical knowledge takes a big stride forward to reach the wholeness, the essence and the internal relations of things, discloses the internal contradictions of the surrounding world, and is therefore capable of grasping the development of the surrounding world in its totality, in the internal relations between all its aspects.

Such a dialectical-materialist theory of the process of development of knowledge, based on practice and proceeding from the superficial to the deep, was not put forward by anybody before the rise of Marxism. Marxist materialism for the first time correctly solved the problem of the process of development of knowledge, pointing out both materialistically and dialectically the deepening process of knowledge, the process of how perceptual knowledge turns into logical knowledge through the complex and regularly recurrent practices of production and class struggle of man in society. Lenin said: "The abstract concept of matter, of a law of nature, of economic value or any other scientific (*i.e.* correct and basic, not false or superficial) abstraction reflects nature more deeply, truly and fully."[3] Marxism-Leninism holds that the characteristics of the two stages of the process of knowledge are that, at the lower stage, knowledge appears in perceptual form, while at the higher stage it appears in logical form; but both stages belong to a single process of knowledge. Perception and reason are different in nature, but not separate from each other; they are united on the basis of practice.

Our practice proves that things perceived cannot be readily understood by us and that only things understood can be more profoundly perceived. Perception only solves the problem of phenomena; reason alone solves the problem of essence. Such problems can never be solved apart from practice. Anyone who wants to know a thing has no way of doing so except by coming into contact with it, *i.e.* by living (practising) in its surroundings.

In feudal society it was impossible to know beforehand the laws of capitalist society, because, with capitalism not yet on the scene, the corresponding practice did not exist. Marxism could only be the product of capitalist society. In the age of free, competitive capitalism, Marx could not have known specifically beforehand some of the special laws pertaining to the era of imperialism, because imperialism—the last stage of capitalism—had not yet emerged and the corresponding practice did not exist; only Lenin and Stalin could take up this task.

Apart from their genius, the reason why Marx, Engels, Lenin and Stalin could work out their theories is mainly their personal participation in the practice of the contemporary class struggle and scientific experimentation; without this no amount of genius could bring success. The saying "a scholar does not step outside his gate, yet knows all the happenings under the sun" was mere empty talk in the technologically undeveloped old times; and although this saying can be realised in the present age of technological development, yet the people with real first-hand knowledge are those engaged in practice, and only when they have obtained "knowledge" through their practice, and when their knowledge, through the medium of writing and technology, reaches the hands of the "scholar", can the "scholar" know indirectly "the happenings under the sun".

If a man wants to know certain things or certain kinds of things directly, it is only through personal participation in the practical struggle to change reality, to change those things or those kinds of things, that he can come into contact with the phenomena of those things or those kinds of things; and it is only during the practical struggle to change reality, in which he personally participates, that he can disclose the essence of those things or those kinds of things and understand them. This is the path to knowledge along which everyone actually travels, only some people, distorting things deliberately, argue to the contrary. The most ridiculous person in the world is the "wiseacre" who, having gained some half-baked knowledge by hearsay, proclaims himself "the world's number one"; this merely shows that he has not taken a proper measure of himself.

The question of knowledge is one of science, and there must not be the least bit of insincerity or conceit; what is required is decidedly the reverse—a sincere and modest attitude. If you want to gain knowledge you must participate in the practice of changing reality. If you want to know the taste of a pear you must change the pear by eating it yourself. If you want to know the composition and properties of atoms you must make experiments in physics and chemistry to change the state of atoms. If you want to know the theory and methods of revolution, you must participate in revolution. All genuine knowledge originates in direct experience. But man cannot have direct experience in everything; as a matter of fact, most of our knowledge comes from indirect experience, *e.g.* all knowledge of ancient times and foreign lands. To the ancients and foreigners, such knowledge comes from direct experience; if, as the direct experience of the ancients and foreigners, such knowledge fulfils the condition of "scientific abstraction" mentioned by Lenin, and scientifically reflects objective things, then it is reliable, otherwise it is not. Hence a man's knowledge consists of two parts and nothing else, of direct experience and indirect experience. And what is indirect experience to me is nevertheless direct experience to other people. Consequently, taking knowledge in its totality, any kind of knowledge is inseparable from direct experience.

The source of all knowledge lies in the perception through man's physical sense organs of the objective world surrounding him; if a person denies such perception, denies direct experience, and denies personal participation in the practice of changing reality, then he is not a materialist. That is why the "wiseacres" are ridiculous. The Chinese have an old saying: "How can one obtain tiger cubs without entering the tiger's lair?" This saying is true of man's practice as well as of the theory of knowledge. There can be no knowledge apart from practice.

To make clear the dialectical-materialist process of knowledge arising from the practice of changing reality—the gradually deepening process of knowledge—a few concrete examples are further given below:

In its knowledge of capitalist society in the first period of its practice—the period of machine-smashing and spontaneous struggle—the proletariat, as yet in the stage of perceptual knowledge, only knew the separate aspects and external relations of the various phenomena of capitalism. At that time the proletariat was what we call a "class in itself". But when this class reached the second period of its practice (the period of conscious, organised, economic struggle and political struggle), when through its practice, through its experiences gained in long-term struggles, and through its education in Marxist theory, which is a summing-up of these experiences by Marx and Engels according to scientific method, it came to understand the essence of capitalist society, the relations of exploitation between social classes, and its own historical task, and then became a "class for itself".

Similarly with the Chinese people's knowledge of imperialism. The first stage was one of superficial, perceptual knowledge, as shown in the indiscriminate anti-foreign struggles of the Movement of the T'aip'ing Heavenly Kingdom, the Boxer Movement, etc. It was only in the second stage that the Chinese people arrived at rational knowledge, when they saw the internal and external contradictions of imperialism, as well as the essence of the oppression and exploitation of China's broad masses by imperialism in alliance with China's compradors and feudal class; such knowledge began only about the time of the May 4 Movement of 1919.

Let us also look at war. If those who direct a war lack war experience, then in the initial stage they will not understand the profound laws for directing a particular war (e.g. our Agrarian Revolutionary War of the past ten years). In the initial stage they merely undergo the experience of a good deal of fighting, and what is more, suffer many defeats. But from such experience (of battles won and especially of battles lost), they are able to understand the inner thread of the whole war, namely, the laws governing that particular war, to understand strategy and tactics, and consequently they are able to direct the war with confidence. At such a time, if an inexperienced person takes over the command, he, too, cannot understand the true laws of war until after he has suffered a number of defeats (after he has gained experience).

We often hear the remark made by a comrade when he has

not the courage to accept an assignment: "I have no confidence." Why has he no confidence? Because he has no systematic understanding of the nature and conditions of the work, or because he has had little or even no contact with this kind of work; hence the laws governing it are beyond him. After a detailed analysis of the nature and conditions of the work, he will feel more confident and become willing to do it. If, after doing the work for some time, this person has gained experience in it, and if moreover he is willing to look at things with an open mind and does not consider problems subjectively, one-sidedly and superficially, he will be able to draw conclusions as to how to proceed with his work and his confidence will be greatly enhanced. Only those are bound to stumble who look at problems subjectively, one-sidedly and superficially and, on arriving at a place, issue orders or directives in a self-complacent manner without considering the circumstances, without viewing things in their totality (their history and their present situation as a whole), and without coming into contact with the essence of things (their qualities and the internal relations between one thing and another).

Thus the first step in the process of knowledge is contact with the things of the external world; this belongs to the stage of perception. The second step is a synthesis of the data of perception by making a rearrangement or a reconstruction; this belongs to the stage of conception, judgment and inference. It is only when the perceptual data are extremely rich (not fragmentary or incomplete) and are in correspondence to reality (not illusory) that we can, on the basis of such data, form valid concepts and carry out correct reasoning.

Here two important points must be emphasised. The first, a point which has been mentioned before, but should be repeated here, is the question of the dependence of rational knowledge upon perceptual knowledge. The person is an idealist who thinks that rational knowledge need not be derived from perceptual knowledge. In the history of philosophy there is the so-called "rationalist" school which admits only the validity of reason, but not the validity of experience, regarding reason alone as reliable and perceptual experience as unreliable; the mistake of this school consists in turning things upside down. The rational is reliable precisely because it has its source in the perceptual, otherwise it would be like water without a source or a tree without roots, something subjective, spontaneous and unreliable. As to the sequence in the process of knowledge, perceptual experience comes first; we emphasise the significance of social practice in the process of knowledge precisely because social practice alone can give rise to man's knowledge and start him on the acquisition of perceptual experience from the objective world surrounding him. For a person who shuts his eyes, stops his ears and totally cuts himself off from the objective world, there can be no knowledge to speak of. Knowledge starts with experience—this is the materialism of the theory of knowledge.

The second point is that knowledge has yet to be deepened, the perceptual stage of knowledge has yet to be developed to the rational stage—this is the dialectics of the theory of knowledge. [4] It would be a repetition of the mistake of "empiricism" in history to hold that knowledge can stop at the lower stage of perception and that perceptual knowledge alone is reliable while rational knowledge is not. This theory errs in failing to recognise that, although the data of perception reflect certain real things of the objective world (I am not speaking here of idealist empiricism which limits experience to so-called introspection), yet they are merely fragmentary and superficial, reflecting things incompletely instead of representing their essence. To reflect a thing fully in its totality, to reflect its essence and its inherent laws, it is necessary, through thinking, to build up a system of concepts and theories by subjecting the abundant perceptual data to a process of remodelling and reconstructing—discarding the crude and selecting the refined, eliminating the false and retaining the true, proceeding from one point to another, and going through the outside into the inside; it is necessary to leap from perceptual knowledge to rational knowledge. Knowledge which is such a reconstruction does not become emptier or less reliable; on the contrary, whatever has been scientifically reconstructed on the basis of practice in the process of knowledge is something which, as Lenin said, reflects objective things more deeply, more truly, more fully. As against this, the vulgar plodders, respecting experience yet despising theory, cannot take a comprehensive view of the entire objective process, lack clear direction and long-range perspective, and are self-complacent with occasional successes and peep-hole views. Were those persons to direct a revolution, they would lead it up a blind alley.

The dialectical-materialist theory of knowledge is that rational knowledge depends upon perceptual knowledge and perceptual knowledge has yet to be developed into rational knowledge. Neither "rationalism" nor "empiricism" in philosophy recognises the historical or dialectical nature of knowledge, and although each contains an aspect of truth (here I am referring to materialist rationalism and empiricism, not to idealist rationalism and empiricism), both are erroneous in the theory of knowledge as a whole. The dialectical-materialist process of knowledge from the perceptual to the rational applies to a minor process of knowledge (*e.g.* knowing a single thing or task) as well as to a major one (*e.g.* knowing a whole society or a revolution).

But the process of knowledge does not end here. The statement that the dialectical-materialist process of knowledge stops at rational knowledge, covers only half the problem. And so far as Marxist philosophy is concerned, it covers only the half that is not particularly important. What Marxist philosophy regards as the most important problem does not lie in understanding the laws of the objective world and thereby becoming capable of explaining it, but in actively changing the world by applying the knowledge of its objective laws. From the Marxist viewpoint, theory is important, and its importance is fully shown in Lenin's statement: "Without a revolutionary theory there can be no revolutionary movement."[5] But Marxism emphasises the importance of theory precisely and only because it can guide action. If we have a correct theory, but merely prate about it, pigeon-hole it, and do not put it into practice, then that theory, however good, has no significance.

Knowledge starts with practice, reaches the theoretical plane via practice, and then has to return to practice. The active function of knowledge not only manifests itself in the active leap from perceptual knowledge to rational knowledge, but also—and this is the more important—in the leap from rational knowledge to revolutionary practice. The knowledge which enables us to grasp the laws of the world must be redirected to the practice of changing the world, that is, it must again be applied in the practice of production, in the practice of the revolutionary class struggle and revolutionary national struggle, as well as in the practice of scientific experimentation. This is the process of testing and developing theory, the continuation of the whole process of knowledge.

The problem of whether theory corresponds to objective reality is not entirely solved in the process of knowledge from the perceptual to the rational as described before, nor can it be completely solved in this way. The only way of solving it completely is to redirect rational knowledge to social practice, to apply theory to practice and see whether it can achieve the anticipated results. Many theories of natural science are considered true, not only because they were so considered when natural scientists originated them, but also because they have been verified in subsequent scientific practice. Similarly, Marxism-Leninism is considered true not only because it was so considered when Marx, Engels, Lenin and Stalin scientifically formulated it but also because it has been verified in the subsequent practice of revolutionary class struggle and revolutionary national struggle. Dialectical materialism is a universal truth because it is impossible for anyone to get away from it in his practice. The history of human knowledge tells us that the truth of many theories is incomplete and that this incompleteness is remedied only through the test of practice. Many theories are incorrect, and it is through the test of practice that their incorrectness will be rectified. This is the reason why practice is called the criterion of truth and why "the standpoint of life, of practice, should be first and fundamental in the theory of knowledge".[6] Stalin well said: "Theory becomes aimless if it is not connected with revolutionary practice, just as practice gropes in the dark if its path is not illumined by revolutionary theory."[7]

When we get to this point, is the process of knowledge completed? Our answer is: it is and yet it is not. When man in society devotes himself to the practice of changing a certain objective process at a certain stage of its development (whether changing a natural or social process), he can, by the reflection of the objective process in his thought and by the functioning of his own subjective activity, advance his knowledge from the perceptual to the rational and bring forth ideas, theories, plans or programmes which on the whole correspond to the laws of that objective process; he then puts these ideas, theories, plans or programmes into practice in the same objective process; and the process of knowledge as regards this concrete process can be considered as completed if, through the practice in that objective process, he can realise his preconceived aim, viz. if he can turn or on the whole turn these preconceived ideas, theories, plans or programmes into facts. For example, in the process of changing nature, such as in the realisation of an engineering plan, the verification of a scientific hypothesis, the production of a utensil or instrument, the reaping of a crop; or in the process of changing society, such as in the victory of a strike, the victory of a war, the fulfilment of an educational plan—all these can be considered as the realisation of pre-conceived aims. But generally speaking, whether in the practice of changing nature or of changing society, people's original ideas, theories, plans or programmes are seldom realised without any change whatever. This is because people engaged in changing reality often suffer from many limitations: they are limited not only by the scientific and technological conditions, but also by the degree of development and revelation of the objective process itself (by the fact that the aspects and essence of the objective process have not yet been fully disclosed). In such a situation, ideas, theories, plans or programmes are often altered partially and sometimes even wholly along with the discovery of unforeseen circumstances during practice. That is to say, it does happen that the original ideas, theories, plans or programmes fail partially or wholly to correspond to reality and are partially or entirely incorrect. In many instances, failures have to be repeated several times before erroneous knowledge can be rectified and made to correspond to the laws of the objective process, so that subjective things can be transformed into objective things, viz. the anticipated results can be achieved in practice. But in any case, at such a point, the process of man's knowledge of a certain objective process at a certain stage of its development is regarded as completed.

As regards man's process of knowledge, however, there can be no end to it. As any process, whether in the natural or social world, advances and develops through its internal contradictions and struggles, man's process of knowledge must also advance and develop accordingly. In terms of social movement, not only must a true revolutionary leader be adept at correcting his ideas, theories, plans or programmes when they are found to be erroneous, as we have seen, but he must also, when a certain objective process has already advanced and changed from one stage of development to another, be adept at making himself and all his fellow revolutionaries advance and revise their subjective ideas accordingly, that is to say, he must propose new revolutionary tasks and new working programmes corresponding to the changes in the new situation. Situations change very rapidly in a revolutionary period; if the knowledge of revolutionaries does not change rapidly in accordance with the changed situation, they cannot lead the revolution towards victory.

It often happens, however, that ideas lag behind actual events; this is because man's knowledge is limited by a great many social conditions. We oppose the die-hards in the revolutionary ranks whose ideas, failing to advance with the changing objective circumstances, manifest themselves historically as Right opportunism. These people do not see that the struggles arising from contradictions have already pushed the objective process forward, while their knowledge has stopped at the old stage. This characterises the ideas of all die-hards. With their ideas divorced from social practice, they cannot serve to guide the chariot-wheels of society; they can only trail behind the chariot grumbling that it goes too fast, and endeavour to drag it back and make it go in the opposite direction.

We also oppose the phrase-mongering of the "Leftists". Their ideas are ahead of a given stage of development of the objective process: some of them regard their fantasies as truth; others, straining to realise at present an ideal which can only be realised in the future, divorce themselves from the practice of the majority of the people at the moment and from the realities of the day and show themselves as adventurist in their actions. Idealism and mechanistic materialism, opportunism and adventurism, are all characterised by a breach between the subjective and the objective, by the separation of knowledge from practice. The Marxist-Leninist theory of knowledge, which is distinguished by its emphasis on social practice as the criterion of scientific truth, cannot but resolutely oppose these incorrect ideologies. The Marxist recognises that in the absolute, total process of the development of the universe, the development of each concrete process is relative; hence, in the great stream of absolute truth, man's knowledge of the concrete process at each given stage of development is only relatively true. The sum total of innumerable relative truths is the absolute truth. [8]

The development of the objective process is one full of contradictions and struggles. The development of the process of man's knowledge is also one full of contradictions and struggles. All the dialectical movements of the objective world can sooner or later be reflected in man's knowledge. As the process of emergence, development and disappearance in social practice is infinite, the process of emergence, development and disappearance in human knowledge is also infinite. As the practice directed towards changing objective reality on the basis of definite ideas, theories, plans or programmes develops farther ahead each time, man's knowledge of objective reality likewise becomes deeper each time. The process of change in the objective world will never end, nor will man's knowledge of truth through practice. Marxism-Leninism has in no way summed up all knowledge of truth, but is ceaselessly opening up, through practice, the road to the knowledge of truth. Our conclusion is for the concrete and historical unity of the subjective and the objective, of theory and practice, and of knowing and doing, and against all incorrect ideologies, whether Right or "Left", which depart from concrete history. With society developed to its present stage, it is upon the shoulders of the proletariat and its party that, from historical necessity, the responsibility for correctly understanding and changing the world has fallen. This process of the practice of changing the world, determined on the basis of scientific knowledge, has already reached a historic moment in the world and in China, a moment of such importance as human history has never before witnessed, *i.e.* a moment for completely dispelling the darkness in the world and in China and bringing about such a world of light as never existed before.

The struggle of the proletariat and revolutionary people in changing the world consists in achieving the following tasks: to remould the objective world as well as their own subjective world—to remould their faculty of knowing as well as the relations between the subjective world and the objective world. Such a remoulding has already been effected in one part of the globe, namely, the Soviet Union. The people there are still expediting this remoulding process. The people of China and the rest of the world are either passing, or will pass, through such a remoulding process. And the objective world which is to be remoulded includes the opponents of remoulding, who must undergo a stage of compulsory remoulding before they can pass to a stage of conscious remoulding. When the whole of mankind consciously remoulds itself and changes the world, the era of world communism will dawn.

To discover truth through practice, and through practice to verify and develop truth. To start from perceptual knowledge and actively develop it into rational knowledge, and then, starting from rational knowledge, actively direct revolutionary practice so as to remould the subjective and the objective world. Practice, knowledge, more practice, more knowledge; the cyclical repetition of this pattern to infinity, and with each cycle, the elevation of the content of practice and knowledge to a higher level. Such is the whole of the dialectical materialist theory of knowledge, and such is the dialectical materialist theory of the unity of knowing and doing.

July 1937.

NOTES

ANALYSIS OF THE CLASSES IN CHINESE SOCIETY

1. A group of unscrupulous fascist-minded politicians who formed the Chinese *Etatiste* Youth League, later renamed the Chinese Youth Party. Subsidised by the imperialists and the reactionary cliques in power, these counter-revolutionaries made a career out of opposing the Communist Party and the Soviet Union. *Etatism* is used to translate *"Kuochia-*ism" to distinguish it from the usual English rendering of Kuomintang which is the *Nationalist* Party. In theory the Chinese *Etatistes* also laid more emphasis on the state than on the people.

2. As a veteran member of the Kuomintang and Chiang Kai-shek's partner in commodity speculation in Shanghai, Tai carried on an anti-Communist agitation after Sun Yat-sen's death in 1925 and prepared the ground ideologically for Chiang Kai-shek's *coup d'état* in 1927. For years he served as Chiang's faithful jackal in counter-revolutionary activities. Driven to despair by the imminent doom of Chiang's régime, he committed suicide in February 1949.

3. Organ of the Association for the Study of Constitutional Government, a political group then supporting the warlords of the Northern clique.

4. With the help of the Chinese Communist Party, Sun Yat-sen decided in 1923 to reorganise the Kuomintang, bring about co-operation between the Kuomintang and the Communist Party, and admit the Communists into his party. Furthermore, in January 1924, he convened the Kuomintang's First National Congress in Canton, and laid down the three cardinal policies of alliance with Russia, co-operation with the Communists, and assistance to the peasants and workers. Comrades Mao Tse-tung, Li Ta-chao, Lin Po-ch'u and Ch'u Ch'iu-pai attended the Congress and played a great role in launching the Kuomintang on the revolutionary path. They were elected regular or alternate members of the Central Executive Committee of the Kuomintang.

5. Here Comrade Mao refers to the middle peasants as later defined in *How to Analyse the Classes in the Rural Areas.*

6. The God of Wealth in Chinese folklore.

7. This refers to the national anti-imperialist movement in protest against the massacre of Chinese people by the British police in Shanghai on May 30, 1925. In May 1925, strikes broke out in the Japanese-owned textile mills in Tsingtao and Shanghai and spread on a gigantic scale. The Japanese imperialists and their jackals, the warlords of the Northern clique, proceeded to suppress them. On May 15 the management of a Japanese mill in Shanghai shot and killed a worker named Ku Cheng-hung and wounded more than ten others. In Tsingtao, eight workers were butchered by the reactionary government on May 28. Thereupon two thousand students in Shanghai started a movement in the foreign concessions on May 30, appealing to the public to support the workers and agitating for the abolition of the concessions. They succeeded in rallying more than ten thousand people in front

of the police headquarters of the British concession, shouting the slogans "Down with imperialism!" and "People of China, unite!" The British police instantly opened fire on the crowd, killing and wounding many students. This was the notorious May 30 Massacre, which immediately aroused the people's indignation throughout the country and led to widespread demonstrations and strikes of workers, students and shopkeepers, culminating in an anti-imperialist movement of enormous dimensions.

8. By the overwhelming majority of the semi-tenant peasants, Comrade Mao here refers to the poor peasants who work partly on their own land and partly on land they rent from others.

9. Shop assistants in China belong to different strata. Here Comrade Mao refers to the largest stratum. Another stratum, whose economic status is even lower, lead the life of the proletariat.

10. *Tou*, a Chinese measure of capacity. A standard (market) *tou* is equivalent to 0·285 bushel; a *sheng* is $\frac{1}{10}$ of a *tou*.

11. In early 1922, seamen at Hongkong and the crews of the Yangtze river steamships went on strike. The seamen held out stubbornly for eight weeks. After a bitter struggle in which much blood was shed, the British imperialist authorities in Hongkong were forced to agree to increase wages, lift the ban on the seamen's union, release the strikers under arrest, and indemnify the families of the martyrs. Shortly afterwards the crews of the Yangtze river steamships began a strike, which lasted two weeks and also ended in victory.

12. Immediately after its founding in 1921 the Chinese Communist Party set about organising the railway workers. In 1922–3 strikes took place under the Party's leadership on all the main lines. The best known is the great strike on the Peking-Hankow railway which began on February 4, 1923 and was a fight for the right to organise a general union for the whole line. On February 7 Wu P'ei-fu and Hsiao Yao-nan, warlords of the Northern clique supported by British imperialism, carried out a ruthless slaughter of the strikers. This is known as the February 7 Massacre.

13. The Kailan strike took place in October 1922. The "Kailan coal mines", an inclusive name for the Kaiping and Lwanchow (Lanchow) coalfields in Hopeh province, form a large, contiguous coal-mining area where over fifty thousand workers were employed at that time. During the Boxer Movement of 1900 the British imperialists wrested the Kaiping mines from China, and the Chinese subsequently organised the Lwanchow Coal Mining Company. Later, when the British secured control of both coalfields, they formed the Kailan Mining Administration by consolidating the two companies.

The Tsiaotso miners struck from July 1 to August 9, 1925. The well-known coal mines of Tsiaotso are in the north-western section of Honan province.

14. Shameen, a section of the city of Canton, was held on lease by the British imperialists. In July 1924 the British imperialist authorities there issued a police decree requiring all Chinese to present passes bearing their photos on leaving or entering the area, while foreigners could move in and out freely. The workers in Shameen struck in protest on July 15 and the British were forced to annul the decree.

15. The general strikes broke out on June 1, 1925 in Shanghai and on June 19 in Hongkong. More than 200,000 workers took part in Shanghai and 250,000 in Hongkong. With the support of the people throughout the country the Hongkong strikers held out for sixteen months and staged the longest strike in the history of the world labour movement.

16. Chihli was the name of the present Hopeh province. The then three north-eastern provinces, Fengtien, Kirin and Heilungkiang now form China's North-east.

17. These secret societies were backward, primitive forms of organisation found among the people. Their members were mainly bankrupt peasants, un-employed handicraftsmen, and *lumpen*-proletarians, who under the feudal conditions of China drew together on the common ground of some religion or superstition and formed numerous organisations of a patriarchal pattern and of different names. Some of these organisations even possessed arms. Through these the *lumpen*-proletarians sought to help each other in social and economic life and on occasions fought the bureaucrats and landlords who oppressed them. Obviously such backward organisations could not provide a way out from their predicament for the peasants and handicraftsmen. Furthermore, they often degenerated into the tools of the landlords and bureaucrats and, because of this and of their wanton destructiveness, some turned into reactionary forces. In his counter-revolutionary *coup d'état* of 1927, Chiang Kai-shek utilised them to disrupt the unity of the toiling masses and to destroy the revolution. Since the rise of the powerful modern proletariat, however, the peasants, under the leadership of the working class, have formed organisations of an entirely new type, and those primitive, backward societies have consequently lost the justification for their existence.

REPORT OF AN INVESTIGATION INTO THE PEASANT MOVEMENT IN HUNAN

1. Hunan was then the storm-centre of the peasant movement in China.

2. Then ruler of Hunan and agent of the warlords of the Northern clique.

3. The revolution that ended the autocratic rule of the Manchu dynasty. On October 10, 1911, under the influence of the bourgeois and petty-bourgeois revolutionary groups, a section of the imperial "New Army" staged an uprising in Wuchang, provincial capital of Hupeh. Similar uprisings in other provinces followed in rapid succession and the Manchu régime soon crumbled. On New Year's Day, 1912, the Provisional Government of the Republic of China was inaugurated in Nanking with Sun Yat-sen as President. This revolution at first triumphed through an alliance of the bourgeoisie with the peasants, the workers and the urban petty bourgeoisie, but finally failed because its leading groups took to compromise. Giving the peasants no real benefits and yielding to the pressure of the imperialist and feudal forces, they let political power slip into the hands of Yuan Shih-k'ai, founder of the Northern clique of warlords.

4. These were the virtues of Confucius, as described by one of his disciples.

5. "Going beyond the proper limit to right a wrong" is an old Chinese phrase. It means that, though the wrong is righted, the proper limit has been exceeded in righting it. This phrase has often been used as a pretext to prevent thorough-going measures and to justify mere patching and tinkering. It implies that the established order of things should not be utterly destroyed, but only certain remedial measures need be introduced for its betterment. Thus it provides a convenient formula for the reformists and the opportunists within the revolutionary ranks. Here Comrade Mao Tse-tung is refuting

such people. When he says in the text, "To right a wrong, we must go beyond the proper limit; otherwise the wrong cannot be righted", he means that mass revolutionary measures, not reformist-revisionist measures, must be taken to end the old feudal order.

6. As Chiang's counter-revolutionary stand was not yet fully revealed when units of the Northern Expedition Army were marching into the Yangtze valley in the winter of 1926 and the spring of 1927, the peasant masses still regarded him as a revolutionary. The landlords and rich peasants disliked him and spread the rumour that the Northern Expedition Army was defeated and Chiang wounded in the leg. It was not until April 12, 1927, when Chiang staged his counter-revolutionary *coup d'état* in Shanghai and elsewhere, and began to massacre the workers, suppress the peasant movement and attack the Communist Party, that he was unmasked as a downright counter-revolutionary. It was also then that the landlords and rich peasants began to support him.

7. Kwangtung was the first revolutionary base to be established in the period of the First Revolutionary Civil War (1924-7).

8. Wu P'ei-fu, one of the best-known warlords of the Northern clique, belonged to the Chihli (Hopeh) faction together with Ts'ao K'un. He supported Ts'ao as his leader and helped him to win the Presidency in 1923 through open bribery of the Parliament. The two were thus generally referred to as "Ts'ao-Wu". Ever since 1920, when he defeated Tuan Ch'i-jui, warlord of the Anhwei faction, Wu P'ei-fu as an agent of Anglo-American imperialism became the real master of the Northern warlord régime at Peking. On February 7, 1923 he ordered the massacre of the workers of the Peking-Hankow railway who were then on strike. In 1924 he was defeated by Chang Tso-lin in the "war between the Chihli and Fengtien factions"—Fengtien, now divided into the provinces of Liaotung and Liaosi, was then the leading province in Chang's domain and thus became the name of his faction. Wu was thus ousted from the Peking régime. In 1926, however, the two adversaries, Wu and Chang, were reconciled by their respective masters, the British and Japanese imperialists, and Wu returned to power. When the Northern Expedition Army fought its way northward from Kwangtung he was the first warlord to be overthrown.

9. The Three People's Principles—Nationalism, Democracy, and the People's Welfare—were proposed by Sun Yat-sen as guiding principles for China's bourgeois-democratic revolution. In the *Manifesto of the First National Congress of the Kuomintang*, issued in 1924, he reinterpreted these principles, defining his Nationalism as the fight against imperialism and pledging active support for the workers' and peasants' movements. The *old* Three People's Principles thus gave way to the *new*, which embody the three cardinal policies of alliance with Russia, co-operation with the Communists, and assistance to the peasants and workers. The *new* Three People's Principles of the three cardinal policies served as the political basis of Kuomintang-Communist co-operation during the First Revolutionary Civil War period. (*See* "On New Democracy", Vol. III of the *Selected Works*.)

10. A leading city in Kiangsi province, on the Yangtze river.

11. The Chinese phrase for "long live" is *wansui*, *i.e.* "ten thousand years", the traditional salute to the emperor which has become a synonym for "emperor".

12. They should not have been allowed to join. In 1927, however, the peasant masses were still unaware of this point.

13. A system of selective service in ancient China.

14. Here Comrade Mao Tse-tung refers to the farm labourers (the rural proletariat) and the *lumpen*-proletarians in the countryside.
15. The rural semi-proletariat.
16. Of the Kuomintang.
17. A warlord of Kweichow. His troops held the western section of Hunan.
18. A deposit in cash or kind, often amounting to a considerable part of the value of the land, was generally placed by a tenant with his landlord as a condition of tenancy. Though supposed to be a guarantee for payment of rent, it actually represented a form of extra exploitation.
19. This was a surcharge imposed on the peasants by the régime of the bullies and the gentry in addition to the regular land tax.
20. Though military head of a province under the régime of the warlords of the Northern clique, the military governor actually controlled both the troops and the civil administration and was virtually dictator in the province. He was always in league with the imperialists and maintained a feudal-militarist independent régime in his province.
21. The house-to-house regular militia was one of the armed forces in the countryside. It was so named because almost every household was obliged to send people into it. After the defeat of the revolution in 1927, the militia was taken over by the landlords and in many places was turned into the armed force of the counter-revolution.
22. Many of the county organisations of the Kuomintang under the leadership of the Kuomintang's Central Executive Committee in Wuhan were then pursuing the three cardinal policies of Dr. Sun Yat-sen. (*See* Note 9 to this article.) They represented the revolutionary alliance of the Communists, the left-wingers of the Kuomintang, and other revolutionaries.
23. Pao Cheng, commonly known as "His Excellency Pao", was once prefect of Kaifeng, capital of the North Sung dynasty (A.D. 960–1127). He was famous in popular legend as an upright official and a fearless, impartial judge who had a knack for passing true judgments on all the cases he tried.
24. This metaphor of archery is from Mencius. Here it means that while Communists should develop the political consciousness of the peasants to the fullest extent, they should leave it to the peasants' own initiative to abolish superstitious and other bad practices.
25. A method of fortune-telling in China by studying the two cyclic characters respectively for the year, month, day and hour of the birth of a person.
26. This refers to the superstitious belief that the location of the ancestors' graves exerts influence on the fortunes of the descendants. The geomancer claims that he can tell whether the site and its surroundings are auspicious.
27. Kuan Yu, a warrior in the epoch of the Three Kingdoms (A.D. 196–264), was widely worshipped by the Chinese as the God of Loyalty and War.
28. Two generals. In the Northern Expedition, T'ang fought on the side of the revolution and Yeh on the side of the warlords of the Northern clique.
29. A warlord whose rule extended over the five provinces of Kiangsu, Chekiang, Fukien, Kiangsi, and Anhwei. He was responsible for the bloody suppression of the insurrections of the Shanghai workers. The Northern Expedition Army crushed his main force in Nanchang and Kiukiang in the winter of 1926.
30. *See* Note 11.
31. In China a dish is served in a bowl or a plate for the whole table, not individually.
32. A folk-song with the refrain "Lotus flowers are falling", very popular among the beggars.

33. The fifteenth day of the seventh month of the Chinese lunar calendar. It usually falls on the full moon in August of the Gregorian calendar.

34. The idea of "Oriental Culture" was advocated by the reactionaries. It means the rejection of modern scientific culture and contentment with the preservation of the backward mode of agricultural production and feudal culture of the Orient.

35. The earliest kings in Chinese history.

36. The secret societies used to adopt as their names those of certain mountains, halls, shrines, or rivers to denote their sectarian affiliations. *Cf.* Note 17 to "Analysis of the Classes in Chinese Society".

37. A *ch'ih* is a Chinese measure of length, a little longer than a foot.

38. About 0·285 bushel.

39. In November 1926, as soon as the Northern Expedition Army captured Nanchang, provincial capital of Kiangsi, Chiang Kai-shek took the opportunity to establish his general headquarters there, and, gathering round him the right-wingers of the Kuomintang and a number of the politicians of the Northern warlord clique, began to plot with the imperialists against revolutionary Wuhan—consisting of the former cities of Wuchang, Hankow and Hanyang in Hupeh province. Finally, on April 12, 1927, he staged his counter-revolutionary *coup d'état* and perpetrated the infamous Shanghai Massacre.

40. One of Chiang's advisers and a right-wing leader of the Kuomintang.

41. Head of an important anti-Communist group in Hunan.

42. As told by Liu Hsiang (76–5 B.C.) in his *Hsin Hsu*, Lord Sheh was so fond of dragons that he adorned his whole palace with drawings and carvings of them. But when a real dragon heard of his infatuation and paid him a visit, he was frightened out of his wits.

WHY CAN CHINA'S RED POLITICAL POWER EXIST?

1. Meaning the national bourgeoisie. For a detailed account of the distinction between this class and the big comprador bourgeoisie, see *On the Tactics of Fighting Japanese Imperialism* (December 1935); and *The Chinese Revolution and the Chinese Communist Party* (December 1939).

2. These four cliques of warlords fought together against Chang Tso-lin and occupied Peking and Tientsin in June 1928.

3. Head of the Fengtien clique of warlords and one-time ruler of China's Northeast which was then divided into the three provinces of Fengtien, Kirin and Heilungkiang. Defeating Wu P'ei-fu in 1924, Chang became the predominant warlord in northern China. In 1926 he and Wu came to terms and jointly occupied Peking. In June 1928 he was defeated by the four cliques of warlords mentioned in the text and was forced to retreat to the North-east. On the way he was killed in the train by a bomb planted by the Japanese imperialists despite the fact that he had always been their obedient tool.

4. Although the national bourgeoisie had followed Chiang Kai-shek in his counter-revolutionary *coup d'état* of 1927, a section of it, in its own interest, gradually formed an opposition to the Chiang régime after the Japanese occupation of Tsinan (*see* next note) and Chiang's disgraceful compromise

with the Japanese. The opportunist counter-revolutionary group headed by Wang Ching-wei and Ch'en Kung-po was active in this opposition movement and became known as the "Reorganisers" within the Kuomintang.

5. With the backing of Anglo-American imperialism, Chiang Kai-shek proceeded north in 1928 to attack Chang Tso-lin (*see* Note 3 above). To check Anglo-American influence from spreading northward, Japanese imperialism dispatched an expeditionary force to occupy Tsinan, capital of Shantung, thereby cutting off the trunk railway line connecting Tientsin and Pukow. On May 3 the Japanese aggressors occupied Tsinan and slaughtered large numbers of Chinese. This is known as the "Tsinan Massacre".

6. The organisational form of China's Red political power was similar to that of Soviet political power. A soviet is a representative council, first introduced as a form of political power by the Russian working class during the revolution of 1905. Lenin and Stalin, on the basis of Marxist theory, drew the conclusion that a soviet republic is the most suitable form of political organisation for a society in the transitional period from capitalism to socialism. During the October Revolution in 1917 a socialist soviet republic, under the leadership of the Bolshevik Party of Lenin and Stalin, came into being for the first time in the history of the world. After the defeat of the 1927 revolution in China, the representative council was adopted as the form of the people's political power in the revolutionary mass uprisings with Comrade Mao Tse-tung at their head and under the leadership of the Chinese Communist Party. At the present stage of the Chinese revolution, however, such political power differs in nature from the political power of the proletarian dictatorship of the Soviet Union in that it is the anti-imperialist, anti-feudal democratic dictatorship of the people, a dictatorship under the leadership of the proletariat during the new-democratic revolution.

7. As a result of the new world situation, Comrade Mao Tse-tung's view on the question of colonies under direct imperialist rule is now different from the one he held in 1928. During the Second World War, a number of colonial countries in the East, formerly held by such imperialist powers as Britain, the United States, France and the Netherlands, came under Japanese occupation. Led by the Communist Parties there, the workers, peasants, the urban petty bourgeoisie and members of the national bourgeoisie, taking advantage of the contradictions between British, American, French and Dutch imperialism on the one hand and Japanese imperialism on the other, organised a broad united front against fascist aggression, established anti-Japanese bases, and firmly carried on an anti-Japanese guerrilla war. Thus the political situation in all these colonies began to change. When Japanese imperialism was driven out at the end of the Second World War, American, British, French and Dutch imperialism attempted to reassert their authority. With armed units of considerable strength formed during the Anti-Japanese War, the colonial peoples would not submit again to the yoke. Furthermore, the whole system of world imperialism is on its last legs as a result of the growing might of the Soviet Union, the downfall or decline of all imperialist powers in the course of the war with the exception of the United States, and the breakdown of the imperialist front in China as a result of the victory of the Chinese revolution. Thus, just as the Chinese people have done, all or at least some of the colonial peoples in the East can hold for an extended period big or small base areas and revolutionary régimes, carry on a protracted revolutionary war to encircle the cities from the countryside, and proceed gradually to take over the cities and win nation-wide victory in their respective countries.

8. That is, 1912.
9. These refer to the first series of counter-attacks which the people under Communist leadership launched in various places against the forces of counter-revolution after Chiang Kai-shek and Wang Ching-wei successively turned traitors to the revolution in 1927. In Canton the workers and revolutionary soldiers jointly staged an uprising and set up a people's political power on December 11, 1927. They fought bitterly against the counter-revolutionary forces directly supported by imperialism, and failed only because the disparity in strength was too great. Peasants in Haifeng and Lufeng along the eastern coast of Kwangtung had started a powerful revolutionary movement during 1923–5 under the Communist leader P'eng Pai; when the National Revolutionary Army based in Canton carried out its two victorious eastward expeditions against the renegade Ch'en Chiung-ming, it received great help from this peasant movement. After Chiang Kai-shek's betrayal of the revolution on April 12, 1927, these peasants staged three uprisings in April, September and October and established a revolutionary régime which held out until April 1928. In eastern Hunan, too, the peasants captured the area embracing the counties of Liuyang, Pingkiang, Liling and Chuchow in September 1927. Meanwhile, tens of thousands of peasants rose in the Siaokan-Macheng-Hwangan area in north-eastern Hupeh and occupied the county town of Hwangan for over thirty days. In January 1928, peasants in the counties of Ichang, Chen, Leiyang, Yunghing, and Tzehing in southern Hunan also rose in revolt and maintained a revolutionary régime for three months.
10. Popular armed units in the revolutionary bases whose members continued to follow their customary employment.
11. See Note 21 to *Report of an Investigation into the Peasant Movement in Hunan*.
12. A big mountain range along the Hunan-Kiangsi border. The Chingkang mountains are in its middle section.
13. Referring to people other than the peasants—handicraftsmen, small merchants, professional people, and petty-bourgeois intellectuals. Though chiefly found in the cities, such social elements are also present in the countryside in quite large numbers. See also *Analysis of the Classes in Chinese Society*.
14. The "Five Wells" is synonymous with the Chingkang mountains. It consists of the rural communities of Big Well, Small Well, Upper Well, Middle Well and Lower Well. Yungsin, Ningkang and Suichwan are in western Kiangsi; Ling county is in eastern Hunan.
15. Chaling is in Hunan. Lienhwa, like Yungsin and Ningkang, is in Kiangsi.

THE STRUGGLE IN THE CHINGKANG MOUNTAINS

1. This war took place in October 1927.
2. This war took place in November and December 1927.
3. The council of soldiers' representatives and soldiers' committees in the Red Army were later abolished. In 1947, however, the People's Liberation Army established armymen's conferences and soldiers' committees under the leadership of officers.
4. These were the troops which staged the Nanchang Uprising of August 1, 1927.

20

They were beaten back in their march on Chaochow and Swatow on the coast of Kwangtung. Thus a part of them, led by Comrades Chu Teh, Lin Piao and Ch'en Yi, withdrew from Kwangtung and entered southern Hunan by way of Kiangsi to carry on guerrilla operations. These troops joined Comrade Mao's forces in the Chingkang mountains in April 1928.

5. Most of the cadres in this regiment were members of the Communist Party. When Wang Ching-wei and his associates in the Wuchang government betrayed the revolution, the regiment left Wuchang at the end of July 1927 to participate in the uprising at Nanchang, Kiangsi. The uprising, however, had taken place before its arrival and the insurrectionary forces had already left the city. The regiment then shifted to Siushiu, western Kiangsi, and joined forces with the peasant army of Pingkiang and Liuyang.

6. In the spring of 1927 peasant armed forces of considerable strength were formed in the area of Pingkiang and Liuyang, Hunan province. On May 21, Hsu K'e-hsiang, a Kuomintang commander, staged a counter-revolutionary *coup d'état* in Changsha and massacred the revolutionaries. To fight back, these peasant forces started a march on Changsha on May 31, but were ordered back by the opportunist Ch'en Tu-hsiu, then at the head of the Communist Party. Thereupon a part of them was reorganised into an independent regiment to engage in guerrilla warfare. After the Nanchang Uprising of August 1, 1927, these armed peasants joined forces at Siushui and Tungku, Kiangsi, and Pingkiang and Liuyang, Hunan, with the Guards Regiment of the Wuchang National Government to stage the Autumn Harvest Uprising, acting in co-ordination with the coal miners of Pingsiang, Kiangsi. In October Comrade Mao led these insurrectionary forces to the Chingkang mountains.

7. In early 1928, while Comrade Chu Teh was directing the revolutionary guerrilla war in southern Hunan, peasant armies were organised in the counties of Ichang, Chen, Leiyang, Yunghing and Tzehing where a foundation had been laid for the peasant movement. Comrade Chu Teh subsequently led these peasant armies to the Chingkang mountains to join Comrade Mao's forces.

8. Shuikowshan of Changning, Hunan, is well known for its lead mines. In 1922 the mine workers' union was organised under the leadership of the Communist Party. The mine workers fought incessantly against the counter-revolution, and many of them joined the Red Army after the Autumn Harvest Uprising of 1927.

9. The Anyuan coal mines in Pingsiang county, Kiangsi, with about twelve thousand workers, were owned by the Han-Yeh-Ping Iron and Steel Company. The Hunan Provincial Committee of the Communist Party began to send organisers there in 1921 to build up the Party organisation and to help the miners organise their union.

10. The Party representative in the Red Army was renamed political commissioner in 1929. The company political commissioner was renamed political director in 1931.

11. This was only a temporary measure to defray part of the army's expenses. With the growth of the army and the expansion of the territory, taxation became necessary and possible.

12. Such a practice, dictated by the then existing circumstances, continued for a long time in the Red Army. Later on, however, officers and men received slightly different treatment according to their ranks.

13. A cash is nominally worth one-thousandth of a silver dollar.

14. Special emphasis is laid here on the necessity of the introduction of a certain amount of democratic life in the revolutionary army, then in the incipient stage of its organisation, in order to call forth the revolutionary zeal of the new peasant recruits and the White troops who had been captured, and to deliver the officers from the influence of warlordism of the reactionary armies. Of course democracy in the army must be confined within the limits of military discipline. It must serve to strengthen, not to weaken, discipline. It should not be confused with the extreme democratisation and utter disregard of discipline which did become a matter of serious concern in the early period of the Red Army and which must be resolutely combated while appropriate forms of democracy are introduced. See *Rectification of Incorrect Ideas in the Party*.

15. Comrade Yeh T'ing commanded an independent regiment during the Northern Expedition of 1926. With Communists as its backbone the regiment became famous as a crack force. It was expanded into the Twenty-fourth Division after the revolutionary army seized Wuchang and into the Eleventh Army after the Nanchang Uprising.

16. Experience has shown that it works out quite well when Party members number about one-third of the complement of the Red Army. This proportion was generally maintained in the Red Army and in the People's Liberation Army.

17. Aided and abetted by Chiang Kai-shek and Wang Ching-wei, the Kuomintang's reactionary army commanders in Hunan, including Hsu K'e-hsiang and Ho Chien, ordered a raid on the provincial headquarters of the trade unions, the peasant associations and other revolutionary organisations in Changsha on May 21, 1927. Communists and revolutionary workers and peasants were arrested and killed *en masse*. This signalised the open collaboration between the two Kuomintang reactionary cliques, the Wuhan clique headed by Wang Ching-wei and the Nanking clique headed by Chiang Kai-shek.

18. This was a provision in the agrarian law promulgated in the Hunan-Kiangsi border area in 1928. Comrade Mao later pointed out that the confiscation of all land, instead of only that of the landlords, was a mistake due to the lack of experience in agrarian struggles. In April 1929 in the agrarian law of Hsingkuo county, Kiangsi, the provision "confiscate all the land" was changed into "confiscate the public land and the land of the landlord classes".

19. Seeing the importance of winning over the intermediate class in the countryside, Comrade Mao soon rectified the erroneous policy of dealing too sharply with this class. Apart from what is contained in this article, his views are also found in his proposals to the Sixth General Assembly of the Red Army (November 1928), including "prohibition of reckless burning and killing" and "protection of the interests of the middle and small merchants". Again in a rhymed proclamation written for the Red Fourth Army (January 1929), he said that merchants in the cities, who had painfully and slowly accumulated their small fortunes, were to be left alone so long as they obeyed the government.

20. With the development of the revolutionary war, the expansion of the revolutionary base areas, and the policy of protecting industry and commerce, this condition could be changed, and in fact was changed later. The important thing was resolutely to protect native industry and commerce and oppose ultra-Left policies.

21. It is incorrect to take the ability to work as the criterion in land redistribution.

For a long time in the Red areas, land was actually redistributed according to the number of persons in each family.

22. The special committee as it was constituted at the First Congress.

23. The special committee as it was constituted at the Second Congress.

24. This is a kind of local counter-revolutionary armed force. "Pacification" is simply a euphemism used by the counter-revolutionaries to conceal their real purpose of "suppressing the Communists".

ON THE RECTIFICATION OF INCORRECT IDEAS IN THE PARTY

1. For a brief period after the defeat of the revolution in 1927, a "Left" adventurist tendency arose in the Communist Party. Regarding the Chinese revolution as a "permanent revolution" and the revolutionary situation in China as one of a "permanent upsurge", the adventurist comrades refused to organise an orderly retreat and, adopting the methods of authoritarianism and relying on a small number of Party members and a small section of the masses, erroneously attempted to stage throughout the country a series of local uprisings which had no prospect of success. Adventurist activities were widespread at the end of 1927, but gradually subsided in the beginning of 1928, though sentiments in favour of adventurism still remained among some comrades.

2. In the guerrilla system of organisation a column corresponded to a division in the regular army, with a much more flexible complement which was usually quite small as compared with that of a regular division.

3. Proverbial Chinese expressions describing the activities of the ringleaders of a rebellion or of outlaws.

4. Leader of the peasant revolts at the end of the T'ang dynasty. In A.D. 875, starting from his home district, Tsaochow (now Hotseh county in Shantung), Huang led armed peasants in victorious battles against the imperial forces. After sweeping in the course of ten years over most of the provinces in the Yellow, Yangtze, Hawai and Pearl river valleys, reaching as far as Kwangsi, he finally broke through the Tung pass, captured the imperial capital of Changan, now Sian in Shensi, and was crowned Emperor of Ch'i. Internal dissensions and attacks by the non-Chinese tribal allies of the T'ang forces compelled Huang to abandon Changan and retreat to his native district, where he committed suicide. His ten-year campaign is one of the best-known peasant wars in Chinese history. China's official historians record that "people suffering from heavy taxes and levies all rallied to him". But as he merely carried on mobile warfare without ever establishing relatively consolidated base areas, his movement is referred to as that of the "roving insurgent hordes".

5. Ch'uang, meaning "dare-all", was the title of Li Tzu-ch'eng, native of Micheh, northern Shensi, who was the leader of a peasant revolt which led to the overthrow of the Ming dynasty. The revolt first took shape in northern Shensi in 1628. Li joined the forces led by Kao Ying-hsiang and campaigned through Honan and Anhwei and back to Shensi. After Kao's death in 1636, Li succeeded to his title of King Ch'uang and campaigned in and out of the provinces of Shensi, Szechwan, Honan and Hupeh. Finally he captured the

imperial capital of Peking in 1644, whereupon the last Ming emperor committed suicide. The chief slogan he propagated among the masses was "support King Ch'uang, and pay no grain taxes". Another slogan of his to enforce discipline among his men ran: "Any murder means the killing of my father, any rape means the violation of my mother." Thus he won the support of the masses and his movement became the main current of the peasant revolts raging all over the country. As he also roamed about without ever establishing relatively consolidated base areas, he was defeated shortly after he took Peking by Wu San-kuei, a general of the Ming dynasty, who allowed the Manchu invaders into China Proper to augment his own forces for the attack on Li.

A SINGLE SPARK CAN START A PRAIRIE FIRE

1. Comrade Fang Chih-min, native of Yiyang, Kiangsi, and member of the Central Committee of the Chinese Communist Party elected at its Sixth National Congress, was the founder of the Red area in north-eastern Kiangsi and of the Red Tenth Army. In 1934 he led the northward march of the Red Army's anti-Japanese advance units. Taken prisoner by the Kuomintang reactionaries in January 1935, he died a martyr's death six months later in Nanchang, Kiangsi.
2. Namely, the organised forces of the revolution.
3. A Kuomintang warlord; he was the Kuomintang governor of Hunan in 1928.
4. Referring to the war fought in March-April 1929 between Chiang Kai-shek, the Kuomintang warlord in Nanking, and Li Tsung-jen and Pai Ch'ung-hsi, the Kuomintang warlords in Kwangsi.
5. Referring to the third occasion on which the Kuomintang warlords in Hunan and Kiangsi invaded the Red Army's base area in the Chingkang mountains. The invasion took place at the end of 1928 and the beginning of 1929.
6. Referring to the brutal measures of slaughter adopted by the counter-revolutionary forces towards the people's revolutionary forces.
7. The Congress, held in July 1928, pointed out that despite the 1927 defeat the Chinese revolution remained a bourgeois-democratic revolution against imperialism and feudalism. It also pointed out that a new revolutionary upsurge was inevitable, but since it had yet to take place, the Party's general line was the winning over of the masses.

   The Congress liquidated Ch'en Tu-hsiu's Right capitulationism of 1927. It also criticised the "Left" adventurism which appeared in the Party immediately after the 1927 defeat, i.e. in late 1927 and early 1928. (See the third part of the *Resolution on Some Historical Problems*, Vol. III of the *Selected Works*.)
8. Author's brackets.
9. In 1929, the Red Army marched eastward from the Chingkang mountains into western Fukien. It established a new revolutionary base and the people's revolutionary political power in the counties of Lungyen, Yungting and Shanghang.
10. Referring to the relatively consolidated revolutionary base areas that were established by the Workers' and Peasants' Red Army.

11. The county town of Chen.
12. Then the Kuomintang commander of the peace preservation corps in Chekiang province.
13. The Kuomintang brigade under Kuo Feng-ming.
14. Two local bandit chiefs whose forces had been incorporated into the Kuomintang army.
15. A Kuomintang divisional commander.
16. Then the Kuomintang governor of Kiangsi.
17. Then a divisional commander of Kuomintang troops in Kiangsi.

WE MUST ATTEND TO ECONOMIC WORK

1. From 1930 to 1934, Chiang Kai-shek launched five large-scale offensives, or campaigns of "encirclement and annihilation", against the Red area with its centre round Juikin, Kiangsi. At the time when this report was made, Chiang was preparing for the fifth campaign which opened two months later.
2. A Chinese unit of weight, approximately one ounce, or $\frac{1}{16}$ of a catty.
3. A measure taken after the agrarian reform to ascertain whether land had been properly redistributed.
4. A democratic campaign in which the broad masses were encouraged to expose any misconduct of the functionaries of the democratic government.

HOW TO ANALYSE THE CLASSES IN THE RURAL AREAS

1. In China's rural areas there are various forms of common ownership of land: land owned by a township or district government, by the ancestral temple of a clan, by a Catholic church or a Buddhist or Taoist temple or a mosque, by a famine relief granary, by a public welfare organisation for the building and maintenance of bridges and roads, or by an educational institution. The land owned by the last is called "school land," hence school rent. Most of such is really controlled by the landlords and rich peasants; only a small section of the peasants can participate in administering it.

OUR ECONOMIC POLICY

1. The temporary decline resulted chiefly from the fact that, as neither land ownership was stabilised nor the new economic order fully established during land redistribution, the peasants could not yet set their minds on production.
2. Based on individual farming, these two kinds of mutual-aid groups were formed by the peasants in the Red areas to facilitate production through a better organisation of labour power. On the principle of voluntary participation and mutual benefit, the members either did an equal amount of work for each other or, when they could not give their fellow members so much help in return, paid the latter according to the difference in working time. In addition to this, members of the mutual-aid working groups extended

assistance to the families of Red Army soldiers on particularly favourable terms. They also worked for bereaved old folk and orphans without any pay except for meals taken in the course of the work.

As these measures of mutual aid were of great help to production and were carried out on a reasonable basis they won the support of the masses. Comrade Mao Tse-tung gave an account of them in his *Survey of Changkang Township* and *Survey of Tsaiki Township*, neither of which is included in the *Selected Works*.

TAKE CARE OF THE LIVING CONDITIONS OF THE MASSES AND ATTEND TO THE METHODS OF WORK

1. A township in Hsingkuo county, Kiangsi province.
2. A township in Shanghang county, Fukien province.
3. Then a county in the Red area in Kiangsi, with its centre at the town of Tungku, south-east of Kian county. It was named after Comrade Huang Kung-lueh, commander of the Red Third Army, who sacrificed his life there in October 1931.
4. As a new tactic for his fifth campaign of "encirclement and annihilation", Chiang Kai-shek decided at a military conference held at the mountain resort of Kuling, Kiangsi, in July 1933, to build blockhouses round the Red areas. It was estimated that 2,900 blockhouses had already been built in Kiangsi by the end of January 1934. The Japanese aggressors later resorted to the same tactic when fighting the Eighth Route and New Fourth Armies. Experience fully proved that this tactic of the counter-revolution could be outmanœuvred and defeated by adhering to Comrade Mao Tse-tung's strategic principles for a people's war.
5. This was a popular jibe at the blockhouses into which the Kuomintang soldiers withdrew when attacked, very much as a tortoise withdraws into its shell.
6. *See* Note 3 to *We Must Attend to Economic Work*.

ON THE TACTICS OF FIGHTING JAPANESE IMPERIALISM

1. Put to the Chinese government headed by Yuan Shih-k'ai on January 18, 1915. On May 7, the Japanese imperialists sent an ultimatum calling for the acceptance of the twenty-one demands within forty-eight hours.

These demands were divided into five parts. The first four contained the following: transference to Japan of the rights Germany had unjustly acquired in Shantung and the granting to Japan of additional rights in Shantung; the Japanese to be allowed to lease or own land in southern Manchuria and eastern Mongolia and to establish residence, engage in industry and commerce, and to have exclusive rights of building railways and mining; the Han-Yeh-Ping Iron and Steel Company in Central China to be reorganised into a Sino-Japanese joint enterprise; and China to abstain from leasing or ceding any harbours or islands along her coastline to any third power.

The fifth part contained the demands that Japan be allowed to control China's government, finance, police and national defence, and that Japan be permitted to build the vital railway lines connecting the provinces of Hupeh, Kiangsi and Kwangtung.

Yuan Shih-k'ai accepted all the demands except those in the fifth part, about which he begged for "further negotiation". Due to the unanimous opposition of the Chinese people, however, these Japanese demands were not carried into effect.

2. Head of the Northern clique of warlords formed during the last years of the Manchu dynasty. When the Manchu régime was overthrown by the Revolution of 1911, the compromising attitude of the bourgeoisie then leading the revolution enabled Yuan to usurp the presidency of the Republic through the support of the imperialists and with the aid of a counter-revolutionary army under his command. He formed the first government of Northern warlords representing the big landlord and big comprador classes. In 1915 he established an imperial régime with himself on the throne and accepted the Twenty-One Demands (*see* note above) of the Japanese imperialists in order to gain their support. An uprising in Yunnan province in December touched off nation-wide rebellion. Yuan was forced to abolish the imperial government in March 1916, and died shortly afterwards in June.

3. In November 1921, the United States government invited China, Britain, France, Italy, Belgium, the Netherlands, Portugal and Japan to a nine-power conference in Washington. It was really a duel between the United States and Japan for hegemony in the Far East. On February 6, 1922, a nine-power treaty was concluded under the U.S.-sponsored principle of the "open door" or "equality of opportunity in China for the trade and industry of all nations". Besides establishing the imperialist powers' joint control of China, this treaty prepared the way for the United States to frustrate Japan's design of exclusive domination and to establish eventually its own monopoly of China.

4. On September 18, 1931, Mukden was seized by the Japanese "Kwantung" army stationed in China's North-east. Under Chiang Kai-shek's order of "absolute non-resistance", the Chinese North-eastern Army in Mukden and elsewhere withdrew to the south of the Great Wall. The Japanese troops were thus able to occupy in rapid succession the former north-eastern provinces of Liaoning, Kirin and Heilungkiang.

5. These refer to a large part of the present Inner Mongolian Autonomous Region and the six provinces in the North-eastern Administrative Area: Liaotung, Liaosi, Kirin, Sungkiang, Heilunkiang and Jehol. The first five provinces and the large part of Inner Mongolia then formed the three provinces mentioned in the preceding note. They were seized by Japan after the Incident of September 18, 1931, and the province of Jehol was seized in 1933.

6. A loose historical-geographical designation of that part of China where provincial administration was set up in the early Manchu dynasty, excluding Manchuria, Sinkiang, Mongolia, Tibet and Chinghai.

7. Aided and abetted by the Japanese, Yin Ju-keng, a Kuomintang collaborator, established on November 25, 1935, the bogus "Eastern Hopeh Anti-Communist Autonomous Administration" over twenty-two counties in eastern Hopeh.

8. These refer to the diplomatic parleys between the Chiang Kai-shek government and the Japanese Government on the so-called "Hirota's three principles": (1) China's suppression of all anti-Japanese movements; (2) Sino-Japanese- "Manchukuan" economic co-operation (Manchukuo being the puppet state set up by Japan in China's North-east); and (3) Sino-Japanese

joint defence against communism. On January 21, 1936, Hirota, Japanese foreign minister, told the Diet that the Chinese government "has accepted the three principles proposed by the Empire".

9. The year 1935 witnessed a new upsurge of the people's nation-wide patriotic movement. Students in Peking, under the leadership of the Chinese Communist Party, organised a patriotic demonstration on December 9, shouting the slogans, "End the civil war!" "Unite against foreign aggression!" and "Down with Japanese imperialism!" The movement broke down the reign of terror imposed by the Kuomintang government in league with the Japanese aggressors and immediately won the support of the people throughout the country, and has since been generally referred to as the "December 9 Movement". After that, changes in class relations in China became manifest and all patriotic people openly advocated, as the only means to save the motherland, the Anti-Japanese National United Front proposed by the Communist Party. The treacherous policies of the Chiang Kai-shek government were thus checkmated.

10. At the time of this report Chiang Kai-shek was giving away North China after giving away the North-east and continuing his frenzied war against the Red Army. Therefore the Chinese Communist Party had to do its utmost to expose him as a traitor. Naturally, Chiang could not in these circumstances be included in the Anti-Japanese National United Front proposed by the Communist Party. In this report, however, Comrade Mao already spoke of a possible disintegration in the camp of the Chinese landlord and comprador classes as a result of the contradictions among the imperialist powers. Serious conflicts did arise later between the Japanese and the Anglo-American imperialists after the former's aggression in North China. In view of the close connection between the Chiang Kai-shek group and Anglo-American imperialism, the Party concluded that Chiang might change his attitude towards Japan at the bidding of his Anglo-American masters, and accordingly adopted the policy of compelling Chiang Kai-shek to turn to resist Japan. In May 1936, upon its return to Northern Shensi from Shansi, the Red Army appealed directly to the Kuomintang government at Nanking for cessation of the civil war and united resistance to Japan. In August of the same year, the Central Committee of the Chinese Communist Party addressed a letter to the Kuomintang's Central Committee asking for a bi-partisan united front against Japan and a parley between the representatives of both sides. But the proposal was rejected by Chiang Kai-shek. It was not until December 1936 that Chiang Kai-shek, detained in Sian by Kuomintang army officers in favour of unity with the Communists to resist Japan, was compelled to accept the Communist Party's demand for internal peace and war against Japan.

11. Ts'ai T'ing-k'ai was deputy commander of the Kuomintang's Nineteenth Route Army and commander of one of its corps, the two other leaders of the Army being Ch'en Ming-shu and Chiang Kuang-nai. This Army had fought the Red Army in Kiangsi and had been transferred to Shanghai after the Incident of September 18. When the Japanese marines attacked Shanghai during the night of January 28, 1932, the Nineteenth Route Army, then garrisoned in Shanghai, under the great impact of the popular anti-Japanese upsurge throughout the country, fought together with the people of Shanghai against the invaders. The campaign was finally lost through betrayal on the part of Chiang Kai-shek and Wang Ching-wei. The army, on Chiang Kai-shek's order, was transferred to Fukien again to fight the Red Army.

But the leaders of the army gradually became awakened to the futility of such fighting. In November 1933, allying themselves with that section of the Kuomintang forces under Li Chi-shen and others, they publicly renounced Chiang Kai-shek, established in Fukien the "People's Revolutionary Government of the Republic of China", and concluded an agreement with the Red Army to attack Chiang Kai-shek and resist Japan. The Nineteenth Route Army and the People's Government of Fukien collapsed under the attacks of Chiang's troops. Henceforth Ts'ai T'ing-k'ai and his associates gradually shifted to a stand for co-operation with the Communist Party.

12. When the revolutionary Northern Expedition Army took Wuhan in September 1926, Feng Yu-hsiang announced in Suiyuan province the end of his alliance with the Northern clique of warlords and joined the revolution. At the beginning of 1927, his troops set out from Shensi to attack Honan province in co-ordination with the Northern Expedition Army. After Chiang Kai-shek and Wang Ching-wei betrayed the revolution in 1927, Feng participated in anti-Communist activities. However, there had been all along a clash of interests between him and the Chiang Kai-shek bloc. After the Incident of September 18 he began to favour resistance to Japan and, in May 1933, joined forces with the Communists to form the Popular Anti-Japanese Allied Armies in Kalgan. This endeavour failed in August under the double pressure of Chiang Kai-shek's forces and the Japanese invaders. In his later years Feng continued to co-operate with the Communist Party.

13. This mutiny, in which more than ten thousand officers and men were involved, occurred in December 1931 in response to the Communist call for resistance to Japan.

14. An officer of the North-eastern army, whose troops were stationed in Heilungkiang. After the Incident of September 18, he and his troops resisted the Japanese invaders driving towards Heilunkiang via Liaoning.

15. A well-known Kuomintang politician. He was an opponent of Dr. Sun Yat-sen's policy of co-operation with the Chinese Communist Party as well as an accomplice of Chiang Kai-shek in the counter-revolutionary *coup d'état* of April 12, 1927. But he was later placed under detention by Chiang Kai-shek as his rival for power. Set free after the Incident of September 18, he went from Nanking to Canton and directed the warlords of Kwangtung and Kwangsi to oppose for a long time Chiang Kai-shek's government in Nanking.

16. This refers to the "Chinese People's Basic Programme for Fighting Japan", proposed by the Communist Party of China in 1934, and published over the signatures of Soong Ch'ing-ling (Mme Sun Yat-sen) and others. The programme consisted of the following items: (1) Mobilise all the sea, land and air forces to fight Japan; (2) Mobilise the people throughout the country; (3) Arm all the people; (4) Confiscate the property of the Japanese imperialists in China and the property of all collaborators to defray war expenses; (5) Establish an all-China committee for armed defence, to be elected by the representatives of workers, peasants, soldiers, students and business men; and (6) Form an alliance with all the forces hostile to the Japanese imperialists, and establish friendly relations with all the countries that observe benevolent neutrality.

17. Referring to the cliques headed respectively by Ch'en Chi-t'ang of Kwangtung and Li Tsung-jen and Pai Ch'ung-hsi of Kwangsi.

18. Chiang Kai-shek's bandit gang called the people "bandits" and their armed attacks upon and their massacre of the revolutionary people "bandit suppression".

19. Veteran member of the Communist Party of China and one of its first organisers. Since the Fifth National Congress of the Party in 1927 he was elected to the Central Committee at each Party Congress. At the Central Committee's plenary session of 1931 (the fourth since the Sixth National Congress), he was elected member of the Political Bureau. In 1933, Comrade Jen served as secretary of the Provincial Committee of the Hunan-Kiangsi Border Region and concurrently as political commissioner of the Sixth Army Group of the Red Army. When the Sixth and Second Army Groups joined their forces to form the Second Front Army, he became its political commissioner. When the Anti-Japanese War began, he was the director of the General Political Department of the Eighth Route Army. In 1940 he began to serve in the Secretariat of the Central Committee of the Chinese Communist Party. At the Central Committee's plenary session of 1945 (the first since the Seventh National Congress), he was elected member of the Committee's Political Bureau and of its secretariat. He died in Peking on October 27, 1950.

20. The Sixth Army Group of the Chinese Workers' and Peasants' Red Army, originally stationed in the base area on the Hunan-Kiangsi border, was ordered by the Party's Central Committee to break through the enemy's siege and shift to other places in August 1934. It joined forces with the Second Army Group led by Comrade Ho Lung in eastern Kweichow in October 1934. These two groups formed the Second Front Army and created the revolutionary base on the Hunan-Hupeh-Szechwan-Kweichow border.

21. In October 1934, the First Front Army, i.e. the Central Red Army (comprising the First, the Third and the Fifth Army Groups) of the Chinese Workers' and Peasants' Red Army embarked on a great strategic shift. Setting out from Changting and Ninghwa, western Fukien, and Juikin and Yutu, southern Kiangsi, the Red Army traversed the eleven provinces of Fukien, Kiangsi, Kwangtung, Hunan, Kwangsi, Kweichow, Szechwan, Yunnan, Sikang, Kansu and Shensi. It climbed over high mountains that were snow-bound the year round and marched across wild marshes where human beings were seldom seen. After having undergone untold tribulations and having repeatedly routed the enemy in his attempts to encircle, pursue or intercept them in a continuous march of 25,000 *li* (12,500 kilometres), the Red Army finally arrived victoriously in the revolutionary base area in northern Shensi in October 1935.

22. This refers to the Fourth Front Army of the Chinese Workers' and Peasants' Red Army which left its base in the Szechwan-Shensi border area in March 1935. Despite the disruption of Chang Kuo-t'ao (*see* note below), a part of it finally arrived in northern Shensi in October 1936 together with the entire body of the Second Front Army. Previously, the latter broke through the enemy siege and left the Hunan-Hupeh-Szechwan-Kweichow border area in June 1936 and joined forces with the former in Sikang.

23. Chang Kuo-t'ao, a renegade of the Chinese revolution, joined the Chinese Communist Party in its early period. He committed numerous mistakes leading to enormous crimes. In 1935, opposed to the northward march of the Red Army, he carried out his defeatist and liquidationist proposal that the Red Army be withdrawn to the regions of the national minorities on the borders of Szechwan and Sikang, thereby causing heavy losses to the Fourth Front Army. At the same time, he openly rebelled against the Party and the Central Committee by establishing a bogus central committee under his own control to disrupt the unity of the Party and the Red Army. Owing to patient educational work by Comrade Mao Tse-tung and the Central Committee,

the rank and file of the Fourth Front Army and the broad masses of its cadres soon turned to the correct leadership of the Central Committee and have since played a splendid role in subsequent struggles. Chang himself proved incorrigible. In the spring of 1938, he fled all alone from the Shensi-Kansu-Ningsia border region and joined the Kuomintang secret service.

24. The Central Red Army, or the First Front Army, refers to the Red Army that was built up in the Kiangsi-Fukien area directly under the leadership of the Central Committee.

25. In Chinese mythology P'an Ku was the creator of the world and the first ruler of mankind. The Three Sovereigns and Five Emperors were legendary rulers in ancient China.

26. The Kuomintang troops started their third campaign of "encirclement and annihilation" against the Shensi-Kansu revolutionary base area in July 1935. In a series of battles, units of the Red Army originally stationed in the base area, together with those arriving from Central China, and the Central Red Army arriving from southern China after the Long March (*see* Note 21), annihilated wholesale regiments and divisions of the Kuomintang troops between the Yellow river on the east and the Shensi-Kansu border on the west. The battle of Chihlo, south-west of Fu county, was the last major engagement in which the Central Red Army took part after its arrival in October and in which one of the enemy divisions was completely annihilated. By November the third campaign of "encirclement and annihilation" was completely smashed.

27. When the main forces of the Red Army in South China moved northward during 1934-5, some guerrilla units were left behind. These guerrillas held out in fourteen base areas in eight provinces: southern Chekiang, northern Fukien, eastern Fukien, southern Fukien, western Fukien, north-eastern Kiangsi, Fukien-Kiangsi border, Kwangtung-Kiangsi border, southern Hunan, Hunan-Kiangsi border, Hunan-Hupeh-Kiangsi border, Hupeh-Hunan-Anhwei border, Tungpeh mountains in southern Honan and Hainan Island off the coast of Kwantgung.

28. Upon Japan's seizure of China's North-east in 1931, the Chinese Communist Party called upon the people there to put up armed resistance. It organised anti-Japanese guerrilla corps and the North-eastern People's Revolutionary Army, and rendered assistance to anti-Japanese volunteer forces of every description. In 1934, all anti-Japanese contingents in the North-east were reorganised under the leadership of the Party into the Anti-Japanese Amalgamated Armies of the North-east with Yang Ching-yu, an outstanding Communist, as Commander-in-Chief. For a long time, the armies kept up anti-Japanese guerrilla activities in the North-east.

In eastern Hopeh the peasants staged an insurrection against Japan in May 1935.

29. This refers to the fight (1918 to 1920) in which the Soviet people under the leadership of the Communist Party beat off the armed intervention of Britain, France, Japan, Poland, the United States, etc., and suppressed the rebellion of the White Guards.

30. The nature of the political authority of a people's republic, together with the policies of such a republic as enunciated here by Comrade Mao, were fully manifested in practice in the people's liberated areas under the leadership of the Communist Party during the Anti-Japanese War. Thus the Communist Party was able to lead the people in the enemy rear to fight victoriously against the Japanese invaders. After Japan's surrender, the Third Revolutionary

Civil War broke out. As the war developed, the people's liberated areas also expanded until the whole country was liberated. The establishment of the unified People's Republic of China in 1949 marked the realisation of Comrade Mao's idea of a people's republic throughout the country.

31. In July 1928, the Sixth National Congress of the Chinese Communist Party adopted the following ten-point programme:

(1) Overthrow the rule of imperialism;

(2) Confiscate all the banks and enterprises of foreign capital;

(3) Unify China and recognise the right to national self-determination;

(4) Overthrow the Kuomintang government of the warlords;

(5) Establish councils of workers', peasants' and soldiers' representatives as the form of government;

(6) Enforce the eight-hour day, increase wages and institute unemployment relief and social insurance;

(7) Confiscate the land of all landlords and redistribute it to the peasants;

(8) Improve the soldiers' living conditions and give land and jobs to the ex-servicemen;

(9) Abolish all exorbitant taxes and miscellaneous assessments and adopt a consolidated progressive tax rate; and

(10) Form an alliance with the proletariat of the world and with the Soviet Union.

32. The Trotskyite group was originally an anti-Leninist faction in the Russian labour movement, and later degenerated into a downright counter-revolutionary gang. In his report to the plenary session of the Central Committee of the C.P.S.U. (B.) in 1937, Comrade Stalin thus explained the course this group of renegades had run: "In the past, seven or eight years ago, Trotskyism was one of such political trends in the working class, an anti-Leninist trend, it is true, and therefore profoundly mistaken, but nevertheless a political trend. . . . Present-day Trotskyism is not a political trend in the working class, but a gang without principle and without ideas, of wreckers and diversionists, intelligence service agents, spies, murderers, a gang of sworn enemies of the working class, working in the pay of the intelligence services of foreign states." After the defeat of the Chinese revolution in 1927, a small number of Trotskyites appeared in China. In 1929, they formed, with Ch'en Tu-hsiu and other renegades, a small counter-revolutionary clique and spread such counter-revolutionary propaganda as that the Kuomintang had already completed the bourgeois-democratic revolution. The Chinese Trotskyites joined the Kuomintang secret service, and became the tool of both the imperialists and the Kuomintang in their oppression of the Chinese people. Acting on the orders of the criminal renegade Trotsky to "not impede occupation of China by the Japanese empire", they began to collaborate with the Japanese secret agents after the Incident of September 18. They received subsidies from the Japanese invaders and engaged in all kinds of activities that facilitated Japanese aggression.

33. From The Book of Mencius. Mencius said this because in the period known as the Era of Spring and Autumn (722–481 B.C.) the feudal princes in China incessantly fought against each other for power.

34. Between 1840 and 1842, in retaliation to the Chinese people's struggle against the opium traffic, the British invaded China under the pretext of protecting their trade. The Chinese army, under the leadership of Lin Tse-hsu, put up resistance. Meanwhile the "Anti-British Corps" which was spontaneously

organised by the citizens of Canton also dealt severe blows to the British aggressors.

35. This refers to the revolutionary war the Chinese peasants waged in the middle of the nineteenth century against the feudalist rule and national oppression of the Manchus. In January 1851, Hung Hsiu-ch'uan, Yang Hsiu-ch'ing and others led the peasants to stage an uprising in Chintien village, Kweiping county, Kwangsi, and established the T'aip'ing Heavenly Kingdom. In 1852 the revolutionary forces embarked on an expedition from Kwangsi. They fought through Hunan, Hupeh, Kiangsi, Anhwei, and took Nanking in 1853. After that, a part of the revolutionary forces was dispatched northward till they reached the vicinity of Tientsin. The T'aip'ing Army, however, did not establish consolidated bases in areas under its occupation, and after Nanking was founded as the capital, its leading bloc committed many political and military blunders. In consequence, it failed to repulse the combined assaults of the Manchus and the British, French and American aggressors, and met with final defeat in 1864.

36. This refers to the vast spontaneous mass movement of the peasants and handicraftsmen in North China in 1900. Forming themselves into secret societies based upon superstitious cults, these peasants and handicraftsmen carried out an armed struggle against imperialism. Presently, the joint forces of eight imperialist powers occupied Peking and Tientsin and suppressed the movement in a most cruel manner.

37. See Note 3 to the *Report of an Investigation into the Peasant Movement in Hunan*.

38. *Cf*. V. I. Lenin, *The War Programme of the Proletarian Revolution*. *Cf*. also *History of the Communist Party of the Soviet Union*, Chapter VI, Section 3.

STRATEGIC PROBLEMS OF CHINA'S REVOLUTIONARY WAR

1. Or Sun Wu, a famous Chinese military scientist in the fifth century B.C. The sentence quoted occurs in *Sun Tzu* (*see* Lionel Giles's translation, Book III, Chapter "The Strategy of Attack").

2. While a professor at the Peking University, Ch'en Tu-hsiu was well known as editor of *New Youth*, an influential magazine which heralded the May 4 Movement. He took part in founding the Chinese Communist Party and, thanks to his reputation as well as the Party's immaturity, became its secretary-general. In the last period of the revolution of 1924–7, the Right opportunism in the Party as represented by him developed into capitulationism. In *The Present Situation and Our Task*, Comrade Mao Tse-tung said that the capitulators at that time "gratuitously relinquished the Party's leadership among the peasant masses, the petty bourgeoisie, the middle bourgeoisie and especially among the armed forces, thus causing the defeat of that revolution". After the defeat in 1927 Ch'en Tu-hsiu and a handful of other capitulators lost their faith in the future of the revolution, and turned liquidationist. He took the reactionary stand of the Trotskyites and formed with them a small faction to oppose the Party. Consequently he was expelled from the Party in November 1929. Ch'en Tu-hsiu died in 1942. For his Right opportunism, *cf*. Editor's Note to *Analysis of the Classes in Chinese Society* (p. 13 of this volume) and to *Report on the Investigation into the Peasant Movement in Hunan* (p. 21 of this volume), and *Introducing the Communist* (Vol. II of the *Selected Works*).

3. This refers to the "Left" opportunist line generally called after its advocate, "Li Li-san's line". It existed in the Party for about four months beginning from June 1930 when Comrade Li Li-san was the most influential leader in the Party centre. Li Li-san's line was opposed to the policy laid down by the Party's Sixth Congress. It denied the need of building up mass strength in the revolution and refused to recognise the unevenness of revolutionary development. Comrade Mao's idea of devoting the main effort for a long period of time to creating rural base areas so that the cities could be encircled with the forces of the countryside and the revolutionary upsurge be accelerated from these base areas, was regarded by it as "extremely erroneous", as "a provincial and conservative view based on peasant ideology". As against this idea, it called for preparations for immediate uprisings throughout the country.

On the basis of this erroneous line, Comrade Li Li-san drew up his adventurist plans for organising immediate armed uprisings in metropolitan cities throughout the country. As he denied the uneven development of the world revolution, so he believed that the general outbreak of the Chinese revolution would necessarily lead to the world revolution, and that without the world revolution the Chinese revolution "could never succeed". As he did not recognise the protracted nature of China's bourgeois-democratic revolution, so he believed that the winning of victory first in one or several provinces would mark the turn towards socialism. A number of inappropriate "Left" adventurist policies were framed on such a basis.

Comrade Mao was opposed to this erroneous line. Great numbers of cadres and the rank and file of the whole Party also demanded its rectification. In September 1930, at a plenary session of the Central Committee (the third since the Sixth National Congress), Comrade Li Li-san admitted his mistakes and subsequently gave up his position of leadership in the Party centre. Having at length thoroughly rectified his erroneous views, he was re-elected to the Central Committee at the Party's Seventh Congress in 1945.

4. The erroneous line of a group of comrades inexperienced in revolutionary struggle whose leaders were Ch'en Shao-yu (known as Wang Ming) and the late Ch'in Pang-hsien (known as Po Ku). It was dominant in the Party from the plenary session of the Central Committee of January 1931 to the Tsunyi meeting of January 1935 when the Central Committee established its new leadership with Comrade Mao at its head. Previously, many effective measures to liquidate Li Li-san's line had been adopted at the Central Committee's plenary session of September 1930 and, for a time, by the reconstituted Party centre. Comrades Ch'en Shao-yu and Ch'in Pang-hsien, however, led their followers to oppose the Central Committee's measures. In a pamphlet entitled *Two Lines* or *Struggle for the Further Bolshevisation of the Chinese Communist Party*, these comrades dwelt on the idea that the danger facing the Party was not "Left" but Right opportunism, and, to justify their own activities, they directed their "criticism" against the "Right tendency" of Li Li-san's line. They put forward a political programme under which Li Li-san's line and other "Left" views and policies were restored, continued and developed under a new situation, and set themselves against the correct line of Comrade Mao Tse-tung.

Comrade Mao Tse-tung wrote this booklet to criticise primarily the military mistakes committed along this new "Left" opportunist line. This opportunist line, which dominated the Party for four years (longer than any previous opportunist line did), brought the heaviest losses to the Party and seriously retarded the progress of the Chinese revolution. Through years of practical experience, however, comrades who erred in this "Left" line have realised and rectified their mistakes and have rendered great service to the Party and the people. On the basis of a common political understanding they have united with all other comrades in the Party under Comrade Mao's leadership. For a detailed summing-up of all aspects of this erroneous line, see *Resolutions on Some Historical Problems* (Appendix, Vol. III of the *Selected Works*), adopted at the plenary session of the Central Committee in April 1945.

5. See Notes 22 and 23 to *On the Tactics of Fighting Japanese Imperialism*.

6. An organisation which Chiang Kai-shek set up in July 1933 in Kuling, a mountain summer resort in Kiukiang, Kiangsi province, to train anti-Communist military cadres. Officers of Chiang's army were sent there in rotation to receive fascist political and military training from German, Italian and American instructors.

7. The strategy of building blockhouses and making slow but steady advance.

8. V. I. Lenin, criticising the Hungarian Communist Bela Kun, said that he "gives up the most essential thing in Marxism, the living soul of Marxism: the concrete analysis of concrete conditions". (*Collected Works*, Russian ed., Moscow, 1950, Vol. XXXI, p. 143.)

9. Held on May 20, 1928, at Maoping of Ningkang county in that border area.

10. See below, p. 238.

11. See Notes 4 and 5 to *Rectification of Incorrect Ideas in the Party*.

12. Predatory behaviour devoid of discipline, organisation and clear political direction.

13. See Note 21 to *On the Tactics of Fighting Japanese Imperialism*.

14. After the defeat of the December uprising of 1905, the revolutionary tide gradually subsided in Russia. *Cf.* the *History of the Communist Party of the Soviet Union*, Chapter 3, Sections 5 and 6.

15. A peace treaty concluded between Soviet Russia and Germany in March 1918. The revolutionary force, confronted with an undisputedly superior enemy force, had to retreat temporarily to prevent the German imperialists from making an attack on the new-born Soviet Republic which as yet had no army of its own. The conclusion of this treaty won time for the Soviet Republic to strengthen the political power of the proletariat, reorganise its economy, and build up its Red Army. The proletariat, having thus consolidated its leadership over the peasantry and accumulated sufficient strength, was able to rout in 1918–20 the White Guards and the armed interventionists from Britain, the United States, France, Japan, Poland and other countries.

16. On October 30, 1927, the peasants of Haifeng and Lufeng in Kwangtung staged their third insurrection under the leadership of the Communist Party. They occupied the Haifeng-Lufeng area, organised the Red Army and established the workers' and peasants' democratic government. The revolutionists were defeated because they under-estimated the enemy's strength.

17. After joining forces in the course of the Long March in autumn 1936, the Second and Fourth Front Armies of the Red Army proceeded north from north-eastern Sikang. Chang Kuo-t'ao, who was in charge of the Fourth Army, persisted in the policy of retreat and liquidation which he had pursued all along. When both Front Armies reached Kansu in October, he organised the Fourth Front Army's advanced units, numbering more than twenty thousand men, into a Western Column to cross the Yellow river and proceed westward to Chinghai. The Western Column was badly beaten in October and was totally defeated in the following March.

18. *See* Karl Marx and Frederick Engels, *Selected Works*, Vol. II, "Marx to Kugel-mann", English ed., p. 421.

19. A famous novel of a peasant war, attributed to Shih Nai-an who flourished about the end of the Yuan dynasty and the beginning of the Ming dynasty (fourteenth century A.D.). There is an English translation by Pearl Buck, entitled *All Men Are Brothers*.

20. Two feudal states in the Chow dynasty (1134–247 B.C.), which occupied in the era of Spring and Autumn (722–481 B.C.) the present-day southern and central Shantung respectively. Ch'i was a country much stronger than Lu. The battle occurred in 684 B.C.

21. Author of *Tso Chuan*, a famous chronicle of the Chow dynasty.

22. The ancient town of Chengkao, to the north-west of the present Chengkao county, Honan province, was of great military importance. At first Hsiang Yu, King of Ch'u, captured it from Liu Pang, King of Han, and almost routed the latter's troops. Having put his army in good shape again, Liu Pang delayed a counter-attack until Hsiang Yu's troops got to midstream in crossing the Chi river. Hsiang Yu suffered a crushing defeat and Liu Pang recaptured Chengkao.

23. Kunyang, now in Yeh county, south-western Honan province, was the place where in 23 B.C., Liu Hsiu, founder of the Eastern Han dynasty, defeated Wang Mang, Emperor of the Hsin dynasty. The numerical disparity between the two forces was 8,000–9,000 on Liu's side against over 400,000 on Wang's side. Taking advantage of the unpreparedness of Wang Mang's generals who under-estimated the enemy, Liu Hsiu routed Wang's main forces with merely three thousand crack troops. Expanding this victory, Liu Hsiu immediately crushed the rest of Wang Mang's forces.

24. Kwantu was in the north-east of the present Chungmow county, Honan province. The battle took place in A.D. 200. Yuan Shao's army was 100,000 strong, while Ts'ao Ts'ao had only a meagre force and was short of supplies. Ts'ao, taking advantage of the lack of vigilance of Yuan's troops, dispatched his light-footed soldiers to spring a surprise attack on them and set their supplies on fire. Yuan's army was thrown into confusion and its main force was wiped out.

25. Wu refers to the forces under Sun Ch'uan, and Wei to those under Ts'ao Ts'ao. Chihpi, to the north-east of Kiayu, Hupeh province, is on the south bank of the Yangtze river. In A.D. 208 Ts'ao Ts'ao led a gigantic force of 500,000, which he claimed to be 800,000 strong, to launch an attack on Sun. Sun Ch'uan, with Ts'ao's antagonist Liu Pei as his ally, mustered a force of barely thirty thousand. Knowing that Ts'ao's army was plagued by epidemic and un-accustomed to action afloat, the allied forces set fire to Ts'ao's fleet and crushed his army.

26. Yiling was to the east of the present Ichang, Hupeh province, where in A.D. 222 Lu Sun, a general of the Kingdom of Wu, defeated the army of Liu Pei, Emperor of Shu. Liu Pei's troops scored successive victories in the beginning. Yet when they arrived in Yiling, they found that they had penetrated five or six hundred *li* into the territory of Wu. Lu Sun avoided battle for over seven months until Liu Pei was at his wits' end and his troops were exhausted and demoralised. Then he crushingly defeated Liu Pei's troops by taking advantage of a wind to set fire to their tents.

27. This battle took place in A.D. 383. Feishui is a river in northern Anhwei province, which separated the forces of the belligerents. Fu Chien, the monarch of Ch'in, had an infantry force of more than 600,000, a cavalry

force of 270,000, and a life-guard corps of about 30,000, while the land and
river forces of Hsieh Hsuan, a general of Eastern Chin, numbered only
80,000. When Fu Chien lined up his troops on the opposite bank, Hsieh
Hsuan, taking advantage of his over-confidence and self-conceit, requested
him to move his troops back so as to leave room for the Eastern Chin troops to
cross the river and fight a battle of decision. Fu Chien complied, but the
withdrawal, once begun, could not be stopped. Hsieh immediately launched
an offensive and defeated the enemy.

28. The Communist Party organised the famous uprising on August 1, 1927 in
Nanchang, Kiangsi, to combat the counter-revolution of Chiang Kai-shek
and Wang Ching-wei and to carry on the revolution of 1924–7. With Comrades
Chou En-lai, Chu Teh, Ho lung and Yeh T'ing as the leaders, an armed force
of more than thirty thousand took part in the uprising. The army of the
uprising withdrew from Nanchang on August 5 as originally planned, but
suffered a defeat when approaching Chaochow and Swatow in Kwangtung
province. Led by Comrades Chu Teh, Ch'en Yi and Lin Piao, a part of the
troops later fought their way to the Chingkang mountains and joined forces
with the First Division of the First Army of the Workers' and Peasants' Revolutionary Army under Comrade Mao Tse-tung.

29. See Note 9 to *Why Can China's Red Political Power Exist?*

30. In September 1927, the people's armed forces of Siushui, Pingsiang, Pingkiang and Liuyang on the Hunan-Kiangsi border carried out the famous
uprising under the leadership of Comrade Mao Tse-tung. These forces,
organised as the First Division of the First Army of the Workers' and Peasants'
Revolutionary Army, were led by Comrade Mao Tse-tung to the Chingkang
mountains and built a revolutionary base there.

31. Abbreviation for "Anti-Bolshevik Group", the English name used by a
counter-revolutionary organisation of the Kuomintang for underground
activities in the Red areas.

32. See V. I. Lenin, *Selected Works*, (two-volume ed.), Vol. II, Moscow, 1947:
"Theses on the Question of the Immediate Conclusion of a Separate and
Annexationist Peace"; "Strange and Monstrous"; "A Serious Lesson and a
Serious Responsibility"; "Report on War and Peace"; and *History of the
Communist Party of the Soviet Union*, Chapter 7, Section 7.

33. The Tibetans in Sikang and the Mohammedans in Chinghai, Kansu and
Sinkiang.

34. The prescribed form of essay in competitive examinations in feudal China
from the fifteenth to the nineteenth century. It is made up of eight parts. The
first four parts (including the three mentioned in the text), serve only as an
introduction and are comparatively short, while the second four parts are the
main body of the essay in which the theme is developed. It is called the
"eight-legged essay" because each of the second four parts contains two
paragraphs forming antithetical "limbs". Comrade Mao Tse-tung uses the
term here to illustrate the various stages in the development of a revolution.
He also employs it on many other occasions to satirise doctrinairism by
stressing its stereotyped, formalistic and doctrinaire character.

35. See Note 11 to *On the Tactics of Fighting Japanese Imperialism*.

36. In Chinese mythology the dragons are the gods of the four seas and their
palaces under water are supposed to be great treasure houses.

A STATEMENT ON CHIANG KAI-SHEK'S STATEMENT

1. The North-eastern Army under Chang Hsueh-liang and the Seventeenth Route Army under Yang Hu-ch'eng, Kuomintang troops which had come under the influence of the anti-Japanese movement of the Red Army and the Chinese people and had accepted the Communist proposal for an Anti-Japanese National United Front, urged Chiang to unite with the Communists and resist Japan. Chiang not only rejected their demands, but even actively prepared to "annihilate the Communists" and massacred a number of patriotic youths in Sian. Under these circumstances Chang Hsueh-liang and Yang Hu-ch'eng arrested him in Sian on December 12, 1936. This was the famous Sian Incident. Finally they released Chiang and let him return to Nanking after he accepted the terms of uniting with the Communists and resisting Japan.

2. They were the pro-Japanese elements and Chiang's rivals in the Kuomintang government in Nanking. With Wang Ching-wei and Ho Ying-ch'in (*see* Notes 4 and 5 below) as their leaders, they advocated a "punitive expedition" against Chang Hsueh-liang and Yang Hu-ch'eng during the Sian Incident. Availing themselves of the incident, they prepared to start a large-scale civil war in order to clear the way for the Japanese invaders and wrest political power from Chiang Kai-shek.

3. The seven leaders of the patriotic anti-Japanese movement in Shanghai were: Shen Chun-ju, Chang Nai-ch'i, Tsou T'ao-fen, Li Kung-p'u, Sha Ch'ien-li, Shih Liang and Wang Tsao-shih. They were arrested by Chiang Kai-shek's government in November 1936 and were released in July 1937.

4. Head of the pro-Japanese clique in the Kuomintang, he had stood consistently for compromise with the Japanese imperialists ever since their invasion of the North-east in 1931. In December 1938 he left Chungking, openly capitulated to the Japanese invaders, and set up a puppet government in Nanking.

5. A Kuomintang warlord and another leader of the pro-Japanese clique in that party. During the Sian Incident he actively plotted civil war by mobilising the Kuomintang troops for an attack on Shensi along the Kansu-Haichow railway. Intending to take over Chiang Kai-shek's position, he even planned to kill Chiang by bombing Sian.

6. A pro-American member of the Kuomintang. On account of the contradiction between American imperialism and Japanese imperialism, then contending for supremacy in the Far East, he also recommended, in the interests of the United States, a peaceful settlement of the Sian Incident.

7. The letter makes a stern and just criticism of the reactionary rule of the Kuomintang and the decisions of the Second Plenary Session of its Central Executive Committee. It also stated the Communist Party's policy of forming an Anti-Japanese National United Front and renewing its co-operation with the Kuomintang. The main part of the letter reads:

"In talking about 'centralisation and unification', the Second Plenary Session of the Central Executive Committee of your party is really putting things somewhat upside down. It must be understood that the ten years' civil war and disunity have been caused entirely by the policy of depending on imperialism pursued by your party and your party's government, a policy

that invites disaster for the nation, and especially by your persistent policy of
non-resistance to Japan ever since the Incident of September 18, 1931. Under
the slogan of 'Internal pacification before resistance to foreign invasion' put
forward by your party and your party's government, you have carried on all
through the years incessant civil wars and innumerable encirclement campaigns against the Red Army, and have spared no effort in suppressing the
patriotic and democratic movement of the people throughout the country.
Even up to recent months you have abandoned North-east and North China
without any qualm and, forgetting that Japanese imperialism is China's
deadliest enemy, you have used all your strength to fight the Red Army and
wage factional struggles within your own party, blocked the Red Army on its
way to fight the Japanese and harassed its rear, neglected the demand of the
people throughout the country for resistance to Japan, and deprived them of
their freedoms and rights. As patriotism is made a crime, innocent prisoners
are in jail all over the country; as treason is rewarded, the collaborators are
congratulating each other on receiving government appointments. To seek
for centralisation and unification by means of this erroneous policy is really
like 'climbing up a tree to look for fish' and will produce the very opposite
result.

"Now we solemnly give you gentlemen a piece of advice: If you do not
fundamentally change your erroneous policy, and if you do not direct your
hatred against the Japanese imperialists but continue to direct it against your
own countrymen, you will find it impossible even to maintain the status quo;
talk about centralisation, unification and the so-called 'modern state' can
only be sheer empty prattle. What the people throughout the country
demand at present is centralisation and unification for fighting Japan and
saving the nation, not centralisation and unification for fawning on the
foreigners and persecuting the people. The people throughout the country
are now eagerly demanding a government that can really save their nation
as well as themselves, a really democratic republic. The people throughout
the country demand a democratic republican government that works for
their interests.

"The principal programme of this government must provide for: First,
resistance to foreign aggression. Secondly, grant of democratic rights to the
people. And thirdly, development of the national economy and alleviation
or even elimination of the hardships in the people's life. In the matter of a
'modern state', only such a programme meets the genuine need of colonial and
semi-colonial China in the present era.

"With eager hopes and firm determination the people throughout the
country are struggling for the realisation of such a programme. But the
policy of your party and your party's government runs counter to these hopes
of the people throughout the country, and thus you will never find it possible
to win their confidence.

"The Chinese Communist Party and the Chinese Red Army hereby solemnly
declare: We approve of the establishment of a unified democratic republic
for the whole country; approve of the convocation of a parliament elected by
universal suffrage; support an anti-Japanese national salvation congress
representative of all the people and all the anti-Japanese armed forces in the
country, and a unified national defence government for the whole country.
We hereby declare: As soon as a unified democratic republic is established
for the whole of China, the Red areas will become one of its component parts,
the representatives of the people of the Red areas will attend the all-China

parliament, and the same democratic system will set be up in the Red areas as in other parts of China.

"We hold that the national defence council, which the Second Plenary Session of the Central Executive Committee of your party has decided to organise, and the national assembly, which your party and your party's government are calling, cannot fulfil the tasks of centralisation and unification for resistance to Japan and national salvation. According to the regulations of the national defence council passed by the Second Plenary Session of the Central Executive Committee of your party, the council will be confined in its composition to a few officials who hold power in your party and your party's government, and its task is merely to serve as an advisory body to your party's government. It is only too clear that such a council cannot achieve anything or win any confidence among the people. Nor, judging by the 'Draft Constitution of the Republic of China' and the 'Organic Law and Election Law of the National Assembly' passed by your party's government, can the national assembly which you gentlemen desire to convoke, because such a national assembly will be merely an organ manipulated by a few officials of your party and your party's government, their appendage and ornament. A national defence council and a national assembly of this kind have absolutely nothing in common with the all-nation congress for resistance to Japan and national salvation (i.e. the national defence council) and the Chinese democratic republic and its parliament that are proposed by our Party.

"We hold that a national defence council for resistance to Japan and national salvation must include the delegates of all parties, all groups, all circles and all armed forces and constitute a real organ of authority capable of deciding on the major policies of resisting Japan and saving the nation, and that a unified national defence government must be formed from this council. And the national assembly must be a parliament elected through nation-wide universal suffrage and must be the supreme organ of authority of the democratic republic of China. Only such a national defence council and such an all-China parliament will secure the welcome, support and participation of the people of the whole country and will be able to place the great cause of saving the nation and the people on a firm, unshakable foundation. Otherwise all high-sounding words will prove utterly useless and will never win the approval of the nation. The failure of the various conferences your party and your party's government have hitherto held affords the best example.

"The declaration of the Second Plenary Session of the Central Executive Committee of your party also stated: 'Dangers and obstacles are only to be expected; but we will never, because of the difficulties and troubles that beset the nation, relax in the fulfilment of our duty.' And again, 'As to the nation's survival, our party will certainly devote all its wisdom and ability and work for it through thick and thin.' True, yours is the ruling party in the largest part of China, and the political responsibility for all past deeds can only rest with you. In view of the fact that the Kuomintang government is under a one-party dictatorship, the Kuomintang can never escape this responsibility. Especially since the Incident of September 18 your party, acting against the wishes of the people throughout the country and against the interests of the whole nation, has pursued an absolutely erroneous policy, resulting in the loss of almost half of China—the responsibility for this can never be foisted on others. As we and the people of the whole country see it, since half of China has been abandoned by your party, we certainly cannot but charge your party with the responsibility of recovering her territory and restoring her sovereignty.

"At the same time, even within your party many men of conscience are now clearly awakened to the horrors of subjugation as well as the inviolability of the people's wishes; they are beginning to turn in a new direction and feel indignant and discontented towards those of their fellow members who have brought disaster both to their party and to the nation. The Chinese Communist Party has full sympathy with this turn, and warmly applauds the noble spirit and awakening of these patriotic and conscientious members of the Kuomintang, their readiness to sacrifice themselves in the struggle, and their courage to introduce reforms when the nation is on the brink of ruin. We know that in your party's central and provincial headquarters, in its central and provincial governments, in educational, scientific, artistic, journalistic, industrial, religious and medical circles, in all kinds of popular organisations, among women, among the police, and especially among the broad ranks of the army and among both old and new members as well as the leaders at various levels of the Kuomintang, there are actually many awakened and patriotic people whose number is daily increasing—this is an unusually gratifying state of affairs. The Chinese Communist Party is always ready to join hands with these members of the Kuomintang and form a solid national united front with them to fight the nation's deadliest enemy—Japanese imperialism. We hope that such members will speedily grow into a dominant force in the Kuomintang and overwhelm those members, namely, the worst and most shameless ones, who, disregarding the interests of the nation, have virtually become agents of the Japanese imperialists and pro-Japanese collaborators—members who are a disgrace to Dr. Sun Yat-sen's memory—so that they may revive the spirit of Dr. Sun's revolutionary Three People's Principles; reaffirm his three cardinal policies of alliance with Russia, co-operation with the Communists, and assistance to the peasants and workers; and devote their 'wisdom and ability' to 'working for' the realisation of the revolutionary Three People's Principles and of the three cardinal policies 'through thick and thin' and to 'working for' the realisation of Dr. Sun's revolutionary Testament 'through thick and thin'. We hope that, together with the patriotic leaders and patriotic people of all parties, all groups, and all circles, they will resolutely shoulder the responsibility of continuing Dr. Sun's revolutionary cause, and resolutely struggle to drive out the Japanese imperialists and to save the Chinese nation from extinction, to win the democratic rights of the people throughout the country, to develop China's national economy in order to relieve the sufferings of the greatest majority of her people, and to bring about the democratic republic of China with a democratic parliament and democratic government.

"The Chinese Communist Party hereby declares to all members of the Kuomintang: If you really do this, we shall resolutely assist you and form with you again a solid revolutionary united front like the one formed against foreign and feudal oppression during China's great revolutionary period of 1924–7— for this is the only correct line today for saving the nation from extinction and ensuring its survival."

THE TASKS OF THE CHINESE COMMUNIST PARTY IN THE PERIOD OF RESISTANCE TO JAPAN

1. This is a blanket name for a series of events in which the Japanese carried on their aggression against North China while the Kuomintang government headed by Chiang Kai-shek surrendered China's sovereignty over the Northern provinces and subjected the whole nation to humiliation. These events were:

    (1) The signing of the "Ho-Umezu" agreement in June 1935 by Ho Ying-ch'in, the Kuomintang government's representative in North China, and Yoshijiro Umezu, commander of Japanese armed forces in North China. In this agreement the Kuomintang government accepted the demand presented by Japan in May, thereby substantially surrendering China's sovereign rights in the provinces of Hopeh and Chahar.

    (2) The Siangho Incident. A group of collaborators under Japanese direction staged a revolt in October in Siangho county, Hopeh province, and occupied the county town.

    (3) The "movement for autonomy in the five northern provinces" in November, which the Japanese aggressors engineered through the collaborators and the subsequent establishment of the puppet "Anti-Communist Autonomous Administration" in eastern Hopeh.

    (4) The formation of the "Political Affairs Commission for Hopeh and Chahar" headed by Sung Che'yuan, a measure taken by the Kuomintang government to meet the Japanese demand for a "special political power in North China".

2. This refers to the Declaration of August 1, 1935. Below are excerpts from it:

    "At this moment when our nation and people are threatened by imminent destruction, the Communist Party once again appeals to all fellow countrymen: Whatever the past or present differences in political opinions and interests among various political parties, whatever the difference in views and interests among the various circles of our countrymen, and whatever the hostile actions once taken or now being taken by the various armies, all should truly awaken and realise that 'brothers quarrelling at home will join forces against attacks from outside'—first and foremost all should endeavour to stop the civil war so that the forces of the nation (man-power, material and financial resources, and armed forces) can be concentrated in the sacred cause of armed resistance and national salvation. Once again the Communist Party solemnly declares: Provided that the Kuomintang troops cease their attacks on the Red Army, or that any armed force carries out resistance to Japan, then regardless of old feuds or present conflicts between them and the Red Army, of differences between them and the Red Army on domestic problems, the Red Army will not only immediately cease its hostile actions against them, but warmly join hands and work together with them to save the country.

    ". . . The Communist Party is willing to initiate this kind of national defence government; it is willing to negotiate about the joint formation of the national defence government with all those political parties and groups, all those organisations (trade unions, peasant associations, student associations, chambers of commerce, educational associations, journalists' associations, school teachers' and staff members' associations, home-town associations, the Chinese Freemasons, the Association for National Armed Self-defence, the anti-Japanese associations, the Association for National Salvation, etc.), all those distinguished personages and scholars, statesmen and local military and administrative bodies, that are willing to take part in the cause of resistance to Japan and salvation of the nation. The national defence government established as a result of the negotiations shall be the provisional organ of leadership for saving the nation from extinction and ensuring its survival. This kind of national defence government shall take steps to call together, in order to discuss more specifically problems concerning the resistance to Japan and the salvation of the nation, a body of delegates truly representative of all our countrymen (delegates to be democratically elected by various circles—workers, peasants, soldiers, government officials and employees, business men and scholars; by all parties and organisations that are willing to resist Japan and save the nation; and by all Chinese overseas and all national groups within China's boundaries). The Communist Party pledges itself to do its utmost to help to convoke such a body representative of all the people and to carry out all its decisions.

"... A united anti-Japanese army should be formed by all troops willing to resist Japan. Its headquarters should be set up under the leadership of the national defence government. Whether the headquarters be made up of delegates elected by the anti-Japanese officers and men of various armed units, or whether it be formed on some other basis, is a question to be decided by representatives from all circles and the consensus of all the people. In order to fulfil its mission to resist Japan and save the nation, the Red Army pledges itself to be the first to join this allied army. To enable the national defence government to discharge effectively the heavy responsibility of national defence and the united anti-Japanese army the heavy responsibility of resisting Japan, the Communist Party appeals to the whole nation: Those who have money give money, those who have guns give guns, those who have food give food, those who have labour power give labour power, and those who have special skill contribute special skill, so that all our fellow countrymen will be mobilised and all ancient and modern weapons used to arm millions upon millions of people."

3. This refers to a resolution adopted at the meeting of the Political Bureau of the Party's Central Committee at Wayaopao, northern Shensi, on December 25, 1935. Entitled "Resolution on the Present Political Situation and the Tasks of the Party", it presented a comprehensive analysis of the international and domestic situation and the changes in class relations that had taken place in China, and defined the policy of the Party. Below are excerpts from the resolution:

"The current situation makes it clear to us that the Japanese attempt to annex China has shocked the whole country and the whole world. Changes have taken place or are taking place in the relations between all classes and strata, all political parties and armed forces in China's political life. Both the national revolutionary front and the national counter-revolutionary front are being reorganised. Therefore, the Party's tactical line is to arouse, unite and organise all the revolutionary forces throughout China to fight the main enemy confronting them—Japanese imperialism and Chiang Kai-shek, the arch traitor. All people, all parties, all armed forces and all classes, in so far as they are opposed to Japanese imperialism and the traitor Chiang Kai-shek, must unite to extend the sacred national revolutionary war to drive the Japanese imperialists out of China and to overthrow their jackals' rule in China in order to achieve China's complete liberation and safeguard her independence and territorial integrity. And it is only by establishing the broadest possible Anti-Japanese National United Front (both at the bottom and at the top) that Japanese imperialism and its jackal, Chiang Kai-shek, can be defeated.

"Of course, various persons, organisations, social classes and strata and armed forces may join the anti-Japanese national revolution out of different motives and from different standpoints. Some join in order to keep their present positions, others to strive for their own hegemony in the movement so that it will not go farther than they will tolerate, and still others to work sincerely for the complete liberation of the Chinese nation. Precisely because their motives and standpoints are different, some may vacillate or turn traitor at the very start of the struggle, other may grow indifferent or withdraw from the front midway, and still others may fight to a finish. Our task, however, is not only to unite all possible basic anti-Japanese forces, but all possible anti-Japanese allies; it is to make all those in the country who have labour power give labour power, those who have money give money, those who have guns give guns, and those who have knowledge contribute knowledge, to make every Chinese patriot join the anti-Japanese front. Such is the general line of the Party's tactics for the broadest possible national united front.

"Only by following such a line can we mobilise the forces of the people of the whole country to deal with the common enemy of the people, Japanese imperialism and Chiang Kai-shek the traitor.

"The Chinese working class and peasantry remain the basic motive forces of the Chinese revolution. The broad masses of the petty bourgeoisie and the revolutionary intellectuals are the most reliable allies in the national revolution. The solid alliance of the workers, the peasants and the petty bourgeoisie will be the main force for defeating Japanese imperialism and the collaborators and traitors. A section of the national bourgeoisie and of the warlords, however much they may disapprove of the agrarian revolution and the Red régime, can be of help in expanding the anti-Japanese front if they show sympathy or maintain friendly neutrality towards the struggle against the Japanese and the collaborators and traitors, or directly participate in the struggle. For this will separate them from the counter-revolutionary forces as a whole and increase the revolutionary forces as a whole. To achieve this end, the Party should adopt all appropriate ways and means to win these forces over to the anti-Japanese front. Moreover, even in the camp of the landlord and comprador classes there is by no means complete solidarity, because many imperialist powers have hitherto contended for China and there have arisen in the service different factions of traitors with contradictions and conflicts between them, hence the Party should employ all means to keep temporarily some of the counter-revolutionary forces from actively opposing the anti-Japanese front. The same tactics apply to imperialist powers other than Japan.

"In arousing, uniting and organising the forces of the people of the whole country to fight their common enemy, the Party should resolutely and unswervingly fight all tendencies towards vacillation, compromise, capitulation and betrayal within the anti-Japanese united front. Those who disrupt the

Chinese people's anti-Japanese movement are collaborators or traitors, and we should all rise to fight them.

"The Communist Party should seek to win leadership in the anti-Japanese front by the resoluteness and correctness of its words and deeds against Japanese imperialism and against the collaborators and traitors. And it is only under the Communist Party's leadership that complete victory can be won for the anti-Japanese movement.

"As to the broad masses in the anti-Japanese war, it is necessary to satisfy their demand in the matter of their basic interests (the peasants' demand for land and the demand for better living conditions on the part of the workers, the soldiers, the poor people and the intellectuals). Only when their demands are satisfied can we mobilise wider sections of the people to join the anti-Japanese front, keep up the anti-Japanese movement, and lead the movement to complete victory. Only thus can we win leadership in the Anti-Japanese War." *Cf. On the Tactics of Fighting Japanese Imperialism.*

4. *See* the circular telegram of May 5, 1936 from the Red Army, which demanded that the Nanking government end the civil war, conclude a peace agreement with the Communists, and unite with the Communists to resist Japan. Its full text reads:

"To the Military Council of the National Government, Nanking; all land, sea and air forces; all parties; all groups; all organisations; all newspapers; and all fellow countrymen unwilling to be slaves of a foreign nation:

"Since the Anti-Japanese Vanguard of the Chinese People's Red Army was organised by the Revolutionary Military Committee of the Chinese Red Army and ordered to cross the Yellow river on an eastward expedition, it won victory wherever it went, thereby causing a nation-wide reverberation. But the moment it occupied the Tatung-Puchow railway and began to prepare energetically for a drive eastward into Hopeh to engage the Japanese imperialists directly, Chiang Kai-shek ordered more than ten divisions to march into Shansi and help Yen Hsi-shan to block it on its way to fight the Japanese, and also ordered the troops under Chang Hsueh-liang and Yang Hu-ch'eng as well as the troops in northern Shensi to thrust into the Shensi-Kansu Red area to harass our anti-Japanese rear.

"In order to attain its objective of directly fighting the Japanese, the Anti-Japanese Vanguard of the Chinese People's Red Army would have had to concentrate all its forces on eliminating Chiang's troops in its way. But after much deliberation the Revolutionary Military Committee of the Red Army held that, in the present national crisis a decisive battle between the two sides, no matter which side should come out the victor, would only, much to the delight of the Japanese imperialists, reduce China's strength for national defence. Furthermore, among Chiang Kai-shek's and Yen Hsi-shan's troops there are quite a number of patriotic officers and men willing to end the civil war and unite against Japan; in blocking the Red Army on its way to fight the Japanese on the orders of Chiang and Yen, they are really acting against their own consciences. Therefore, in order to keep intact China's strength for national defence and thereby expedite the Anti-Japanese War, to carry out resolutely the declaration we have repeatedly made to the nation on cessation of the civil war and unity against Japan, and to urge Chiang Kai-shek and the patriotic officers and men in his army to awaken at long last, the Revolutionary Military Committee of the Red Army voluntarily withdrew the people's Anti-Japanese Vanguard to the west of the Yellow river, in spite of its numerous victories in Shansi.

"With this action as a pledge of good faith to the Nanking government, to all land, sea and air forces of the country, and to the people of the whole country, we are willing to hold, within a month, cease-fire and peace negotiations with all the armed units attacking the anti-Japanese Red Army in order to end the civil war and resist Japan.

"The Revolutionary Military Committee of the Red Army hereby solemnly advises the gentlemen of the Nanking government that at this critical moment of the threat of immediate destruction to the nation and the people, you ought, in all reason, to break with your past and, in the spirit of the maxim, 'Brothers quarrelling at home will join forces against attacks from outside', to stop the nation-wide civil war, first of all stop the war in Shensi, Kansu and Shansi, so that both sides can send delegates to discuss specific measures for resisting Japan and saving the nation. This will not only be for your own good, but also a blessing to the nation and the country. If, however, you obstinately refuse to awaken to reason and want to become collaborators and traitors, then your rule will certainly collapse in the end, and you will certainly be spurned and overthrown by the people of the whole country. The old saying has it, 'Pointed at by a thousand accusing fingers, one dies even though in perfect health.' And again, 'The butcher becomes a Buddha the moment he drops his cleaver.' These are words for you gentlemen to digest and ponder.

"Further, the Revolutionary Military Committee of the Red Army calls upon all organisations, all parties and the people of the whole country, who are unwilling to be slaves of a foreign nation, to support our proposal for a cease-fire and peace negotiations and for solidarity against Japan, and to organise a committee to hasten the cessation of the civil war by sending delegates to the front to stop the firing on both sides and to see to it that this proposal is completely carried out."

5. *See* Note 7 to *A Statement on Chiang Kai-shek's Statement.*

6. This refers to the Central Committee's "Resolution on the New Situation in the Movement to Resist Japan and Save the Nation, and on the Democratic Republic", in which specific explanations were given on the slogan of a democratic republic. This slogan was proposed in the "Resolution on the Present Political Situation and the Tasks of the Party", adopted by the Political Bureau of the Central Committee, and in Comrade Mao's report, "On the Tactics of Fighting Japanese Imperialism". Later, the Party adopted, as was made imperative by the situation, the policy of forcing Chiang Kai-shek to resist Japan and, as the slogan for the people's republic would be unacceptable to his clique, the Party's Central Committee, in a letter to the Kuomintang in August 1936, changed the slogan into "for a democratic republic". The two slogans meant essentially the same thing despite the difference in wording. Below are excerpts from the "Resolution on the New Situation in the Movement to Resist Japan and to Save the Nation and on the Democratic Republic", September 1936:

"The Central Committee holds that in the current situation it is necessary to put forward the slogan for establishing a democratic republic, because this is the best way to unite all anti-Japanese forces to guarantee China's territorial integrity and to save the Chinese people from the calamity of genocide and national destruction, and because this is also the most appropriate slogan for the united front based on the democratic demands of the broad sections of the people.

"The democratic republic means a democracy which is geographically more extensive than that of the workers' and peasants' democratic dictatorship

on a part of China's territory, and a political system which is far more progressive than the Kuomintang's one-party dictatorship in the main sections
of China; it can therefore better guarantee the extensive development and
complete victory of the Anti-Japanese War. Moreover, the democratic
republic will not only enable the broadest sections of the masses of the Chinese
people to take part in the country's political life, thereby enhancing their
political consciousness and increasing their organised strength, but will also
set the stage for the unfettered activity of the Chinese proletariat and its
leader, the Communist Party, in their struggle for the victory of socialism in
future. Therefore the Chinese Communist Party declares that it actively
supports the movement for a democratic republic. It also declares that when
the democratic republic embracing the whole nation is established and a
parliament elected by universal suffrage is actually convened, the Red areas
will be made a component part of the republic, the people of the Red areas
will elect their representatives to the parliament, and one and the same
democratic system will be put into practice in the Red areas.

"... The Central Committee points out emphatically that it is only by
continuing to expand the Chinese people's movement for resisting Japan and
saving the nation, by broadening the Anti-Japanese National United Front
of all parties, all groups, all circles and all armies, by strengthening the
Chinese Communist Party's role of political leadership in the Anti-Japanese
National United Front, by greatly consolidating the Red political power and
the Red Army, and by waging a determined struggle against all words and
deeds which undermine our sovereignty and humiliate our nation or weaken
the national front, that we can press the Nanking government of the Kuomintang to resist Japan and secure the prerequisites for the democratic republic.
Without a bitter persistent struggle, without the awakening of all the Chinese
people, and without a revolutionary upsurge, the democratic republic cannot
be established. In the course of the struggle for the democratic republic, the
Chinese Communist Party should see to it that the democratic republic
proceeds on the Ten-Point Programme for Resistance to Japan and Salvation
of the Nation proposed by our Party until the basic tasks of the Chinese
bourgeois-democratic revolution are thoroughly accomplished."

7. This telegram, dispatched on February 10, 1937, reads:

"Gentlemen of the Third Plenary Session of the Central Executive Committee of the Kuomintang:

"The peaceful settlement of the Sian Incident has been celebrated throughout the country; it is indeed fortunate for the nation that henceforth the line
of peace and unification and solidarity against foreign aggression can be
carried out. At this moment when the Japanese invaders are running amuck
and the survival of the Chinese nation hangs by a thread, our Party eagerly
hopes that in accordance with this line the Third Plenary Session of the
Central Executive Committee of your party will lay down the following as
the national policy:

"(1) end all civil wars and concentrate the nation's strength to cope unitedly
with foreign aggression;

"(2) guarantee the freedom of speech, assembly and association and
release all political prisoners;

"(3) call a conference of representatives of all parties, all groups, all circles
and all armies, and concentrate the nation's talents for common
endeavour to save the country;

"(4) complete speedily all preparations for resisting Japan; and

"(5) improve the living conditions of the people.

"If the Third Plenary Session of your Central Executive Committee resolutely and firmly lays down the above as the national policy, then, in order to show our good faith in solidarity for resisting foreign aggression, our Party will pledge the following:

"(1) all over the country the policy of armed insurrection for overthrowing the National Government will be discontinued;

"(2) the workers' and peasants' democratic government will be renamed as the government of the special region of the Republic of China, and the Red Army will be designated as a unit of the National Revolutionary Army, and will accept guidance directly from the Central government in Nanking and its Military Council respectively;

"(3) in the areas under the government of the special region, a thoroughly democratic system based on universal suffrage will be put into effect; and

"(4) the policy of confiscating the land of the landlords will be discontinued and the common programme of the Anti-Japanese National United Front resolutely carried out."

8. In November and December 1936, a strike broke out among 45,000 workers in twenty-six Japanese and Chinese textile mills in Shanghai. In December all the workers in the Japanese textile mills in Tsingtao struck in sympathy. The Shanghai workers subsequently won a five per cent increase in wages and the employers agreed not to discharge workers arbitrarily or to assault or abuse the workers. The strike in Tsingtao, however, was suppressed by the Japanese marines.

9. Britain and the United States began to change their attitude towards Japan as their interests in North and Central China were directly jeopardised by Japan's occupation in 1933 of the Shanghai pass at the eastern terminal of the Great Wall on the sea coast, by her penetration into North China, and especially by the "Ho-Umezu" agreement of 1935 (*see* Note 1 above). Consequently they exerted an influence on the policy of the Chiang Kai-shek government towards Japan. When the Sian Incident occurred in 1936, Britain suggested the rejection of such Japanese demands as were detrimental to British interests in China. She even intimated that, provided the Chiang Kai-shek government could maintain its rule over the Chinese people, it might as well "form some sort of alliance with the Communist Party" in order to checkmate the Japanese policy of aggression.

10. In June 1936, under the pretext of "resisting Japan and saving the nation", Li Tsung-jen and Pai Ch'ung-hsi, warlords of Kwangsi, and Ch'en Chi-t'ang, warlord of Kwangtung, jointly declared their opposition to Chiang Kai-shek. By August the opposition was crushed by Chiang Kai-shek through bribery and the tactics of "divide and rule".

11. The Japanese and Chinese puppet troops began their invasion of Suiyuan in August 1936. In November, the Chinese troops quartered in the province fought back and the people throughout the country started a movement to support the fight.

12. After the "Ho-Umezu" agreement of 1935 (*see* Note 1 above), under the impact of the upsurge of anti-Japanese sentiment among the Chinese people and the influence of the stiffening policy towards Japan on the part of Britain and the United States, the Kuomintang government somewhat stiffened its

attitude towards Japan. It deliberately dragged out the talks for four months
(from September to December 1936) and rendered them fruitless.

13. The session began in Nanking on February 15, 1937.

14. Ah Q is the leading character in the *Authentic Biography of Ah Q*, a famous
novel by the great Chinese writer Lu Hsun (1881–1936). Lu Hsun made him
the type of all who seek compensation for the failures and setbacks in real life
by regarding them as moral or spiritual victories.

15. In the stage of China's bourgeois-democratic revolution, the Communists
agreed with the basic points of Sun Yat-sen's principles or programme of
nationalism, democracy and the people's welfare. Therefore they co-operated
with him. But they disagreed with the bourgeois and petty-bourgeois world
outlook or ideological system he stood for. The Chinese Communists, as the
vanguard of the Chinese proletariat, view national and other problems in the
light of an entirely different ideology. *Cf.* "On New Democracy", Vol. III,
of the *Selected Works*.

16. Reorganised by Sun Yat-sen in 1924, the Kuomintang became a revolutionary
alliance of several classes, in which the Communists joined as individuals.
After betraying the revolution in 1927, it started a nation-wide massacre of the
Communists and many of the left-wingers in the Kuomintang who were
genuine supporters of Sun Yat-sen's three cardinal policies. This was called
by the Kuomintang a campaign to "purge the party". It marked the beginning of the Kuomintang's transformation into a counter-revolutionary political
party of the big landlord and big bourgeois classes.

17. This refers to the situation created by the opportunist leadership of the
Central Committee of the Party in the first half of 1927.

STRIVE TO WIN OVER MILLIONS UPON MILLIONS OF THE MASSES TO THE ANTI-JAPANESE NATIONAL UNITED FRONT

1. After the Sian Incident, Japanese imperialism for a time assumed a concilia-
tory attitude in order to induce the Kuomintang authorities to disrupt the
national peace and the Anti-Japanese National United Front that were being
established in China. Thus, in December 1936 and again in March 1937, the
puppet autonomous government of Inner Mongolia, under Japan's orders,
sent two circular telegrams pledging allegiance to the Kuomintang government in Nanking; Sato, the Japanese foreign minister, set out to lure Chiang
Kai-shek by declaring that the relations between China and Japan could be
improved and that Japan would help China in her political unification and
economic recovery; and an "Economic Study Group" headed by one of
Japan's financial magnates, Kenji Kodama, came to China for the ostensible
purpose of helping China to "complete the organisation of a modern state".
These schemes formed the so-called "Sato's diplomacy", or "Japan's retreat"
in the eyes of the deluded people.

2. This refers to the trial of the seven patriotic leaders in Shanghai. (*See* Note 3
to *A Statement on Chiang Kai-shek's Statement.*) They were tried by the High
Court in Soochow in April 1937 on the charge of "endangering the Republic",
the usual indictment trumped up by the reactionary Kuomintang authorities
against all patriotic movements.

3. Prior to the Sian Incident, the North-eastern Army was stationed on the border between Shensi and Kansu and was in direct contact with the Red Army in northern Shensi. Profoundly influenced by the Red Army, it finally staged the Sian Incident. To cut off its contact with the Red Army and sow discord among its ranks, the Kuomintang reactionaries ordered it to move eastward to Honan and Anhwei in March 1937.

4. A military leader in China's North-west who staged the Sian Incident together with Chang Hsueh-liang. Thus the names of the prime movers of this incident were hyphenated in popular parlance as "Chang-Yang". While Chang was put into prison immediately after he accompanied Chiang Kai-shek to Nanking, Yang was deposed and forced by the Kuomintang reactionaries to go abroad. When the War of Resistance began, Yang returned to China to offer his services, only to be interned by Chiang Kai-shek for the rest of his life. In September 1949, when the People's Liberation Army was driving near Chungking, Chiang had him murdered in a concentration camp there.

5. Tung pass or Tungkwan is a gateway of strategic importance on the borders of Shensi, Honan and Shansi. At the time of the Sian Incident the main forces of Chiang Kai-shek's Kuomintang troops were quartered on both sides of it.

People reputed in the Party to be "Lefts", like Chang Kuo-t'ao, advocated that the Red Army should "fight its way out of Tung pass". By this they meant the opening of an offensive on the Kuomintang troops. This proposal ran counter to the Party centre's policy for a peaceful settlement of the Sian Incident.

6. For a long time after the October Revolution in Russia, French imperialism persisted in a hostile policy towards the Soviet Union. From 1918 to 1920, the French government took an active part in the armed intervention carried out by fourteen powers against the Soviet Union. It continued to pursue the reactionary policy of isolating the Soviet Union even after the intervention proved a failure. It was not until May 1935 that, owing to the influence of the Soviet Union's peace policy among the French people and to the menace of fascist Germany, France concluded a pact of mutual assistance with the Soviet Union, a pact which her reactionary government failed to observe in good faith.

7. Referring to the students' patriotic demonstration in Peking on December 9, 1935 under the leadership of the Chinese Communist Party. The movement called for the cessation of civil war and armed resistance to Japan and won nation-wide support.

8. This refers to the so-called "Sino-Japanese economic collaboration".

9. *Cf.* Marx and Engels, *The Communist Manifesto*, Part IV; V. I. Lenin, *Two Tactics of Social-Democracy in the Democratic Revolution*, Part XII and Part XIII; *History of the Communist Party of the Soviet Union*, Chapter III, Section 3.

10. *Cf.* J. V. Stalin, *The Foundations of Leninism*, III; *The October Revolution and the Tactics of the Russian Communists*, II; *On the Problems of Leninism*, III.

11. *See* J. V. Stalin, "Address to the Graduates from the Red Army Academies" (*Problems of Leninism*, in which he said:
". . . of all the valuable capital the world possesses, the most valuable and most decisive is people, cadres. It must be realised that under our present conditions 'cadres decide everything.' . . ."

12. This refers to the difference which existed during 1935–6 between the Party centre's line and Chang Kuo-t'ao's line of retreat (*cf.* Note 23 to *On the Tactics of Fighting Japanese Imperialism*). Comrade Mao's statement here that "the old

difference has been settled" was based on the fact that the Fourth Front Army of the Red Army, which was under Chang Kuo-t'ao's leadership, had by that time joined forces with Red Army units under the direct leadership of the Party centre. As to Chang Kuo-t'ao's subsequent desertion from the Party to become an open counter-revolutionary traitor, it was a personal act of treachery and had nothing to do with any differences over the lines of leadership.

ON PRACTICE

1. V. I. Lenin, *Philosophical Notebooks*, Russian edition, Moscow 1947, p. 185.
2. *Cf.* Karl Marx, *Theses on Feuerbach*, published as an Appendix in Frederick Engels's *Ludwig Feuerbach and the End of Classical German Philosophy*; and V. I. Lenin, *Materialism and Empirio-Criticism*, Chapter III, Section 6.
3. V. I. Lenin, *loc. cit.*, p. 146.
4. *Cf.* Lenin, *loc. cit.*, p. 146: "For the sake of knowing, one must start to know, to study, on the basis of experience and rise from experience to general knowledge."
5. V. I. Lenin, *What Is To Be Done?*
6. V. I. Lenin, *Materialism and Empirio-Criticism*, Chapter II, Section 6.
7. Joseph Stalin, *Foundations of Leninism*.
8. *Cf.* V. I. Lenin, *Materialism and Empirio-Criticism*, Chapter II, Section 5.